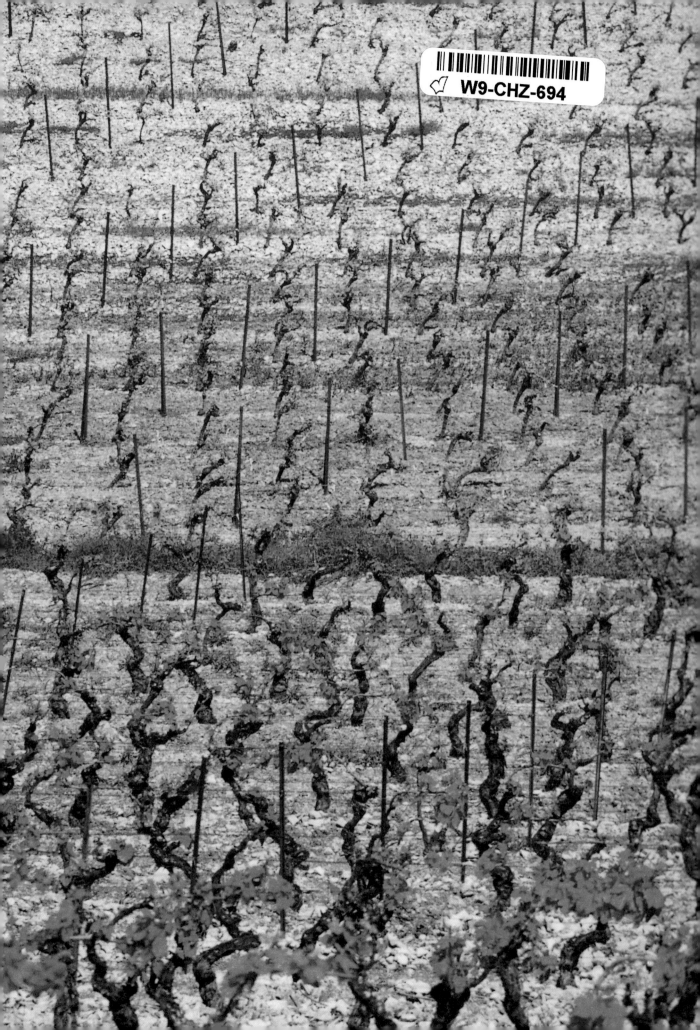

LANGUEDOC
THE WINES & WINEMAKERS
ROUSSILLON

LANGUEDOC
THE WINES & WINEMAKERS
ROUSSILLON

PAUL STRANG   PHOTOGRAPHY BY JASON SHENAI

MITCHELL BEAZLEY

for Tony and Lucia

LANGUEDOC-ROUSSILLON
THE WINES & WINEMAKERS
by Paul Strang

First published in Great Britain in 2002 by Mitchell Beazley,
an imprint of Octopus Publishing Group Ltd,
2–4 Heron Quays, London E14 4JP

ISBN 1 84000 500 9

A CIP catalogue record for this book is available from the
British Library. The author and publisher will be grateful for
any information that will assist them in keeping future
editions up to date. Although all reasonable care has been
taken in the preparation of this book, neither the publisher
nor the author can accept liability for any consequences
arising from the use thereof, or from the information
contained therein.

Photographs by Jason Shenai
Commissioning Editors Rebecca Spry, Hilary Lumsden
Executive Art Editor Yasia Williams
Managing Editor Emma Rice
Designer Colin Goody
Editor Susan Keevil
Production Angela Couchman
Index Ann Parry

Typeset in Berkeley Book and Helvetica

Printed and bound in China

guide to the producer listings

Where appellation rules require the presence of grape varieties in given percentages, these do not relate to individual wines, but to the grower's whole vineyard covered by the rules in question.

Appellation wines and vins de pays made by the same producer are dealt with together. Producers making only vins de pays are described in the section corresponding geographically to their vineyards. Growers whose wines are described in detail adopt the best vineyard practices outlined on page 17 unless otherwise mentioned.

Growers are divided into four categories, with price ranges from A (cheapest) to D (most expensive). The range within which a grower falls is usually determined by the price of his best-selling wine. Stars against the names of wines are intended to suggest quality between wines of the same district, not necessarily Languedoc-Roussillon as a whole; nor do the stars take price into account. Stars may reflect general opinion as well as the author's personal predilictions.

Telephone numbers in France change as often as anywhere else. Those listed are believed up-to-date as of going to press. It is sensible as well as polite to telephone before visiting growers, especially the smaller ones who may not have round-the-clock reception facilities. Map references appear before each grower's name, and in some cases will refer to maps in other sections. The price categories after the telephone number or internet address.

contents

introduction

Languedoc-Roussillon is the largest vineyard in the world, its production exceeding that of Australia or Bordeaux. Until the last quarter of the twentieth century, little save very poor wine was made here, nearly all "plonk". Today there are hundreds of serious growers of quality wine, some rivalling the best in France or the New World.

But how did the region plumb such profound depths in the first place? And how did it climb out of them? The terroirs and the climate are constant. Only the intervention of man has been responsible for such swings in quality.

greeks and romans

Evidence discovered in Marseilles, and on wrecked ships raised from the seabed offshore, proves that Marseilles was an active wine port when it was founded by the Greeks six centuries BC. But the Greeks made little attempt to develop the rest of this southern coastline.

The Romans were bolder: their lines of communication were shorter, they had stronger armies, a more sophisticated administration, and they were not frightened of the local inhabitants who at once showed an insatiable thirst for wine; their drunkenness became proverbial. The Romans were quick to plant vines in their new colonies and profit from the market which they had unwittingly uncovered. Loyal military and administrative service was rewarded by the grant of lands for the purpose.

Rome's expansion west of the Rhône resulted in a colony which became known as the Province of Narbonne. It extended up both banks of the Rhône as far as Vienne, westward as far as modern Montauban, and south to the Pyrenees. It thus included the whole of what we now know as Languedoc-Roussillon, as well as the Côtes du Rhône and Gaillac.

Avoiding the insuperable barrier presented by the Massif Central, viticulture nevertheless spread via the Rhône until it reached almost the whole of Eastern France, and down the valley of the Tarn and into the River Garonne, which gave access to the Atlantic at what is today Bordeaux. The development of more grape varieties, hardier than those which the Romans originally brought with them, coupled with what seems to have been a gradual warming of the climate, enabled cultivation of the vine to spread to most of the present-day vine-growing areas of France.

wine and the church

The Roman Empire declined and fell but, despite successive invasions by barbarians from Eastern Europe and later by the Saracens, the vineyards survived and even thrived. Wine was no longer just a crop to be traded like olives or cereals: the vine itself was regarded as having an intrinsic value quite apart from the religious associations within the rites of the fast-expanding Christian Church. It was an important badge of culture, one of the obvious expressions of the quality of life. It was a sign to the outside world that the Church was looking after the interests of the citizens on a secular as well as a spiritual level.

Wine was also an important source of Church revenue. Its vineyards expanded to supply outlying parishes and smaller churches with wine for sacramental purposes. The Church carried out many of the functions of today's catering industry, receiving pilgrims en route to holy places, or merely giving travellers refreshment and rest. Wine was core to such activities: vineyards sprang up round the monasteries and abbey churches. Valmagne (Pézenas), Fontfroide (Corbières), Caunes (Minervois), Saint-Gilles (Nîmes), and Saint-Hilaire (Limoux) became, among others, the centres of what to this day remain productive wine regions.

left flood waters from severe storms are carried away by gullies cut into the vineyards of Roussillon

FRANCE

Languedoc-
Roussillon

CLAIRETTE D[U]
LANGUEDOC

Bédarieux

Clermont
l'Hérault

FAUGÈRES

COTEAUX DU
LANGUEDOC

Pézenas

ST-CHINIAN

St-Jean
de Minervois

Béziers

Agde

MINERVOIS

CABARDÈS

D11

Aude

Sérignan

Bram

Carcassonne

Trèbes

N13

Narbonne

A61

CÔTES DE LA
MALEPÈRE

Lézignan-
Corbières

A9

Orbieu

CORBIÈRES

Limoux

Port–La-Nouvelle

LIMOUX

N9

D118

FITOU

FITOU

Cap des Frères

MAURY

Étang de
Leucate
ou de
Salses

D117

Agly

Rivesaltes

RIVESALTES

Têt

St–Estève

Perpignan

CÔTES DU
ROUSSILLON

Étang de Canet
et de St–Nazaire

Ille–sur–Têt

N116

Prades

A9

N9

N
↑

0   5   10 km
0   3   6 miles

Elne

Tech

Côte
Vermeille

Collioure
Port-Vendres

D618

N114

Céret

D115

BANYULS & COLLIOURE

ESPAÑA

Barcelona

revolt and protest 1

The religious struggles which engulfed Languedoc from the Middle Ages onward slowed its development, leaving scars which still have not healed. The Cathar movement was inspired largely by resentment at the corruption and luxurious decadence of the Church. The Cathar heresy, which struck at the heart of Catholic doctrine in fundamental respects, spread like wildfire among the people of Languedoc. They saw in it not only a way of purifying the Church, but of standing against the combined power of the then foreign French King, bent on securing the total subjugation of Languedoc to the French crown, and the Pope in Rome, determined to exterminate heresy. After many years of resistance and persecution, the last of the Cathars, confined to almost impregnable fortresses in the mountains of the South, were gradually eliminated by torture or massacre in one of the most shameful episodes in Christian history, the horrors of which still resonate eight hundred years later.

The Cathar story is a living part of Languedoc tradition, like the Protestant influence round Nîmes and in the Cévennes, countered just as determinedly if with less cruelty. The people of the Midi, though conservative in character, are dissident politically. Languedoc is reluctant to promote or accept change, but votes solidly Left to this day.

Elsewhere in France the newer vineyards were consolidating their position, securing virtually all the overseas markets. Languedoc had only two routes by which to compete: the historical corridors established by the Romans, unattractive because of the exaction of greedy tolls which made the wines uncompetitive, or a sea voyage round the south of Spain, which was expensive and liable to ruin the wines, except the vins doux naturels fortified with added alcohol.

a slow and gradual development

The seventeenth century heralded a much greater political and economic stability in France. The apogee of the *ancien régime* under Louis XIV should have brought with it a corresponding economic expansion, but the King's luxurious court and territorial wars sucked the economic blood from the provinces, and Languedoc suffered with the rest. A system of tax-collection was introduced, administered locally by tax-farmers many of whom have left a legacy of fine châteaux and vineyards behind them, usually close to larger cities such as Montpellier.

Until the building of the Canal du Midi, little of the wine produced in Languedoc was exported either to the rest of France or abroad, and virtually none from Roussillon, which until about that time was not even part of France. It might be thought that the opening of the canal would have brought an immediate boost in trade, but in fact what was really needed was the ability to compete on equal terms with the rest of the French vineyards. This could not happen until the abolition in 1776 of the tolls and privileges enjoyed by Bordeaux. Nevertheless the eighteenth century did see the development of an important trade in brandies which were distilled from the local vineyards and shipped down the canal to Sète. Brandy would travel well and did not mind how long it was in transit.

boom...

The burgeoning trade in eaux-de-vie and the abolition of the privileges of Bordeaux, which gave Languedoc access to the Atlantic, resulted in a frenzy of vine-planting in the region after the Revolution. Vines, until then grown mostly on the higher and poorer soils, spread downward to the plains. Gradually they became the principal Languedoc crop. A drop in the price of wheat induced the better-off growers to plant more and more vineyards; high-yielding grapes such as Aramon or those of high alcoholic potential, Clairette especially. At the same time, the market for brandy was flourishing, Languedoc making in 1805 about two-fifths of all spirits produced in France. In the *département* of Hérault alone there were over 1,000 distilleries. During the first half of the nineteenth century, shipments of brandy trebled, while exports of wine also increased, particularly to Germany, the Netherlands, Switzerland, and Italy.

The boom was further fuelled by the rise of a new industrial proletariat generated by the Industrial Revolution. Gradually the larger landowners were able to concentrate on the vine as a monoculture. The Canal du Midi then came into its own.

the canal du midi

This extraordinary feat of civil engineering was conceived in the middle of the seventeenth century by Paul Riquet, born in Béziers in 1604. His vision was to create a link between the Atlantic and the Mediterranean so that boats did not have to go round the Straits of Gibraltar. The concept coincided with the unquenchable appetite of the Sun King for prestige, and the ambition of his cunning Finance Minister, Colbert, to develop France into a merchant nation.

The idea was not new, but previous schemes had foundered on the difficulty of feeding a canal with water in such a way that it would fall toward both

Toulouse to the west, and the Mediterranean in the east. Riquet's solution was to locate the high point of the canal, as it crossed the watershed between the two seas, at a spot where it could be fed by the waters coming off the Black Mountain.

The project received the royal go-ahead in 1666. The canal took 12,000 labourers and twelve years to build. The lack of a port on the Mediterranean to serve as the eastern terminus was solved by creating from scratch what is today the town of Sète.

The canal, with its ninety-nine locks and 45,000 trees planted specially along its banks, was opened in 1681. Sadly Riquet had died just six months earlier.

The first eighty years of the nineteenth century were a golden age for the Languedoc, made even more golden by the coming of the railways. In this heyday, Languedoc had very nearly 300,000 hectares under vine, yielding sometimes more than 100 hectolitres per hectare in the plain. In Roussillon the yields were lower, because of the more ungrateful terroir. In Hérault, the area under vine doubled between 1850 and 1870. What had become an important industry became increasingly exposed to the laws of the market.

The phylloxera suddenly struck everywhere in the 1870s. Chemistry could do nothing to defeat this aphid, and the only solution was to replant the wholly destroyed vineyards with immune American rootstocks, on which traditional French varieties would be grafted. This was a disaster for many smaller growers because only the larger estates could afford the necessary reinvestment. Discontent developed a markedly political overtone. But still the demand for more cheap wine increased, and the Government even promoted the creation of supplementary vineyards over the sea in Algeria.

revolt and protest 2

Languedoc entered a period of rapid decline. At first there was not enough wine to satisfy the demand of the market, so the shortfall was imported from Algeria to stretch the supply. Sète became a net importer instead of an exporter. Fraud was rife, too, from areas outside the Languedoc; wines were artificially produced in the North by adding raisins or sugar to sour, inferior juices. Eaux-de-vie made cheaply from sugar-beet, maize, and potatoes flooded the market. This led to demonstrations in the streets

right starkly outlined against the backdrop of a cold autumn day, the vines are prepared for the onslaught of winter

of Perpignan, Narbonne, and Montpellier as early as 1893. Discontent was muffled by a recovery at the end of the 1890s, though radical politico-vignerons continued to press for protection and law-reform.

As the newly replanted vines started to yield, business began once again to flourish, responding to the ever-increasing demand for cheap wine from the industrial working-class. Aramon and Alicante vines, capable of yielding 120 hectolitres of wine to the hectare, dominated vineyards in the plains, though Carignan and Grenache were introduced from Spain into the better quality vineyards.

By the turn of the century over-production had become the real danger. Certainly too much wine was being made in France as a whole, despite consumer demand. Prices between 1880 and 1901 had fallen by three quarters. A brief temporary recovery served only to exacerbate the disasters

about to supervene, because the big landowners did not restore the cuts in wages which had been imposed during the worst years.

In 1903/4 the vineyard workers went on strike. They were successful because they had effectively unionized themselves. They naturally had the support of the radical politicians and press.

The second collapse of wine prices in three years (1904) had the ironic effect of uniting the bosses and workers. Now the big estates suffered equally with their employees. Social unrest led to mass demonstrations and riots in 1907. Meetings in the big cities culminated with a gathering of 600,000 people in Montpellier. Government troops were sent to keep order, but such was their sympathy with the growers that 600 of them mutinied and "sat down" in the streets of Béziers. The general in command refused to discipline them.

This episode is little publicized today, but in 1907 it had profound consequences, boosting the embryonic coopérative movement in Languedoc. Legislation was introduced to suppress fraud and to protect the distilleries of the South. New measures encouraged the replanting of land with better quality grapes, the reduction of the total area under vine, and the introduction of mechanization.

Thus the seeds for the later renaissance were sown earlier than is generally supposed, but the people of the South are slow to respond to change, and the effects were felt only very gradually. One factor inhibiting a switch from quantity to quality was the continuing rise in French wine consumption, which by 1926 had reached 136 litres per year per person, men, women, and children included.

For the greater part of the twentieth century, at least until 1970, it was business as usual. Growers made no effort to cut production in the interests of quality. The policy was to make as much wine as possible. To make it saleable they beefed it up with strong, dark-coloured Algerian and Moroccan wines. The blends were bottled, given plastic stoppers, and marketed throughout France at a knock-down price. Nearly as much money could be had back on the bottle as the cost of the wine inside. The quantity sold made up for the lack of quality, at least for a time.

rebirth

It is surprising that the growers had not learned the lessons of history: overproduction eventually gave the same results it had in the 1900s – poor returns. This time more radical treatments were needed, and they were inspired from outside the region.

The market for wine was gradually changing: 1959–89 saw the first lasting economic revival in France for nearly a century. Consumers started to look for better quality wine, while others started to switch to beer. Today about half the French nation does not drink wine at all, a far cry from 1926.

While Algeria remained in French hands, the import of African wine had continued. But Algerian independence in the 1960s had important effects. The new Muslim rulers stopped the export of wine to France, so the blenders and dealers in Languedoc had nothing with which to cover up the weaknesses of their own product. Although making and consuming wine in Algeria was not illegal, many of the French growers there felt either not wanted, perhaps even in actual danger, or at best they saw little future for themselves. Many repatriated themselves to France, bringing back with them techniques which they had developed in Africa. A spirit of innovation was about and a generation of growers began to emerge alongside the established bulk-growers, coopératives, and négociants – a new movement which saw that the survival of Languedoc depended on a search for better quality.

At the same time, there was the problem of what to do with the ever-increasing "wine-lake" caused by over-production in France and Italy. Growers were offered grants to dig up inferior rootstocks and either to replant with quality grapes or diversify into other crops. In total, 100,000 hectares of vines disappeared as a result, though you would hardly guess as much from the apparently interminable

left today a tranquil waterway for holiday-makers, the Canal du Midi was once a thriving trade route, carrying wine between the Atlantic and the Mediterranean

landscape of vines which still greets the visitor today. Statutes of Appellation d'Origine Contrôlée (AOC) were decreed throughout the region, setting out the terms on which wines could enjoy protection (and thus the better chance of a market) as long as they complied with certain requirements as to terroir, grape variety, and limitation of production. There had been no controls over production at all in the bad old days.

Vignerons' sons and daughters took themselves off to college and studied winemaking techniques. These days it is rare for a young vigneron to take over from his or her parents, or to acquire a vineyard of his or her own, without technical qualification. The new generation has set new standards as well as teaching its parents new tricks. More and more have left the coopératives, a tendency which looks set to continue into this new century. Every year sees fresh names enter the lists of independent growers.

the structure of the wine trade

Before the First World War, the vineyards had belonged largely to the big landed estates, whose owners would have a manager and workers regularly employed in the vineyards and the *chais*. There were some lesser proprietors who operated similarly but on a smaller scale. The mass of people engaged in the industry were paid workers.

The picture has changed fundamentally. There are still a few large estates, but they are far less important than they used to be. Many of them belong to the coopératives who still dominate the bulk of the production. Some coopératives work to a much higher standard than others. As a general rule the best are to be found in the areas of AOC.

The second half of the last century also saw the growth of a number of big négociants. These may work in different ways. The traditional dealer will buy in wine which has been made by growers who are not members of a coopérative but do not have ageing or bottling facilities of their own; they may even buy in wine from each other or from coopératives. They then blend their wines and either sell them on to other traders, or make them up into blends for supermarkets.

Some négociants have several regular suppliers, perhaps of single varietal wines such as Chardonnay or Viognier, which they either bottle

as they are, or mix with the wines of other growers of the same grape varieties in order to achieve the best blend they can.

Others may have their own domaines, or at least work with independent growers who may or may not have their own *chais*, but who do not mind sacrificing a certain amount of their independence in order to achieve the market which the négociant is able to provide. These are usually the best of the négociants. The names of Skalli Fortant de France, Delta, Bessières, Jeanjean, and Comte Cathare come to mind instantly. They make and sell good wines, but the most characterful wines will nearly always be the single product of an independent grower who makes, bottles, and markets his own wine.

AOC and non-AOC

The French wine authorities have identified areas within Languedoc-Roussillon which have historically made good wines or which have a distinctive terroir which sets the wines apart in style. These are the areas of Appellation d'Origine Contrôlée (AOC). Even within them not all the land qualifies for the right to call itself by the appellation. The parcels which do are also separately identified. AOC winemakers are restricted to the grape varieties which they may use, to the amount of wine which they may legally produce, to its minimum alcoholic content, and the density at which the vines must be planted. This system was initiated nearly a hundred years ago, and was designed to ensure that a bottle of wine labelled X should correspond in style (not necessarily quality) with any other wine called X.

Enquiring spirits have questioned the value of the rules initially set up to protect them. In particular they have been experimenting with grape varieties forbidden by the appellations; not the old high-yielders, but noble varieties such as Cabernet Sauvignon, Merlot, Pinot Noir, Chardonnay, and Sauvignon, varieties which had previously not been grown in quantity in Languedoc. These grapes are today used either to produce varietal wines (i.e. wines which are the product of one single grape variety rather than a blend) and which the French call "*vins de cépage*"; or blended with each other or with the traditional grapes of the region to produce vins de pays or vins de table.

Vins de pays do not qualify for AOC; they may contain non-AOC grape varieties, or come from land outside the AOC areas. They do, however, bear an indication of origin, and will be submitted to a test by tasting. They must also comply with yield limitations, less strict than in areas of AOC, and attain specified alcoholic strength. The choice of permitted grape varieties is larger than in the AOCs. The concept of terroir and compliance with custom are less important. Geographical identification may be by reference to the widest possible area, e.g. Vins de Pays d'Oc; county (e.g. Vin de Pays de l'Hérault); or a smaller zone within a *département*, such as Vin de Pays de la Côte Vermeille.

Vins de table are unregulated and somewhat unpredictable. There are a few good wines, mostly from quality winemakers who take a pride in not being subject to control.

The movement to work outside the appellation rules has been given added impetus by the so-called "flying winemakers", and other outsiders wishing to profit from the climate and cheap land prices, by making *vins de cépage* or vins de pays in the style of the New World – from which most of them have come. The big négociants also make vins de pays of a style more in tune with the requirements of export markets. The coopératives, too, have followed suit.

terroir

This one word carries, for the French, a wealth of associations which makes it almost untranslatable into any other language, summed up in a feeling that a wine has come from one particular place, just as every artist has a unique style which determines the character of his or her work. It is a combination of the kind of soil and subsoil to be found in the vineyard, the way the ground faces, how it is drained, the gradient on which the grapes grow, the micro-climate which it enjoys, all these factors influencing the choice of grape varieties which will succeed there, and the way they are grown and pruned.

Thus there is no single terroir common to any wine region in the South. But there are certain factors which give the area a sense of unity.

The first is geographical. The whole area is sandwiched almost without break between mountains and the Mediterranean. Behind the entire coastline, running from the Camargue to

the Spanish frontier, the vineyards start almost at the water's edge and gradually climb into the mountains until either the geology or the altitude make viticulture impossible.

Climate is another unifying element. The popular picture of hot, uninterrupted sunshine throughout the year is sometimes true. Certainly, the summers are torrid and annual rainfall figures are low everywhere in the region. Winters can be mild but frosts are not unknown, and the occasional downpour is tropically ferocious. The autumns in particular can be stormy and turbulent. The stoney beds of the rivers can be turned instantly into raging torrents, and flooding is frequent. The growers in the Corbières and the Minervois will long remember the terrible floods of the last winter of the old millennium. Generally speaking, however, the reality lives up to the idyll and there are few bad vintages. Some are just better than others.

The most striking feature of the climate is the almost incessant wind. Near Nîmes the Mistral blows from the north, dry and cold. Further west the wind from the Cévennes is called le Tramontane, and is again a drying wind. Toward the Minervois the wind often blows from the northwest and is called the Cers, and in Corbières and Roussillon the Tramontane blows with renewed vigour. These winds are good for the grapes because they dry off any moisture quickly, and so reduce the number of chemical treatments which a grower needs to apply to prevent disease.

The wind from the sea brings moisture: it can shroud the plain in mist on summer mornings, yielding as much water as a good shower. This wind, le Marin, brings rain in spring and autumn.

The grape varieties also lend a kind of unity to the whole of Languedoc-Roussillon and give the key to the general style of wine. Red AOC wines derive from Syrah, Mourvèdre, Grenache, Carignan, and Cinsault. Other kinds are sometimes permitted but rarely seen in practice.

White wines represent only a small proportion of the total production, but the list of white AOC grape varieties is longer than that of the reds, with more variation from one district to another.

For the vins de pays made outside the appellations, the permitted red grapes include Merlot and the two Cabernets (Sauvignon and

Franc), Pinot Noir being planted occasionally in the less torrid areas. The AOC varieties are also permitted, as are Cot (Malbec) and Portan. For rosés, Cinsault is a mainstay everywhere. White counterparts include Chardonnay and Sauvignon of course, but also the increasingly popular Viognier – the grape imported from the cult Rhône vineyards of Condrieu – Chenin, Mauzac, Colombard, Sémillon, and all the varieties appropriate to AOC wines of the area.

All AOC red wines in the region and many whites too are required by law to be a blend of at least two grapes, three in Roussillon. They cannot be *vins de cépage*. Vins de pays may be *vins de cépage* or blends of two or more varieties. In the latter case, the grape variety first mentioned on the label must be the principal ingredient, but the second must not be less than thirty per cent of the *assemblage*.

best vineyard practices

Important, today, is a movement toward organic production, not necessarily in the purest sense of that term, but in recognition of the virtues which it entails. The so-called *culture raisonnée* is a half-way house to strict organic principles, recognizing the superiority of natural fertilizers and composts to chemical ones, and of natural ways of keeping down undesirable insects to the use of chemical insecticides. It has the advantage of leaving the door open to growers to have recourse to bad old practices if otherwise irretrievable disaster overcomes their vineyards.

The tendency is to work the soil by hand rather than machine, thereby properly aerating the upper part of the root system while avoiding the main roots of the plants. The wise vigneron today has learnt the lesson that good wine can come only from small crops of grapes. The smaller the yield the higher the concentration within the fruit. The grower will therefore prune his vines very hard, whether they are grown in *gobelet* form, as is usually the case with Carignan and Grenache, or on a wire, which is the norm for Syrah. Just before grapes start to turn colour, the vigneron carries out a *vendange verte*, by removing and sacrificing all but a few of the best bunches on the plant. It is easy to imagine how much persuasion was required to impose this technique on small producers who were traditionally remunerated only by the quantity of grapes they produced. The grower will also remove some of the leaves round the remaining bunches, while carefully nurturing the foliage of the upper part of the vegetation – the "motor" of the vine – and which ensures a proper feeding of the roots for the following season.

harvesting

Picking has to be by hand if grapes are to be vinified by *macération carbonique*, and the ubiquitous Carignan is frequently processed this way. In quality vineyards the harvesting of other grapes tends also to be manual. Smaller growers can often twist the arms of their friends and relations to pick with them; sometimes they take on students and holiday-makers on an ad hoc basis. Larger producers have teams which they hire, sometimes through Spanish agents who specialize in this eclectic kind of fixing.

The grapes tend to be brought from the vineyard to the *chais* in small rather than larger containers. The use of these small *cagettes* reduces the pressure from the weight of the grapes and ensures that the fruit reaches its destination in perfect condition. Speed is also essential so as to avoid the oxidization of the grape juice on the way. Harvesting is sometimes done at night, or at least as early as possible in the morning, before the heat of the sun increases the risk of oxidization. Fussy growers discard inferior fruit before it has a chance to get into the baskets, and the grapes are further examined on a specially manned table at the entrance to the *chais* where unripe or rotten fruit is eliminated.

winemaking practices

Macération carbonique is no longer just a method of making fruity and quick maturing wines; it has become a sophisticated way of extracting flavours which balance the characteristics of the other grapes in a blend, while at the same time making a wine which is capable of long ageing. It involves hand-harvesting to avoid the grapes being bruised by the machines, because the grapes must go, without their skins being broken, straight into the tanks where they are covered in a layer of carbonic gas. Fermentation is by explosion from within. This technique accentuates fruit flavours particularly in the

Carignan grape, and is sometimes applied to Syrah. *Macération pelliculaire*, as applied to white wines, consists of allowing the grapes to rest with the skins in the *cuve* before fermentation begins. This is carried out under refrigeration and is calculated to develop maximum freshness of fruit. Other wines are fermented in barrel, much in the New World style, and some are allowed a malolactic fermentation to develop richness and complexity, though sometimes at the expense of freshness and fruit.

Temperature control has always been one of the bugbears of winemakers in the South. Inside the *chais*, elaborate systems, some computer-controlled, have been evolved to maintain temperatures at a constant and desired level, ensuring a disciplined and regular vinification. Sometimes this means the introduction of gentle refrigeration in the case of white and rosé wines.

The vinification tanks nowadays tend to be made either of stainless steel or concrete lined with epoxy resin. Some growers are loath to part with their old concrete tanks, which are enjoying a comeback; concrete as a storage medium is less liable to temperature fluctuation than steel. Corresponding improvements have been made in the conditions in which wines are matured and then stored, often, where geological conditions permit, by the construction of underground cellars, the best of them air-conditioned.

oak-ageing

Languedoc-Roussillon has embraced the general fashion of raising at least part of its production in new oak barrels. This is thought to correspond with public demand, as created by the media and pundits. Professional judges tend to promote oaked above non-oaked wines automatically, and so the oaked ones get the medals. The French, particularly, swear by medals, and so it is conventionally believed that there is an inherent merit in oaking wines. Research also shows that younger people and newcomers to wine generally prefer the oaked style.

Largely it is a question of taste whether one prefers oak to no oak, but most growers use new oak for only a small percentage of their production, because it increases the price of wine substantially.

The price of over £300 ($200) for a 225-litre barrel has to be passed on to the consumer, as does the additional labour in overseeing the ageing of wine in so many small containers. Sometimes growers oak their wines because they feel they have to. All the same, there is a reaction against the over-oaking which was common in the 1990s. Many growers will tell you that they seek to avoid the taste of wood in the wine, but value oak for the extra complexity and richness it adds. Certainly it is now common for brand-new oak to be used mainly for white wines, before being passed on in its second and subsequent seasons to the reds.

the wine-lover

Languedoc-Roussillon is producing wine in huge quantities; much of it is mediocre or worse. But such is also the case in Bordeaux and Australia. The emergence of truly fine wines in the closing years of the last century has been indisputable. The problem for the consumer is to sort the good from the bad.

Anglophones, accustomed to the marketing styles of the New World, are especially attracted by *vins de cépage*. The name Chardonnay or Cabernet on a bottle will help sell a wine whether it comes from Australia or from Languedoc. But so many excellent wines from Languedoc are sold under the Appellation d'Origine Contrôlée system (Minervois, Faugères, Banyuls, etc.); these are usually blends. Here the new generation of independent growers often excels.

Many believe that the long-term future of the region lies with the AOC production. For them *vins de cépage* are beginning to look hackneyed. Others, largely supported by the legions of journalists and guide-writers, regard the Appellation system as outdated if not dead. The tension between these two schools of thought is the same as that which lies behind the debate about globalization and terroir, between those who promote the standardization of wine from one region or country to another, and those who believe that wine is not a product like Coca-Cola, and that its excitement lies in its sense of origin, and its unpredictability from one vintage – and even from one bottle – to the next. Why should all bottles of wine marked Merlot taste the same?

In truth these distinctions are unreal. There are only two kinds of wine: good and bad. Even so, this book concentrates on the creativity of the individual grower, whether of AOC wines or of others, which it prefers to the undoubted skill of the blender or the chemist. A real winemaker will inevitably be a person who regards his *métier* as a way of life rather than the production of just another crop. Good wine is a product of passion not the test tube.

price

"Value for money" has become a catchphrase which has sadly come to concentrate more on the money than the value. More often than not "cheapest is best". A Languedoc Merlot priced at £X may be better or worse than a Chilean Merlot priced at £Y. The cheaper may or may not be better, but the average shopper will more likely than not choose it.

At the same time many growers in Languedoc-Roussillon are getting too greedy too soon, profiting from media attention, the medals they have won, or the buzz which those who have a talent for marketing can create with their personalities: but their wine can also be very good. So the question of value for money must be addressed from the point of view of quality as well as price.

left it is a mistake to think that all the Languedoc is flat. Here a grower extolls the virtues of the steep slopes

principal AOC grape varieties

Languedoc-Roussillon is a huge region, but the selection of original grape varieties grown there today – red and white – is relatively small. Many of the traditional Languedoc-Roussillon grapes survive only as a reminder of the region's inglorious past, nowadays overshadowed by their modern rivals.

red varieties

Though some producers cling onto the old red varieties, these have largely been replaced by grapes native to Spain or the Rhône Valley.

syrah is the noble grape from which Hermitage and Côte Rôtie are made. The Australians call it Shiraz. Although it has always been present in Languedoc-Roussillon, until recently comparatively little has been grown. Now it is suddenly fashionable. It is one of the two so-called "*cépages améliorateurs*", considered by the authorities as a necessary antidote to more traditional grapes such as Carignan and Cinsault. Its complex tannins give concentration and structure, deep colour, sometimes a roasted, smokey character, and some finesse. When mature it can suggest game and mushrooms, even burnt rubber or tar. Usually grown on wire with short pruning, Syrah's leaves have five lobes with deep sinuses. The berries are small. It grows less well in excessive heat.

mourvèdre (sometimes called **mataro**), Catalan by birth, is mainstay of the wines of Bandol and contributes pepper and spice flavours. It makes structured, deeply coloured, robust wine, with good acidity. Most often found as a supporting grape, it is not easy to grow and takes time to come to maturity, just as its wine needs ageing. It thrives in only some terrains, needing moisture as well as heat, so is particularly suited to maritime conditions. It is the second "*cépage améliorateur*". Its leaves are round with noticeable teeth and the clusters are quite large.

grenache is the main red grape of the South, absent from few vineyards, though a relative newcomer planted after the phylloxera plague. It gives good fruit and alcohol, though it is low in acidity and oxidizes fast. It lacks colour and tannin too, but is invaluable for blending. It is the backbone of red vins doux naturels in particular, preferring gravelly to limestone soils. Prone to disease, Grenache is often given a mild pre-winter pruning, the serious heavy pruning being deferred until late spring so that the vegetal cycle is delayed until the danger of disease has passed. Usually grown *en gobelet*. The leaves are curly and the lobes pronounced. The grape-clusters are large-ish.

lladoner (also **lledoner**) **pelut** is a close relative of Grenache and is for most purposes interchangeable and not differentiated. It is rather rare today.

carignan is another post-phylloxera Spanish import, suited to poor soils such as schist, and resistant to the strong winds of the South. Dark and alcoholically generous, but tannic and sometimes lacking in fruit and softness, it is generally vinified by *macération carbonique*, a technique which maximizes fruit flavours. It is usually blended, though some growers make a varietal wine from it. The leaves are rather large and curly and the plant is usually grown *en gobelet*. Scorned by the authorities who have spent much energy and money persuading producers to dig it up, Carignan is making a comeback and could even be called fashionable.

cinsau(l)t is another frowned-on grape, although with the longest history of all in the Languedoc. It will give fruity, pleasant, soft wines if yields are kept low and the soil is poor enough. Lighter in colour than any of the foregoing, it is much valued for

making rosé wines, and for moderating the power of Grenache. Cinsault usually has poor ageing potential, though. The powers that be in Paris are trying to reduce its presence but tradition dies hard in the South. The plants are not vigorous and sometimes seem to droop. The leaves are sharply indented and the berries very large.

white varieties

Traditionally sweet, today, producers have adopted new techniques to make dry-style whites, sometimes with varieties imported from other regions.

muscat appears in two forms in the South – "Alexandria", in practice limited to the vins doux naturels of Rivesaltes, and "Petits Grains", found in all the vins doux naturels of Languedoc-Roussillon. There is a fashion for dry Muscat too. Muscat is one of the few wines to taste of grapes. Its leaves have sharp teeth. Petits Grains has small clusters and grows well on chalky soil. Much beloved by birds,

bees, and wasps, it ripens early. It is generally considered finer than Alexandria, which has large bunches and does better on gravelly or acid ground, maturing later.

mauzac is recognizable in the vineyard by the downy-white underside of its leaves, and in the glass by its aromas of apples and pears. Acidity weakens as the grapes mature, so it is sometimes beefed up in Limoux by blending with Chenin and Chardonnay fruit. The leaves are round and rather rough in texture. Mauzac does best where there is some chalk in the soil.

mac(c)abeu (or mac(c)abeo) is another Catalan grape – still important in Spanish sparkling wines – principally to be found no further east than Minervois. The plant is vigorous but easily snapped by strong winds; it makes a surprisingly pale wine, with pronounced floral character when unblended, though sometimes weak in acidity. Maccabeu is

above in the post-phylloxera era, Spanish grape varieties were imported to improve the vineyards

choosy about terrain: it does not like soils that are either too dry or humid. The leaves have long pointed lobes and the bunches and the berries are big.

roussanne is a native of the Rhône Valley, and is a newcomer to Languedoc-Roussillon where it has settled down well. It likes poor stony soils with good exposure to the sun. The wines are fine and complex with flavours of honey, flowers, and apricot. Good acidity and strength ensure that they keep well. The plant is easily recognized by its leaves which have pronounced, almost circular lobes, separated from each other by deep sinuses. Clusters and berries are rather small.

marsanne does not quite enjoy the same status as Roussanne with which it is often blended, but the wines can be good, with some acidity, and attractive bouquet. The plant is vigorous and fertile and needs sharp pruning to limit its yields. The leaves are very rough and have practically no teeth, and the lobes, while distinguishable, have very shallow sinuses. The clusters are large but the berries, which turn deep golden or reddish when fully ripe, are small.

vermentino (also called **rolle**) is probably of Italian or Corsican origin. It is resistant to drought and thrives in poor soils. The juice is pale, sometimes lacking in acidity, but can make well-balanced wines, said to have hawthorn and pear aromas. The leaves have deep sinuses and sharp teeth, and hard pruning is needed to control yield. The bunches and the berries are rather large.

piquepoul blanc is the sole constituent of the increasingly popular Picpoul de Pinet wines, which are dry and fresh, with good fruit. Grown close to the sea in sandy or chalky ground, the grapes make a wine which is perfect with the oysters and mussels of Bouzigues and Sète. The leaves of the plant have five or seven distinct lobes with teeth, and the grape clusters are large. Piquepoul Blanc is also used widely as a supporting variety.

grenache blanc is the white cousin of Grenache Noir. It is very similar except in colour, though it has an earlier cycle. It is well-adapted to drought and wind but likes magnesium in the soil. The grapes can give either sweet or dry wine, the latter being soft and full but sometimes high in acidity and alcohol. Grenache Blanc is the backbone of many a wine from the South. Its other cousin, Grenache Gris, is less well-esteemed, but in good hands can be excellent.

chasan is a modern, early maturing cross between Chardonnay and Listan (better known as Palomino, the sherry grape). Chasan is well adapted to cooler soil, its acidity dropping fast as the grapes come to maturity. It oxidizes fairly quickly but is valuable for its aromatic qualities. It is recognizable in the vineyard by its clearly lobed leaves with deep sinuses and very long teeth. The clusters are very large.

terret is grown chiefly in mid-Languedoc and makes crisp dry wine which can transcend the ordinary in the hands of good growers. Mildly fashionable. The grapes are medium-sized and elliptical, the bunches large, compact, late-ripening, and prone to mildew.

viognier is not a variety yet permitted in AOC areas, but the day must soon come when it will be. Currently all the rage in Languedoc, just as Chardonnay was a few years ago. It needs high density of planting and careful pruning. It is also sensitive to wind. It buds early, so fears spring frosts. The wines are very aromatic and complex, with notes of peach, apricot, and tropical fruits. The grapes are naturally high in sugar, but sometimes lacking in acidity. They need careful vinification to avoid vulgarity and coarseness. Viognier produces small clusters and grapes. The leaves are roughish and curly at the margin.

left an old artistic rendering of a bunch of grapes adds a whimsical note to this attractive and sun-drenched vineyard

bourboulenc (also called **malvoisie** or **tourbat**) is a rustic variety that ripens late and needs warmth. Delicate rather than powerful, the wines are fine, aromatic, and high in alcohol. The plants tend to droop so need pruning and regular tying-in. The leaves have three lobes and are rough in texture. The clusters are large, mildew sensitive, but rot resistant.

clairette is formerly the chief white grape of the Midi, and its presence has been cut by eighty per cent during the last half-century. At its best in the AOC regions bearing its name. It likes dry, shallow, chalky ground. The wines are alcoholic but at times a touch hard. Apple aromas are common. Sweet and dry wines can be made from the grapes. Lack of acidity calls for early drinking. When mature, they are distinguishable by their olive shape.

costières de nîmes

The Costières are on the cultural border between Provence and Languedoc. Geographically they mark the point at which the garrigue and the Cévennes hills behind swing westwards away from the Rhône basin and start to run parallel with the Mediterranean coast. The vineyards rank among the oldest in France.

The area of the Costières is lozenge-shaped, running parallel on one side with the canal linking the Rhône to the port of Sète, and on the other with the A9 motorway. At its southern tip is the ancient port of Saint-Gilles, an embarkation point for the Crusaders in the Middle Ages, near the medieval fortress of Aigues-Mortes. Beyond are the marshy lands of the Camargue, and then the Mediterranean coastline – where vins de pays are made from grapes grown literally on the sand and therefore called *vins de sable*.

The Costières constitute a low-lying plateau between the prehistoric course of the River Rhône – which ran approximately past present-day Nîmes and Montpellier – and the present-day estuary to the south. Nîmes was the first city to be built by the Romans when they expanded their empire by crossing the River Rhône. Its buildings are famous: the Maison Carrée, the vast arena in the centre of the city, and above all the world-famous Port-du-Gard, which used to carry the water supply to the city from the hills beyond.

The countryside round Nîmes is statistically one of the hottest regions in all of France, but the Mediterranean climate is somewhat qualified by the wind. The Mistral can blow hard here, but it quickly clears the sky and dries the vines after summer storms. Further geographical advantage is provided by the thick protective layers of pebbles which prevent the sub-soils from drying out altogether in the summer, enabling vine-roots to plunge deep into the ground. These stones are called "*galets roulés*". They were washed down the Rhône Valley when the Alps burst forth from the earth's heart in prehistoric times.

The local growers claim these stones are the same kind – sometimes coloured red from their iron content – as that which constitutes the vineyards at Châteauneuf-du-Pape. The stones are to be found in various vineyards in the hills north of Nîmes, sometimes on the *causses* above the rivers of the Southwest, but rarely elswhere. They are usually large, and thus have the capacity to retain the heat

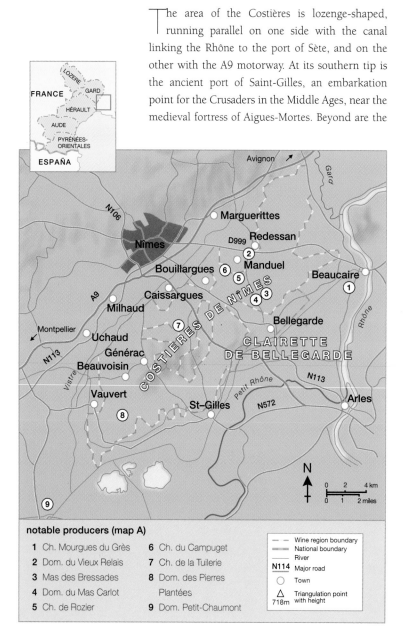

notable producers (map A)

1 Ch. Mourgues du Grès	**6** Ch. du Campuget
2 Dom. du Vieux Relais	**7** Ch. de la Tuilerie
3 Mas des Bressades	**8** Dom. des Pierres
4 Dom. du Mas Carlot	Plantées
5 Ch. de Rozier	**9** Dom. Petit-Chaumont

- – – Wine region boundary
- ▬▬▬ National boundary
- —— River
- N114 Major road
- ○ Town
- △ Triangulation point
- 718m with height

of the midday sun and reflect it back onto the grapes during the night, so hastening the ripening of the fruit. The rain, though it comes seldom, buckets down on the few wet days there are. It quickly sinks through the *galets*, and forms an underground reservoir of damp which prevents the plants burning in the sun.

The wines of Nîmes are among the oldest in France. They quenched the thirst of the Popes during their residence in Avignon in the thirteenth century. They were exported widely from the sixteenth century onwards, and were much admired by early writers such as Philip de Serre and the great Doctor Guyot, who likened them in style with those of the Rhône Valley. After the phylloxera plagues and until the middle of the twentieth century, they suffered a decline, like other wines of the South, because of the production of excessive yields. The renaissance started as recently as 1950 when a certain Philippe Lamour was inspired to lead a return to quality.

Today it is all change. As well as mirroring the improvements elsewhere in the South, a study in depth of the geology and the hydrology of the region has made planning for the future easier. AOC status was granted in 1986 just before the change of name in 1989. The appellation was re-baptised Costières de Nîmes (from being Costières du Gard) to distinguish it from the vins de pays which still carry the name Gard.

Until recently this appellation lagged behind the others, perhaps uncertain whether it belonged with the wines of the Côtes du Rhône or with its neighbours in the Languedoc. Politically and administratively it is part of the former, the vineyards being in the *département* of the Gard. Ask a local grower whether he is a Provençal or a Languedocien, and he will reply that he is Rhodanien (a man from the Rhône Valley). But in so many other respects it fits better into the Languedoc.

There are eighty or so independent producers of whom about a quarter are producing really good wine. And there are seventeen coopératives showing the usual range of variable standards. Only a quarter or so of the planted area of the vineyard is AOC, though the proportion is rising as the quality of the product improves. Investment from outside is also helping to raise the status of the appellation.

The presentation of the wines, certainly the best of them, is today in bottles called "*nîmoises*", not unlike a Burgundy bottle in shape, many of which bear the logo of the city of Nîmes, created by the fashionable designer Philippe Starck.

Among the red grape varieties grown here, Carignan is still the most important although its presence is diminishing gradually in the face of the advances made by Syrah and Grenache. Furthermore, many growers think that Carignan does not really succeed on this terroir. One might expect a greater emphasis on the virtues of Mourvèdre instead, but, despite the nearness of the sea, this moisture-loving grape does not always do well either. What Cinsault there is is usually used for the rosé wines.

On the other hand, the white wines are more faithful to their Languedoc history; Clairette and Maccabeu complement the newcomers Marsanne and Roussanne, while Grenache Blanc is often the most important grape for producing single-varietal wines. However, the production of white wine is a tiny four per cent of the total AOC output.

A small part of the Nîmes appellation also qualifies for the separate appellation Clairette de Bellegarde. Only one Nîmes grower, apparently, makes both these wines, Domaine du Mas Carlot (see page 32).

Today's reds can be drunk young, when they are best served at cellar temperature or even slightly chilled. The better ones will age for a few years and the best reward more cellarage. The rosé wines – a quarter of the total production – are particularly attractive. The whites are floral and fruity, excellent with the local goat's cheeses called *pélardons*. The bulk of the region's production is vins de pays, whether du Gard or simply d'Oc.

special features of costières de nîmes

AOC area 24 communes between Beaucaire, Saint-Gilles, and Vauvert of which 25,000 hectares are classified AOC; 12,000 are presently planted.

the soil consists mostly of unusually large round pebbles, like those found at Châteauneuf-du-Pape.

climate dry; not everywhere suitable for the Mourvèdre grape.

above new wine into old barrels – not in this case

right a modern transport network manages not to spoil the peace and tranquility of traditional properties such as La Tuilerie

notable producers

A6 Jean-Lin Dalle

CHATEAU DU CAMPUGET
(also Château de l'Amarine)
30129 Manduel
☎ 04-66-20-20-15
Ⓦ www.campuget.com A/B

Jean-Lin Dalle's father had been a Flemish lawyer before he bought Campuget and its 160 hectares of vines in 1941. With absolutely no experience of winemaking, he must have been a bold man.

Today, son has succeeded father and added to the family portfolio the thirty-five hectares of nearby Château de l'Amarine. The combined output these days is big business indeed. It is surprising that the wines of Campuget are among the appellation's best, production on this scale rarely going hand in hand with quality.

The old plants which Dalle found here would not, today, dare speak their name. Now the grape varieties and the winemaking are modern, though new wood is sparingly used. The range which most growers would call "Tradition" is labelled Campuget, while the *cuvées prestiges* bear the l'Amarine label. All the wines are made and aged at Campuget.

Of the Campuget range, the white★★ is a pale gold, floral and spicy on the nose, round and lively on the palate, best drunk at cellar temperature and no colder. The fresh and elegant rosé★ suggests raspberries and peaches. The red★★ comes from very ripe fruit (Grenache), and shows cassis (Syrah) and spices (Mourvèdre). There is a special red called "Sommelière"★★ mainly from Syrah, raised in oak, some old some new. It needs keeping.

The red l'Amarine★★, a range which is subtitled "Cuvée de Bernis", is also discreetly oaked. The white★★ has more Marsanne than its Campuget counterpart. This grape gives extra richness to the Grenache Blanc, which comes from very old vines.

A3 Cyril Marès

MAS DES BRESSADES
30129 Manduel
☎ 04-66-01-66-00 B

Cyril is proud of his vinous ancestors. One, a friend of Louis Pasteur, discovered the use of sulphur in treating vines against disease. Another set up a Bordeaux vineyard which is today managed by Cyril's father. Cyril himself will doubtless found a dynasty in the Costières, having married his neighbouring *vigneronne*, the dynamic Nathalie, who runs Domaine de Mas Carlot down the road (q.v.).

Cyril is as contemporary, dapper, and *soigné* as the new underground *cave* which he himself has built to house his precious oak barrels: Cyril is a great lover of new wood. The wines here feel like a personal credo of the maker.

His twenty-two hectares of Rhône pebbles he describes modestly as a small property: it is, when you compare it with, say, Campuget. The Rhône is not far away, so the Mistral blows hard here, windbreaks of spruce and cypress break up the surface of the level plateau and add a few verticals to the horizontal lines of the landscape.

Cyril made his name with a vin de pays, a 70% Cabernet/Syrah blend★, generously aged in oak. It won instant awards and critical acclaim. Better today are the AOC wines: scarcely a year goes by without Cyril collecting at least three medals to put on his walls.

His "Tradition" range, in all three colours, is aged in tank, the "Excellence", red and white, in wood. Cyril makes twice as much red Tradition★★★ as Excellence★★, because it is his best wine: mainly Syrah/Grenache with a touch of Cinsault, brilliantly clear of aspect, it strongly suggests mushrooms, game, and leather: concentrated but not over-extracted, and very long. The Excellence, almost entirely from Syrah, distinctly recalls preserved fruits. The oaking is very discreet: one year in barrels, none of them new.

Cyril prefers a pale style of rosé★★, and his is one of the best in the region: he keeps the Syrah content to 20% because the grape tends to produce deeply coloured juice.

The unoaked white★, largely from Grenache Blanc with 25% Roussanne, is almondy, rather delicate. The very different oaked version★★ is vinified and aged in new wood for five months with frequent *bâtonnage*. The Roussanne (80%) gives a richness to the wine; the wood adds to it the kind of depth which calls out for cheese rather than fish.

A1 Anne et François Collard

CHATEAU MOURGUES DU GRES
30300 Beaucaire
☎ 04-66-59-46-10 A

Agronomist, oenologist, journalist, and finally six months hands-on at Château Lafite-Rothschild. Such is François Collard's curriculum vitae. You would expect his wines to be good; many say they are the best of the appellation.

His thirty-five hectares are close to the Rhône, and aspire to emulate the best of the Rhône Valley's reds. The vines enjoy a perfect southern exposure, bearing out the motto, shared with Prieuré Saint-Jean-de-Bébian, which graces the sundial on the façade of the *mas*: "*sine sole nihil*" (nothing without sunshine).

The estate was once a farm attached to a former convent. Come the Revolution the property was sold off. Collard *père* bought it in 1963 and François, who took over in 1994, has done much to put the wines on the map. Although he has a limited palette of grape varieties, he is always keen to experiment. He will plant Viognier when the rules allow this grape variety into the appellation.

1999 saw the first experiments in whites: one for early drinking★ in the range called "Galets" (80% Grenache Blanc/20% Roussanne) is immediately attractive; the other★★ in the range called "Terre d'Argence" being more serious and having greater length and depth, and in which the proportion of the grape varieties is reversed.

There are two much admired rosés. The first★★, "Galets", is *saigné* from 70% Syrah/30% Grenache, developing a remarkable bouquet of strawberries, and other red fruits which carry through to the palate. The wine is full and surprisingly long. The second ★★ is part of a new top range called "Les Capitelles" and is made from 70% Mourvèdre: *élevage* in oak stresses the complex spices associated with the grape variety.

There are three grand reds. "The Galets"★★, relatively light, fresh and to be drunk on the fruit; the "Terre d'Argence" ★★★ from thirty-five year-old vines. a wine full of concentration and spices which overlay the substantial fruit like a fine sauce; finally "Les Capitelles" (80% Syrah/20% Grenache)★★★, aged for one year in oak barrels, of which half are new, and bottled unfiltered. Les Capitelles is big, rich, and intense, slightly smoky on the nose, with lots of cassis, spices, and a good deal of the garrigue. Biteable, plump, and long in the mouth, this wine is better than many prestigious Rhônes that cost three times the price.

A5 Louis de Belair

CHATEAU DE ROZIER
30129 Manduel
☎ **04-66-01-11-87 A/B**

Would that all bank managers were as kindly as Louis de Belair. Such was his career until 1981 when he inherited this spacious *mas* from a great-aunt, gave up the world of finance, and set about growing asparagus, peaches, and tomatoes. Disappointed by the financial return, he switched to vines. He now has twenty-two hectares, from which he makes only red wine.

He is very proud of his ancestors, one of whom, a certain Mitiffiot, burnt the Turkish fleet at Smyrna in the Middle Ages. Today, Louis is setting the Costières alight with his wines, particularly his red *tête de cuvée* –

right Louis de Belair of Château de Rozier; his bottles are a picture too

called simply Mitiffiot★★★ – matured in mostly old oak. For this his Syrah and Grenache vines yield only twenty-five hectolitres per hectare; the wine is neither filtered nor fined. Firm structure and good round tannins promise long life.

The "Tradition" style red★★ which has more Grenache than Syrah, is unoaked, but full-bodied, spicy, and elegant, with plenty of curranty fruit flavour. A third wine, intended for early drinking, is sold as "Dauphin de Rozier"★.

Louis sells half of his wine *en vrac*, the other half in bottles, sixty per cent of which are exported.

A7 Chantal et Pierre-Yves Comte

CHATEAU DE LA TUILERIE
route de Sainte-Gilles
31000 Nîmes
☎ **04-66-70-07-52**
Ⓦ **www.chateautuilerie.com B**

Chantal Comte has won many commendations. She was Top Exporter of Languedoc-Roussillon 1986, Wine Woman of the Year 1988, and Oenological Person of the Year 1989. Today she presides over many wine-related organizations and charities.

Chantal comes from a creative family. Her mother – an artist who worked successfully in Paris – ornamented the concrete *cuves* in the *chais* in her eightieth year, with saucy drawings of goings-on in the vineyards. More demure drawings on the walls of the tasting-room of the château are themselves also worth a visit.

In addition to their table wines, the Comtes sell a range of elixirs and old rums which they import from connections in Martinique. They also sell the produce of their extensive orchards in which they

left Eric Comte of Château de la Tuilerie contemplates the task of pruning grow no less than eighty different varieties of peach and twenty of apricot.

Tuilerie is a real château, complete with "pepperpot" turret, conveniently close to the Nîmes-Garons airport. There are seventy hectares of vines, which produce a little red vin de pays from Merlot and Cabernet, and white from Viognier; otherwise the production is entirely AOC. Unusually, most of the vines face north, which the Comtes consider gives their grapes a better balance of acid to sugar in this climate.

The old *chais* goes back to the nineteenth century and is still in use, but the family have recently invested in state-of-the-art equipment, including new receiving bays, air-conditioning throughout, a bottling plant which can handle 3,000 bottles an hour, and a new store to hold 600 barrels.

The wines are not blockbusters: the characteristics, even of the oaked wines, are finesse and elegance, cleanness, aromaticity, and expressiveness. The white from old vines★★ has *gras*, but it is not heavy, while the top wine, "Cuvée Eole"★★, is lightened with 20% Rolle, giving a bouquet of old roses.

The red "Vieilles Vignes"★★★ has concentrated spices from the Syrah grape, dark fruits and liquorice on the nose; Madame's son Eric says that in the mouth it is "a wine to get your teeth into, velvety and sumptuous…with subtle hints of cocoa". The Cuvée Eole red★★, given a maceration of up to five weeks in a good year, is "very substantial, with rich mellow tannins giving good structure. Also, mature, oaky vanilla, and spice aromas".

A2 Pierre Bardin

DOMAINE DU VIEUX RELAIS
30129 Redessan
☎ 04-66-20-07-69 A

Monsieur Bardin may be the doyen of the Costières, but his eyes are young, twinkling with mischief. They glow with passion for his old vines. The domaine opens off the Via Domitia, the old Roman road linking

Provence with the west. Today this former staging post is a cross between a village pub and a sub-post office. Monsieur Bardin stands behind the bar-counter with a few bottles and glasses, dispensing his charmingly artisan wines with disarming generosity and Old World charm, as locals come and fill up their *bidons* with his *vrac* wine.

Pierre is proud of his polycultural tradition: he still grows the melons and other fruit which his father and grandfather before him sent to Covent Garden. But his wines are fully worthy to rank beside the more sophisticated productions of his younger colleagues.

For the *vendange* he gets help; otherwise he and his wife do all the work with just a little extra assistance at pruning-time. It is a hard life for veteran winemakers, but such passionate ones as these bear out the adage that a good grower never really retires.

Pierre makes just two red wines. The first red ★★, mainly Syrah and Grenache with just a little Carignan, is everything that a grower's basic wine should be: immediately attractive but with a depth and a potential for ageing which is unusual.

A more serious second red★★★ is Mourvèdre based, with Grenache to make up the complement. It is a splendidly deep and complex wine which shows off the character of Mourvèdre extremely well.

other good costières growers

Madame Jacqueline Boyer
Château Beaubois,
Franquevaux,
30640 Beauvoisin
☎ 04-66-73-30-59

Bertrand du Tremblay
Domaine de Belle Coste,
30132 Caissargues
☎ 04-66-20-26-48

SCEA Castillon et fils
Château de l'Ermitage,
30800 Saint-Gilles
☎ 04-66-87-04-49

GAEC Grande Cassagne
Château Grande Cassagne,
30800 Saint-Gilles
☎ 04-66-87-32-90 or
04-66-87-07-29

Denis Fournier
Domaine du Haut Plateau,
30129 Manduel
☎ 04-66-20-31-78

Monsieur Grangette
Domaine Haute Cassagne,
route de Générac,
30800 Saint-Gilles
☎ 04-66-87-18-44

Olivier Gibelin
Château Mas Neuf des Costières,
Gallician, 30600 Vauvert
☎ 04-66-73-33-23

EARL Roger Gassier
Château de Nages,
30132 Caissargues
☎ 04-66-38-44-20

SCEA Cep de Diane
Château d'Or et de Guèle,
Domaine de la Petite Cassagne,
30800 Saint-Gilles
☎ 04-66-87-39-11

Roger, Françoise, et Annie Molinier
Château Roubaud, Gallician,
30600 Vauvert
☎ 04-66-73-30-64

Guy de Mercurio
Château Saint-Cyrgues,
30800 Saint-Gilles
☎ 04-66-87-31-72

Guilhem et Hervé Durand
Château des Tourelles,
4294 route de Bellegarde,
30300 Beaucaire
☎ 04-66-59-19-72

Dominique Ricome
Château Valcombe,
30510 Générac
☎ 04-66-01-32-20

Cos de la Belle
30800 Saint-Gilles
☎ 04-66-81-45-83
(Vins de Pays du Gard)

(*See also* Roc d'Anglade, Côteaux du Languedoc, page 41.)

clairette de bellegarde AOC

This is one of the last outposts of the Clairette grape, here limited to three small areas to the north of the village of Bellegarde, not far from Saint-Gilles. No other grape variety may be used in making Clairette de Bellegarde.

There are four coopératives but seemingly only one independent producer, Nathalie Blanc-Marès, though she says that the Mayor of Bellegarde is about to have a go at making this rare wine too.

A4 Nathalie Blanc-Marès

DOMAINE DU MAS CARLOT
30127 Bellegarde
☎ 04-66-01-11-83 **B**

Nathalie's Clairette is an attractive straw colour, with a bouquet dominated by lime and orange blossom. It is big and generous on the palate with a very more-ish touch of bitterness about it. Aromatic and lively in character with a hint of the wild fennel which grows everywhere here. It is dry but feels rich.

Perhaps this is why Nathalie keeps her Clairette quite apart from the mainstream of her production, as if it was made from a different fruit, like the olives which she also grows; or as if it were the equivalent of Grandma's parsnip wine. Her publicity material does not mention Clairette, nor does the Press take any notice of it although she wins medals for it regularly. Nevertheless three-quarters of her white wine production is Clairette.

Nathalie's father, Paul Blanc, from whom she took over in 1986 has given his name to the AOC Costières wines, which are lightly oaked. The Mas Carlot range is not. All the wines here would qualify as AOC, but

Nathalie prefers to market some as vins de pays under the domaine rather than the family name, because her customers like to see the name of the grape on the label, something which is forbidden under AOC rules. The styles of the two ranges also remain distinct.

The vins de pays go for freshness and aromatics, for early drinking. The AOC wines are more substantial: the white is vinified in barrel but aged in tank. The wood for it is new and is then passed onto the red wines. These are round, but have good attack and the right kind of tannins, some acidity and a good finish. Altogether ★★ quality.

vin de pays des sables du golfe de lion

A9 GAEC Bruel

DOMAINE DU PETIT-CHAUMONT
30220 Aigues-Mortes
☎ 04-66-53-60-63 **A**

You do not have to be an agronomist, an engineer, a chemist, a do-it-yourself-builder, and a winemaker all in one to appreciate a visit to Monsieur Bruel; but it certainly helps. After crash-courses in land-drainage, the recycling of carbonic gas, time-and-motion techniques in the *cave*, as well as a guided tour through the minefields of local wine-politics, he will reward visitors with his delicious vins de pays. For all this, allow plenty of time.

Alain Bruel is certainly the best known of all the producers of vins de sables; he spends his time with vines literally grown in the same sand as you will find on the nearby beaches of the Camargue. The phylloxera bug never got through the sand to attack the vine roots in this region, many of which survived into old age – certainly until most of the other vineyards were replanted with respectable phylloxera-resistant grape varieties.

Alain's father was in the wine business in Algeria before he come back to mainland France in 1962. Alain himself has travelled

all over the world and considers his main claim to fame to be the part he played in introducing harvesting machines to Australia and California.

On their return from Algeria, the Bruels bought this estate of 200 hectares. Today, 120 are planted with vines, making this a big enough vineyard to contain just about every grape variety in the book, from Alicante to Tempranillo, Clairette to Cabernet Sauvignon, all the result of massive reorganization between 1973 and 1985.

Visitors can expect to be offered anything and everything, because the permutations and combinations of Alain's different blends are infinite. On the other hand, you may enjoy a pure Chardonnay★★, clean, dry, and not too fat, with just a touch of butter and not over alcoholic; or perhaps a 100% Alicante, partly vinified like a white wine, which gives it a touch of the acidity often lacking in this sometimes dull grape.

Blends might include a 70% Clairette★★ with the balance made up equally of Sauvignon Blanc and Chardonnay, a wine specially designed to accompany dishes of fish in sauce; or an oaked mix of Syrah, Merlot, and Cabernet Sauvignon straight from the cask. All highly fascinating and amazingly unpredictable.

vin de table

A8 Gilles Perraudin

DOMAINE DES PIERRES PLANTEES
Chemin des Salines
30600 Vauvert
☎ 04-66-73-17-00 **B/C**

Gilles is a distinguished architect, a lecturer at Montpellier University, with his private practice based at this vineyard address. His second passion is wine, especially wine made from the Viognier grape.

This terroir, situated on a raised plateau (costière) east of Vauvert and overlooking the Camargue, has just the right amount of clay to suit the grape, and the night mists which

rise from the sea refresh the stones in the soil as well as the vines. The grapes here develop just the right amount of the acidity and vivacity that are needed to counterbalance the fatness and fruit character that are commonly found in Viognier grown at this latitude.

In 1991, when Gilles arrived here, there was nothing except a few hectares of all the wrong grapes. His architectural skill was put to building a combined *chais/* architectural office. Somehow he came by a few old stones from the Pont du Gard and these, supplemented by many more from a local quarry, served as an inspiration for a unique stucture combining the geometry of Corbusier with the rectangles of Thebes – some have been likened the inner cloister to Agamemnon's tomb!

Perraudin has three-and-a-half hectares under cultivation, with another two-and-a-half

waiting to be planted. His beloved Viognier plants were grafted for him in Condrieu.

He also has a little Chardonnay and Sauvignon Blanc. Gilles makes just two *cuvées*. One called by the old name of the vineyard, "Sud de la Cabane Magnan"★★★, made to keep, like Condrieu itself. This is unusual for a white wine from so far south. The other is called after the present name of the domaine★★★ and is meant for earlier drinking.

The *assemblages* each year depend on the performance of the unpredictable Viognier. It always dominates, however it must be said that the hallmarks of these wines are finesse and elegance.

Vinification is partly in steel, partly in barrique; in the latter case there is the now-common technique of *bâtonnage*, but no malolactic fermentation or filtration. For the most part the steel tanks hold only

above Gilles Perraudin, an architect, specialises in wine from the Viognier grape

forty hectolitres, and there are a dozen or so barrels each containing about 400 litres.

This means that production is on a miniature scale and to the very highest of standards, so as to emulate as far as possible the standards of perfection inspired by Château Grillet in Condrieu, whose wines are the apotheosis of the viognier grape.

With two and half hectares still awaiting their destiny, will Perraudin plant more Viognier, or will he perhaps experiment with some Syrah, that other great grape from the Northern Rhône?

Meanwhile this domaine remains a benchmark for Viognier wines in the Languedoc-Roussillon. More's the pity that their production is small and the are wines difficult to find.

coteaux du languedoc

Certainly the most diffuse and varied appellation of Languedoc-Roussillon, Coteaux du Languedoc is an amalgam of vastly differing landscapes and terroirs; the wines made there are equally diverse in style. But in each region there is bound to be a handful of growers succeeding in making some of the best wines of the South.

The identification of the various terroirs and *climats* listed opposite stems from the heterogeneous nature of this appellation. The Coteaux du Languedoc is not so much an identifiable vineyard as a mixture of various Southern wine-styles; the producers feel that each component district has its own typical character – or *typicité*. In the Pic Saint-Loup, for example, growers believe rightly that they have one of the most privileged terroirs in the South; they do not want their wines lumped together with those of others, who, with all the skill in the world, are never going to obtain the quality possible on the best terroirs.

On the other hand, over-hierarchization confuses the consumer, and makes the job of marketing the wines of Languedoc that much harder, which explains why some of the larger négociants would like to see one single appellation in the South: "Languedoc" pure and simple.

The French wine authorities seem to be listening to both points of view, because consideration is being given to amalgamating many of the smaller terroirs and *climats* under larger groupings – thus, for example, Grès de Montpellier will probably include Saint-Christol, Vérargues, La Méjanelle, Saint-Drézéry, and Saint-Georges-d'Orques. But this is the kind of compromise which may end up pleasing no-one.

Those unfamiliar with the region are therefore best advised to concentrate on the names of the best producers, and not to worry whether growers are producing wine under this or that terroir or *climat*. Some excellent growers are outside the terroirs altogether. Furthermore, some of the very best négociants have been concentrating on varietal wines, often from grapes forbidden to appellation wines, and they tend not to be concerned with the niceties of origin. The centre of the appellation Coteaux du Languedoc is historically the home of these blenders and dealers, where they have continued to benefit from modern transport systems. It should not be thought that, although this book concentrates on independent producers, all wines from bulk makers are poor. It is just that many of them lack personality or character; taste them blind and they could often come from California or Australia, and this, it has to be said, is why they strike a chord with many consumers.

Despite the overall size of Coteaux du Languedoc, the average area of a landholding under vine is a mere three hectares, which explains why many producers grow other crops as well as grapes, why some of them belong to one of the ninety-four coopératives, and why some sell *en négoce* either to the big blenders or other bulk merchants. For these growers, grapes tend to be just one crop, much like the others they produce. The old belief that the more grapes you can produce, the more money you can earn, has not yet completely died out. Growers are still producing grapes for vins de pays at the rate of eighty hectolitres to the hectare and more, compared with average yields of half that for appellation wines.

The more forward-looking coopératives are trying to instigate positive change: they are starting to grade the prices they pay their members according to the improvements resulting from lower-yields, but all too often quantity still rules the roost at the expense of quality.

The result is that the poorer bulk wines of the South are impossible to sell at anything but a knockdown price, a state of affairs aggravated by

the competition from New World countries such as Chile, where the cost of production is so much less, and the quality even at basic level can be high. This explains the intermittent eruption of violence by small-time growers against the bulk-négociants and dealers who are accused of flooding the market with cheap imports and not supporting the indigenous product. In the absence of a market for these bottom-level wines, there is little case for continued subsidy, but the immediate removal of all government and European support for the growers of the Midi would result in a terrible hardship and severe social problems.

Perhaps the answer is to go back to the days before the wine-boom of the nineteenth-century, when the plains of Languedoc were producing crops other than wine. The financing of the introduction of modern irrigation would perhaps enable the hack-growers to turn to other cultures like their fellow-countrymen in the Roussillon, where fruit-orchards have replaced the vineyards in the plains, and the vines are grown in the terrain which suits them best – on the higher ground in the foothills of the mountains.

The Coteaux du Languedoc stretch from the Costières de Nîmes to the east as far as Narbonne

special features of coteaux du languedoc

the wines red (73%), rosé (14%), and white (13%).

AOC area 157 communes in Hérault and Aude not covered by other appellations, but not including all areas where wines are grown. Outside the appellation area, the vins de pays come into their own. Inside it the vins de pays often take second place.

terroirs and climats within the AOC area, 17 zones have been identified as special, either because of their terroir or the climate, and may use the name on their wines. Picpoul de Pinet is a separate AOC for white wines only.

extent about 8,400 hectares are under vine in the coteaux.

growers there are 2,800 or so producers. Of these 415 are independent, bottling and marketing at least some of their wine.

annual production about 380,000 hectolitres (the equivalent of 50 million bottles), which, after Corbières, makes CL the largest appellation of the south.

yield Average is 45/50 hectolitres to the hectare.

cartagène an apéritif made from unfermented grape juice, fortified with eau-de-vie (rather after the style of Pineau de Charentes), is an old regional tradition and often appears on restaurant wine lists. Manufacture is mostly artisanal.

the 9 terroirs

Saint-Christol
Vérargues
Saint-Drézéry
La Méjanelle
Saint-Georges-d'Orques
Montpeyroux
Saint-Saturnin
Cabrières
Quatourze

the 8 climats

Terre de Sommières
Grès de Montpellier
Pic Saint-Loup
Terrasses du Larzac
Picpoul de Pinet
La Clape
Terrasses de Béziers
Pézenas

the west. The AOC includes wines grown just below the limestone *causses* of the Massif Central, some grown in the foothills of the Cévennes, and others grown almost on the beaches of the Mediterranean. Not all of the vineyard land comprised in this area, however, qualifies for AOC status; certain areas only have been admitted, and the remainder of the growers are obliged to market their wines as vins de pays or vins de table. Generalization becomes impossible except in the very widest terms.

The wines from the higher ground are apt to have more finesse and complexity than those made on the plains. Many of the special zones listed above are in the hills. A little lower down, the wines are often said to borrow aroma and flavour from the "garrigue" – the heathlands between mountain and sea on which little will grow except wild thyme, bay, rosemary, fennel, dill, and other wild herbs; sometimes the wines carry a suggestion of saffron, aniseed, cloves, juniper berries, and, above all liquorice. On the plains, and nearer to the Mediterranean, the wines tend to become rather more ordinary, except in the areas specially identified below.

The geology is varied. In general there is a lot of schist or shale in the hills, chalk on the garrigue, and a deal of gravelly chalk washed down by former tributary branches of the Rhône closer to the coast.

The famous quintet of red wine grapes being the only ones to be found generally, and in some areas there is a minimum percentage covering Syrah, Mourvèdre, and Grenache (either singly or in any combination) – ninety per cent in Pic Saint-Loup and seventy per cent in La Clape for example – reducing the presence of Carignan and Cinsault in these wines to a minimum. The development of the growth of Syrah, Mourvèdre, and Grenache grapes (for red wines) has been phenomenal. These are varieties which are thought to produce wines to suit the modern taste and today's market. Their adoption has often been at the expense of traditional Languedoc varieties such as Carignan and Cinsault, which some growers are beginning to regret that they have been persuaded to dig up.

On the other hand, experiments are under way to marry the different *cépages* to different terroirs. Trials are going ahead with the Carignan grape, perhaps in response to certain growers who value it highly and do not like to see it giving place to other New World varieties. Perhaps this is a sop thrown out to them as the authorities pursue in parallel a hard line in favour of the so-called "*cépages améliorateurs*".

The variety of wines to be found within the Coteaux is infinite. There are wines beefy and masculine, or round and soft, well-structured, or simply fruity and lively. Every district has a wine to suit its character.

Above all other wine-growing areas, this is one to discover with little haste and much patience. An agreeable exploration can be made via the Canal du Midi, once a busy highway for the wine-dealers, but today a watery idyll for those seeking the slow life and a holiday of relaxation on a barge. There is always the prospect of making your own exciting discoveries, of wines not listed in the magazines, newspapers, or books – even this one – and there are several waterside *auberges* where interesting local bottles can usually be found.

Where the Authorities have excluded land from the appellation, the growers are constrained to call their wines vins de pays or vins de table. Sometimes these are made from the traditional grapes of the South, sometimes from imported noble varieties, sometimes a blend of the two styles. Outside the Appellation a grower is free to decide which of these options to follow.

These wines may well be of a standard equal to many appellation wines. Sometimes, as in Aniane for example, micro-terroirs may call for grape varieties which are not permitted in appellation wines, even if the vineyard itself is within a qualifying area. In the appellation areas themselves, however, growers tend to make vins de pays as a way of turning out a quick euro – these are wines that are intended to be drunk young, on their fruit, and as such they usually tend to be a deal cheaper than the more thoughtfully made appellation wines from the same growers.

Of all the thousands of wines to choose from in this far-flung appellation, those listed below – representing all price-levels – should provide benchmarks for quality, whether they be appellation wines, vins de pays, or vins de table.

notable producers (map B)

1	Roc d'Anglade	**18**	Dom. de Mortiès	**34**	Mas des Brousses	**51**	Le Prieuré de Saint-Jean-de-Bébian
2	Dom. Arnal	**19**	Ch. de l'Engarran	**35**	Dom. des Conquêtes	**52**	Ch. Saint-André
3	Dom. de la Croix-Saint-Roch	**20**	Dom. Henry	**36**	La Grange des Pères	**53**	Dom. Deshenrys
4	Ch. de la Devèze	**21**	Dom. de la Prose	**37**	Mas de Daumas Gassac	**54**	Dom. Mont Rose
5	Dom. de la Coste	**22**	Dom. Belles Pierres	**38**	Dom. de Granoupiac	**55**	Dom. La Condamine l'Evêque
6	Cellier du Mas Montel	**23**	Dom. de la Capelle	**39**	Dom. Font Caude	**56**	Dom. de l'Arjolle
7	Ch. Puech-Haut	**24**	Terre Mégère	**40**	Dom. de l'Aiguelière	**57**	Dom. La Croix-Belle
8	Dom. Saint-Jean de l'Arbousier	**25**	Le Mas d'Aimé	**41**	Dom. Saint-Andrieu	**58**	Les Chemins de Bassac
9	Dom. de Clavel	**26**	Ch. de la Peyrade	**42**	Dom. d'Aupilhac	**59**	Dom. de la Colombette
10	Ch. de Flaugergues	**27**	Dom. Peyre Rose	**43**	Dom. Les Thérons	**60**	Dom. de Raissac
11	Ch. de l'Euzière	**28**	Abbaye de Valmagne	**44**	Ch. de Jonquières	**61**	Dom. Perdiguier
12	Ch. La Roque	**29**	Mas Saint-Laurent	**45**	Mas Cal Demoura	**62**	Dom. d'Espagnac
13	Clos Marie	**30**	Dom. Morin-Langaran	**46**	Mas Jullien	**63**	Ch. Le Thou
14	Ch. de Cazeneuve	**31**	Dom. Félines-Jourdan	**47**	Mas des Chimères	**64**	Dom. du Nouveau Monde
15	Ermitage du Pic Saint-Loup	**32**	Vignobles Montfreux de Fages	**48**	Dom. du Temple		
16	Mas Bruguière	**33**	Cuvée Ludovic Gaujal	**49**	Dom. Fontedicto		
17	Dom. de l'Hortus			**50**	Dom. La Croix-Vanel		

notable producers

terre de sommières

This hilly area to the north-east of Montpellier is partly on chalk mixed with clay, partly also on the large round pebbles found in the Costières de Nîmes and the Rhône Valley.

B2 Henri et Frédéric Arnal

DOMAINE ARNAL
251 Chemin des Aires
30980 Langlade
☎ 04-66-81-31-37 B

The Arnal family have been here since 1910. Henri took over in 1985 and was joined ten years later by his brother Frédéric. Between them they have enlarged the vineyard by digging up garrigue on the higher ground above the village and levelling the soil. Today they have thirty-five hectares on very stoney ground.

The Arnal specialty is the Mourvèdre grape, which suits the local terroir very well. Mourvèdre is much prized by those who can grow it, and the Arnals cannot grow enough. At 150 metres (500 feet) or so their vineyards get just enough rain and moisture from the sea to balance the fierce summer heat.

As part of the topographical division of Coteaux du Languedoc, the Arnals are lobbying to get Langlade designated as a special terroir. They hope that the rules will ensure that at least forty or fifty per cent of the encépagement in every vineyard using the Langlade name consists of Mourvèdre. There are 650 hectares of AOC vines in Langlade, so the project sounds interesting.

If other growers can make such good wines with their Mourvèdre as the Arnals, Langlade is going to put itself on the map with a splash. Their red wine★★ has just 20% Syrah to balance the Mourvèdre, and the result can be wonderfully spicy, deep, and flavoursome, while cask samples promise extraordinarily sweet and forward fruit for future bottles.

The use of oak here is very careful. The Arnals plan gradually to phase out the normal 225-litre barrels and replace them with demi-muids therefore proportionally reducing the surface area of wood in contact with the wine. Even today, no new barrels are used for the red wine, only those which have already seen one or more wines, usually the domaine's own white★ from Roussanne – a wine which has some citrus flavours and what the French call *bonbons anglais* (pear drops).

Twenty-two of the thirty-five hectares enjoy appellation status; the other thirteen produce a delightful vin de pays★ for early drinking.

B6 Dominique et Jean-Philippe Granier

CELLIER DU MAS MONTEL
Aspères
30250 Sommières
☎ 04-66-80-01-21 B

Like most of the *mas* in the area, Montel was formerly a farm belonging to the church – in this case the Prieuré d'Aspères, in turn attached to the abbey of Psalmodi. The original cellar here can trace itself back to the eighth century. Marcel Granier bought the property in 1945 with its present *cave* which was previously an olive-mill; with it came the magnificent battery of old *foudres* which are still used to age the red wines of today. They can hold nearly 300,000 litres.

When the parcels of land were identified for inclusion in the appellation, the vineyards of this property were somehow omitted, and it took the Graniers until 1997 to have this rectified by the authorities. Today they have fifty-five hectares of which twenty are AOC and are sold as Mas Granier, while the remaining thirty-five produce vins de pays under the name of Mas Montel. The lower ground around the *mas* is chalky clay, while on the wild hillsides behind, which command wonderful views west to the sea, the ground is much stonier and the best quality AOC grapes are grown.

Marcel Granier celebrated being mayor of Aspères for forty years in 2001, when he retired, having already handed over the vineyards to his two sons. Jean-Philippe is a highly respected consultant oenologist. Not surprisingly, he is in charge of the production, while his brother Dominique, a qualified economist, looks after the promotion, sales, and business side: "*faire du vin c'est bien, le faire connaître c'est mieux,*" he says, as he conducts a tasting round a splendid log fire in the spacious office-cum-sitting-room.

The *encépagement* is what you would expect for the red wines; and for the whites Grenache Blanc and Roussanne for the AOC wines, but also some Carignan Blanc (rare), Muscat, and Chardonnay. The red grapes are fermented in tanks lined with glazed bricks, the whites more conventionally in enamelled *cuves*.

Of the two red vins de pays, the first called "Psalmodi"★ is a blend of Merlot, Grenache, and Syrah, vinified traditionally for twelve days in tank, and which results in an excellent early and easy drinking style. The "Cuvée Jéricho"★★ is an altogether more serious wine, a modern Languedoc blend of 80% Syrah-20%-Grenache, from low-yielding vines, vinified by *macération carbonique* and aged in the old *foudres* for eighteen months.

The AOC white called "Les Marnes"★★ made from Viognier and Grenache Blanc grapes, is partly oak-aged. There are two AOC reds, both given a *cuvaison* of twenty-two days: the "Tradition"★★★ aged in the *foudres*, the other, "Les Grès"★★★, aged in small Allier-oak barrels and demi-muids for sixteen months. These red wines are real keepers, particularly the Allier-oaked wine. Both have pronounced perfumes of the surrounding garrigue, good structure, fine tannins, rich fruit, and great length. Both are outstanding.

B1 SCEA Pédréno et Rostaing

ROC D'ANGLADE
30980 Langlade
☎ 04-66-81-45-83 D

"They're from the hand of a great winemaker", says Rémy Pédréno's English distributor of these wines. He would say that of course, but for once the words are true.

Rémy Pédréno's first vintage at Langlade, where he rents his six hectares of vines and borrows his *chais d'élevage* from friends, was as recently as 1999. The promise of that first effort is fully fulfilled in his more recent wine, of which he makes only one version, which is red★★★, and usually blends two-thirds Syrah to one-third Grenache. If you tell him that his Syrah is like a Côte Rôtie, you will not be the first to do so, and you could also tell him his Grenache might be mistaken for a fine old burgundy, such is its finesse and elegance. Either way he will give you one of his beatific smiles.

Rémy's rapid arrival at the top of the Languedoc tree is all the more surprising given that his family had no vines, nor had he had any training in oenology or winemaking – although he is now studying for a degree so that he can qualify for planting rights, which are strictly controlled so as to limit over-production of wine. Rémy also has vines near Saint-Gilles, where his first efforts (one lonely barrique) were made from Syrah in 1996. five barriques were made in 1997, and twenty-five in 1998, by which time he had managed to attract the attention of the French press. *Vins de garage* indeed!

The work in the vineyards is copybook organic, though Rémy does not find it necessary to sign up formally to these tenets. Yields average only twenty-three hectolitres to the hectare. Grape selection is done on the vine, one picker managing to bring in only 300 kilos a day. The grapes are taken to the *cave* in tiny *cagettes* each holding only thirteen kilos of grapes each. This prevents bruising on the way.

above there is nothing foxy about the wines of the Granier family at Mas Montel

There is no destalking, and *cuvaisons* may last anything between two and five weeks, depending on the level of extraction required and the vintage. The wine is put into barrel two days after the *cuvaison* is finished; 80% of the barrels have already seen one wine, while 20% are brand new, and highly toasted at that. Nevertheless the wood, judging by the taste of the final *assemblage*, is very discreetly handled.

This wine fully justifies its high praise and price. Rémy's future is both bright and certain.

other good sommières growers

Christian Faure
Domaine Faurmarie,
route de Sommières,
34160 Galargues
S 04-67-86-94-25

saint-christol

This small terroir is north-east of Montpellier. It is likely to be absorbed into the proposed regrouping called Grès de Montpellier.

B5 Elisabeth et Luc Moynier

DOMAINE DE LA COSTE
34400 Saint-Christol
☎ 04-67-86-02-10 A

"Coste" is the local word for the ubiquitous round stones, the same as those found in the Costières. Here there is also a deal of rather scruffy looking red sandstone. Together these provide an ideal terroir for the Mourvèdre for which the Moyniers are fanatics. The soil is so poor here that the yields are never anything but tiny, and this obviates the necessity for *vendanges vertes* during the summer. Furthermore, the grapes are usually so ripe that destalking becomes unnecessary because there is no greenness or woodiness to the *rafle*.

Luc Moynier is a mustachioed giant, and he was largely responsible for the designation of the special terroir of Saint-Christol. He is unexpectedly quiet and modest, almost apologizing for the excellent quality of his characterful wines. He is also generous to a fault with visitors, showing them bottle after bottle of all the vintages and *cuvées* he can lay his hands on, as well as samples from the cask and tank. This will be a long visit.

The property has been in the family for several generations and Luc has been winning medals since 1984. There are seventy-five hectares of vines of which thirty are AOC. No white wine is made at all. He has the usual red grapes except Carignan. Fifteen per cent of production is rosé, of which he makes two kinds: a salmon-pink Mourvèdre ★★ which has depth and is excellent, and a more floral Grenache-Cinsault blend★ which lovers of the *bonbons anglais* style will appreciate.

left a rare centenarian cork tree ages gracefully beside a road in the Languedoc

The vins de pays are sold under the name "Domaine des Brus", and the red varietal Merlot★★ is good. Of the AOC reds, there can be as many as four in any year, depending on the *assemblages* which Luc chooses to make. A wine which any other maker might call "Tradition"★★ may mix all the Languedoc grapes, with plenty of Mourvèdre. Another called "Cuvée Sélectionnée"★ could be nearly all Syrah with just a little Grenache, and will probably need keeping. At four years old it still shows strong tannins, but plenty of fruit to see them off in another year or two. The "Cuvée Prestige"★★ brings the Mourvèdre to the fore again, with just a little Syrah to moderate it, spicy as you would expect, but with a strong presence of wild violets. This wine, too, needs time, the 1997 showing a little ahead of the 1996 at the same tasting. The star of the show is Luc's pure Mourvèdre which he calls "Merlette"★★★. Quite surprisingly it seems to soften out and become round and friendly much earlier than Luc's other wines. Luc is not interested in new wood.

vérargues

This is another cru of the Coteaux to the northeast of Montpellier, likely to be absorbed into Grès de Montpellier. The name is little used in practice today.

B4 Les Héritiers Navarro

CHATEAU DE LA DEVEZE
34400 Vérargues
☎ 04-67-86-00-47 B

It is surprising how the sudden demise of a paterfamilias can cause such a hiccough in the fortunes of a quality vineyard. Louis Navarro's sudden death in 1999 has thrown the affairs of this beautiful estate into sudden uncertainty. French inheritances are notoriously complicated and long-winded, and this one may run longer than the average; Madame Navarro meanwhile will find it hard to make the investment necessary to maintain the vineyards, let alone replace the twenty-two hectares or so which had recently been dug up. In the immediate term, it looks as if Laurent Gourdon, with experience already of running a similar estate in Provence, will be a safe pair of hands as *régisseur*. He has no illusions about the tasks ahead, but has the quiet determination of one who is prepared to accept difficult challenges.

Devèze has always managed to hold its place at the head of wines of this region north of Montpellier. No doubt it will continue to do so despite the appearance of flashier newcomers, literally on the horizon. Of the seventy-eight hectares currently in production sixteen are given over to the Muscat grape, from which a good Muscat de Lunel★ is made. Fourteen hectares of Merlot and Cabernet are planted in the richer soils of the dips between the folds in the hills. These go to make attractive vins de pays. There is an irresistible Cinsault-based rosé★, light, pale and delicate with just a touch of Grenache. But it is the AOC red wines on which the Devèze reputation rests. Old Carignan goes into the "Tradition"★★, along with 50% Syrah and 20% Grenache to make a fresh, fruity, and immediately attractive wine. An oaked version★★ omits the Carignan, and the Syrah outweighs the Grenache 3:1. The bunches are selected on the vines so as to eliminate all but the best. The wine is given a *cuvaison* of about 25 days and the wood is renewed on a three-year cycle. It is not at all prominent. Nor is it in a one-off wine called "Cuvée 2000"★★★, a keeper made in 1998 to honour the Millennium. It is pure Syrah aged entirely in new oak, and the result is surprisingly unwoody.

other good vérargues growers

Jean Clave
Mas les Catalognes,
4 place de la Champagne, 34670 Saint-Brès
☎ 04-67-70-27-76

(*See also* La Croix Saint-Roch, page 180.)

saint-drézery

Another candidate for the Montpellier amalgam. Most producers consider the present name unattractive commercially.

B7 Gérard Bru

CHATEAU PUECH-HAUT
34160 Saint-Drézery
☎ 04-67-86-94-07 C

Approaching down the long drive, lined on both sides with vines, it is unbelievable that, as recently as 1984, there was nothing here but scrub and a few olive-trees. Today, Puech-Haut is one of the finest estates in Languedoc, and its wines among the best the region produces.

The owner is as unusual as the domaine. At the tender age of twenty-five he had already established an exceptionally successful business and made a substantial personal fortune.

Blood is thicker than water, and wine is thicker than both. Perhaps his childhood in the Minervois, where his father had some vines, persuaded Gérard that he should reinvest in wine the fruits of his early retirement. In the 1980s he bought his first twenty-five hectares at Saint-Drézery, having seen its potential: no house, no *cave*, no plant. Gérard Bru started this domaine completely from scratch.

Gérard has achieved his ambition of having a hundred hectares under vine, all *dans un seul tenant*, surrounding the house. He built an elegant home – or rather had a pretty Montpellier town house dismantled and re-erected here stone by stone – a *cave* too, and one of the finest state-of-the-art wineries (no other word will do) in the Languedoc, of which even the owner of a *cru classé* in Bordeaux would be proud.

Although there is nothing ostentatious about Gérard Bru himself, the sight of so much gleaming stainless steel, the battery of purpose-built modern *foudres*, and the air-conditioned *chais d'élevage* with its 600 new oak barrels, make the eyes and the mouth water equally.

To justify such investment, the wines would have had to be good, and they certainly are. The range is surprisingly small, just the one white★★★, a touch of Viognier giving the Roussanne and Marsanne more than a hint of exoticism, emphasized by a *macération pelliculaire*. Fermentation is in new barrels with frequent *bâtonnage* over three months. An hectare of grapes yields as little as twenty hectolitres of this wine. In the glass, the bouquet confirms masterly control of the wood, and continues through to the palate with plenty of dried fruit and New World complexity.

"Prestige"★★ is what others would call their "Tradition". The emphasis is on elegance rather than power, though the wine has substantial body and structure. The tannins are velvety and the finish long. It is aged in oak of which one third is new each year. This is a wine that is good to drink four years or so after the vintage; it will last considerably longer.

The "Tête de Cuvée"★★★ sports 25% Carignan vinified by *macération carbonique*. Deep in colour, its bouquet proclaims at once the use of only the ripest fruit. It spends fourteen months in barrels, two-thirds of which are new each year. The resulting wine is rich, powerful, and complex, needing as much as six to ten years' ageing. With all this splendour, it is easy to overlook the rosés★★. Don't: they are particularly good and win gold medals regularly.

B8 Jean-Luc et Cathérine Viguier

DOMAINE SAINT-JEAN DE L' ARBOUSIER
34160 Castries
☎ 04-67-87-04-13 A/B

An "*arbousier*" is a Languedoc tree bearing strawberry-like fruit in autumn. Here, mixed with old umbrella pines, they surround the forty-six hectares of this fine domaine. Jean-Luc follows his father and grandfather in winemaking, and his wife Cathérine is an oenologist, with dual American-French nationality. They have been independent of the local coopératives since 1983.

The wines are made either simply as Coteaux du Languedoc without suffix, or as vins de pays. The suffix "Saint-Drézery" does not interest the Viguiers. The wines all come from vineyards which surround round the domaine and comprise more sandstone and chalky clay mixed in with the round pebbles than usual.

There are two *caves* here: one where the wines are made, which is called Mas Nau, a little way from the domaine. The other is at Saint-Jean itself, where the wines are aged. The vineyards have been continuously developed as the "better" grape varieties have been introduced. Cathérine models her taste on the Rhône Valley, from where she once brought back a number of varietal samples, on which she performed her own blending trials. The formula that she liked the best has been adopted as a benchmark at this vineyard.

The Viguiers are also keen on preserving some of the old Languedoc grape varieties on which the authorities have been frowning for some years: for example the Mourastelle. Their version differs from most in that it has white flesh and is thus used for making white wine. (There is still one hectare left of the black grape version at the Abbey of Valmagne, q.v.)

The Viguiers have some Rolle and Viognier in addition to the usual white grapes. The white AOC★★ has some of all of these, which goes to make an explosively aromatic cocktail. Perfumes of flowers give way to peaches and pineapple.

The same intensity of flavours on the palate is a feature of the red AOC★★, with blackcurrants, spices, good structure, and backbone, fruit and depth. Some ageing is required to allow the bouquet to develop. This wine has much more keeping potential than the 100% Cabernet vin de pays.

la méjanelle

The citizens of Montpellier are proud of this cru which survives within the city boundaries, an oasis amid the suburban sprawl. Two growers in particular are special.

B9 Pierre Clavel

DOMAINE DE CLAVEL
Mas de Périé
34820 Assas
☎ **04-67-86-97-36**
Ⓦ **www.vins-clavel.fr B**

Clavel's training is unusual for such an innovative winemaker, even if his father was a founding father of the Syndicat of Languedoc producers and an eminent wine-historian. Pierre left school at sixteen for the solitude of the Cévennes, where he grew his hair long and became a goatherd. There, he met Georges Dardé, then in charge of the coopérative at Roquebrun. Georges kindled in Pierre the passion for wine which somehow Pierre's father had not managed to ignite.

After a spell as a salesman of gastronomic foods, then working on a fishing boat, Pierre suddenly decided he was going to be a winemaker. At the age of twenty-five he rented thirty-seven hectares in the suburbs of Montpellier. His new fief was called La Calage, and it seemed like a version of paradise, completely hidden amid the urban jungle of autoroutes and dual carriageways.

Today, Pierre has cut his hair short, which accentuates his roguish grin and infectious laughter. He has no ambition to become a man of property, and views with philosophical resignation the possibility that his landlord will cash in on Pierre's success when the lease expires. Pierre has, however, taken precautions and has bought twelve hectares of vines up in the hills near Saint-Christol. Here he will plant the same Syrah, Grenache, and Mourvèdre with which he

right Pierre Clavel; from goatherd to food salesman to master-winemaker

replaced the old Aramon and Alicante he found at Montpellier. Here, too, he has managed to get all his operation under one roof in a new purpose-built *chais*. So, whatever happens at La Calage, we will be hearing a lot more of Pierre Clavel.

Today, he makes an exotic white called "Cascaille"★★ from Rolle, Roussanne, and Grenache Blanc; and rosé "Mescladis"★, but their production is small compared with his reds: an easy-to-drink "Le Mas" ★, a rather more substantial "Les Garrigues"★★, and the top-of-the-range "La Copa Santa"★★★, an astonishingly rich fruity wine, aged for upwards of a year in second-hand barrels and bottled without filtration. This brilliant wine needs five years or so in bottle to show its complexity.

Pierre exports no less than eighty-eight per cent of his production, largely to the USA.

B10 Henri Comte de Colbert

CHATEAU DE FLAUGERGUES
1744 avenue Albert Einstein
34000 Montpellier
☎ 04-99-52-66-37
Ⓦ www.flaugergues.com B

Montpellier is surrounded by follies, many built by tax-farmers and other dignitaries before the Revolution: they were the new aristocracy. Etienne de Flaugergues had taste, and this very Tuscan mansion, with its many cypress trees remains unchanged architecturally since the 1740s. The architect is unknown, but the building is remarkable for its internal iron staircase which at first sight appears to have no visible support.

Visitors cannot fail to be impressed by the magnificent furniture and furnishings, particularly the tapestries which adorn the staircase. A fine library includes a mouth-watering book on old grape varieties.

The tour is a long one, especially for those who thought they were visiting a vineyard. But Monsieur le Comte is as

left divine and fall: after the equinox, the autumns are often hot and sunny

charming as he is erudite, and the thirsty should be patient.

Built on the site of an old smallholding, the estate has kept its agricultural character, despite being surrounded almost entirely by modern Montpellier. Only the occasional aeroplane recalls the outside world. The gardens include a bamboo plantation and a lovingly collected assortment of wild plants from the garrigue. Monsieur le Comte, who seems more English than Mediterranean, is careful to keep a just balance between the heritage of this estate, and the wine-business which helps to support it. The vines and olives go back to Roman times. The vineyards were replanted little by little from 1976 onwards.

Some rather unremarkable white wine is made, and fractionally more rosé, but it is the reds that people come for. Not always the over-oaked "Cuvée en Fûts"★, but rather the "Cuvée Sommelière"★★ from 70% Syrah and 30% Grenache which is given a *cuvaison* of up to four weeks. Dark to look at, very rich and southern on the nose, the wine is full and firm. The long finish suggests bay leaf and liquorice. The "Sélection Rouge"★★ is for drinking young, though it will develop in bottle and would be good with grills and cheese. "The Tradition"★ is for younger drinking still, given only eight to ten days on skins at cooler temperatures than the other wines.

saint-georges-d'orques

Today, Saint-Georges-d'Orques could so easily become a western suburb of Montpellier, but its reputation for good wine goes back to a time when it was lost in unspoilt undulating hills. The growers therefore jealously guard their terroir, resisting temptation to dig up its old vines.

These are coteaux wines. The soil is in part chalky clay with large pebbles toward the village of Murviel, and red ferrous limestone further north. The wines of Saint-Georges-d'Orques have had knowing and distinguished admirers, including Thomas Jefferson and the French wine-historian André Jullien. About 300 hectares are currently in production.

B22 Damien Coste

DOMAINE BELLES PIERRES
24 rue des Clauzes
34570 Murviel-lès-Montpellier
☎ 04-67-47-40-33 A/C

Damien's father was once a *coopérateur*, but, tired of its lack of dynamism, he left the group in 1989. Damien worked alongside his father for some while but eventually took over in 1999 and re-named the property which used to be called Domaine des Clauzes. Father is another of those vignerons who never quite retires, and he is invaluable at harvest time.

When he started, Damien specialized in white wines, producing two outside appellation rules: "Cuvée Mosaique"★ is mostly Sauvignon, with some Viognier; "Ineptie"★★, sometimes breaking the saccharometer, and thereby falling foul of the AOC rules, is based on 60% Roussanne, 30% Viognier, and the rest Muscat. The legitimate appellation wine is called "Les Clauzes de Jo"★★ (literally "the vineyards of Jo", his father), a name applied also to a red★★ which Damien started to make in 1998 when he had acquired his own *égrappoir*. A version raised in new barrels is called "Chant des Ames"★★.

The most original of all Damien's creations is his Jurançon lookalike called Passidore★★★ made from Petit Manseng with some Grenache Blanc added: a luscious dessert wine, raised in oak and perhaps the finest sweet wine without added alcohol currently being made in the Languedoc.

These wines are strictly artisanal, Damien having but fifteen hectares scattered around Murviel. The Petit Manseng is grown in a sheltered bowl of land, surrounded by wooded hills which protect the vines from the cold and the damp. Damien uses barriques, but the new ones are reserved for his beloved vin doux and the Chant des Ames, mostly older wood being used for the rest of his production. The oak is well-handled: it is allowed to develop and soften the tannins in the red wines and the sugar in the white, but without imposing the taste of the wood itself.

B19 SCEA du Château de l'Engarran

34880 Saint-Georges-d'Orques
☎ 04-67-47-00-02 B

Another tax-farmer's folly, this one was built in the Classical style by Jean Vassal toward the end of the eighteenth century, replacing the former building put up by Henri Engarran 150 years before. The splendid iron gates, even though bearing the Vassal coat of arms, come from another property, their fleur-de-lys added when a visit from royalty was hoped for but never materialized.

The flagship wine here is named after a Canadian called Quetton who bought the property in the 1830s, and whose widow started a long line of lady-vignerons. Today it is home to the Grill's: Marguérite Bertrand in the 1920s, her daughter Francine Grill, and now Francine's two daughters continue the tradition. Francine was responsible for the switch to quality. Bottling at the Château started in 1978.

It is her daughter Diane who will probably greet visitors today: a qualified agronomist, dynamic, chic, and not a person to stand any nonsense, she could not, like many other scions of wine-growers, resist the call of the vines, giving up a well-paid job to come home and work with her mother. Her sister Constance, a professional head-hunter, was herself head-hunted by Diane to come back too. They suffered a terrible tornado in autumn 1999 just as the new *primeur* was about to be bottled. The tempest ripped away most of the roof of the *chais*, but the bottling went on just the same, the workers wearing hard hats. The ill wind did blow some good: a new insulated roof was paid for with the insurance.

There are forty hectares of vines at Saint-Georges and another twenty in nearby Pignan. Of the five red wines, "Les Garrigues d'Engarran"★, a red vin de pays with 90% Carignan, is seductive. The red "Cuvée Sainte Cécile"★ is an excellent straight AOC to be enjoyed young, on its fruit.

The Saint-Georges d'Orques name is reserved for the "Tradition"★★, nearly 50% Syrah, and raised in splendid *foudres*. The top red "Quetton Saint Georges"★★ is part matured in tank, part in oak, 25% of which is new each year. Good though these reds are, don't miss the white, a varietal Sauvignon ★★★, bright gold, with a bouquet of pineapples and mandarins, fresh hay, and cut flowers: grapefruit joins in on the palate. Unlike many Sauvignons, this one keeps.

B20 François Henry

DOMAINE HENRY
Avenue d'Occitanie
34680 Saint-Georges-d'Orques
☎ 04-67-45-57-74 B/C

Family inheritance share-outs can promote apparently insuperable difficulties. For François Henry, the ill Marin when his father died blew some good, because today he has fifteen hectares of prime vineyard site in Saint-Georges-d'Orques, and a fine winery opposite the football ground.

François' family have been winemakers for ten generations, going back almost as far as the reputation of Saint-Georges itself. François has vines in each of the three different types of terroir: his *tête de cuvée* is named "Les Chailles"★ after the sharp silex stones which crop up haphazardly over the area; here François bows delicately and tentatively in the direction of new oak, but basically all his wines are aged in *cuve*, and this is no exception. This is a wine for keeping, longer than the classical "Saint-Georges"★★, whose make-up includes some Cinsault over eighty years old.

There is a quicker-maturing, easy-to-drink red called "Paradines"★★ made from younger vines and given a shorter *cuvaison* and which earns no fewer medals than the other reds. There is also a pure Carignan, which François describes as "simple but authentic" though the grape variety is not his *truc*, he says; and a huge rosé, to be opened an hour ahead of drinking, and a good Chardonnay. But these vins de pays are eclipsed by an extraordinary sweet unfortified "Grenache wine"★★★ from very late-picked grapes allowed to shrivel on

above the Abbaye de Valmagne, founded in 1138, is one of the historic cradles of Languedoc winemaking

the vines. This is a style to be found elsewhere perhaps only at Château Viranel in St-Chinian.

B21 Alexandre et Patricia de Mortillet

DOMAINE DE LA PROSE
BP 25
34570 Pignan
☎ 04-67-03-08-30 C

The signpost is small and keeps getting used by *la chasse* for target practice, but

the turning is almost into Saint-Georges, just beyond a strange abbey church. A long rough road leads up into the garrigue where the Mortillets have built a spanking new *chais* into the hillside, so that the vinification and storage are done in the cool. They were helped by the fact that Alexandre is a surveyor by profession, though his family had cultivated the vine for some generations.

The new construction, which Alexandre designed, was necessary so that he could vinify the wines from grapes which he had previously sent to the coopérative. The building was completed, and Mortillet became fully independent in 1999, along with a

further twenty-eight hectares of vineyards.

Bertrand, Alexandre's son, had meanwhile been to wine-college in Bordeaux and also studied at Château Montrose in Saint-Estèphe, and in Burgundy. Still in his twenties, he is now in complete charge of the winemaking, and very talented he is too.

A feature here is the excellent duo of white wines: the classic "Cadières"★★ is a blend of Grenache Blanc and Vermentino grapes, the latter being a throwback to Corsica where Alexandre's father had once farmed. Fresh and floral with a finish reminiscent of roses, this is unoaked, unlike the "Grande Cuvée" ★★★ that also contains some Roussanne

and Viognier. The wood is very gentle and by no means masks the fruit lingers on the palate. These are gentle and vivacious whites, brilliant and lively.

The reds are no less successful: the "Cadières"★★ is an excellent "Classique" wine, aged in tank; "Les Embruns"★★ (the name means sea-spray) is aged in wood which has already seen the top wine, the "Grande Cuvée" ★★★, which is itself nothing but sumptuous.

Bearing in mind the fact that Bertrand was only let loose in the new *cave* in 1999, progress so far shows he is clearly going to make a great career for himself.

other good saint-georges growers

Madame Lise Fons-Vincent
Château de Fourques, 34990 Juvignac
☎ 04-67-47-90-87

Thierry Hazard
Domaime de la Marfée,
34570 Murviel-lès-Montpellier
☎ unavailable

Geneviève Ponson-Nicot
Château Perry, 34980 Murles
☎ 04-67-84-40-89

Claude Tourette
Chemin du Mas de Buisson,
34680 Saint-Georges-d'Orques
☎ 04-67-75-56-01

grès de montpellier

Beyond Saint-Georges, a belt of vineyards
extends in the direction of Béziers, mostly
planted in the undulating hills where the
garrigue has been dug up to allow the planting
of vines. The name of this terroir is likely to
become used in the future to include a variety
of the small crus round the city of Montpellier.

B28 Le Baron d'Allaines

ABBAYE DE VALMAGNE
34560 Villeveyrac
☎ 04-67-78-06-09 vdp A; AOC B

Monsieur le Baron Gaudart d'Allaines might
excuse visitors who say that his wines are
splendid but his abbey is even more so.
This must be one of the historic cradles of
Languedoc winemaking, founded in 1138
and gradually becoming one of the richest
Cistercian establishments in the South.
During various upheavals in the Church,
Valmagne survived largely because of the
abbey's use as a wine warehouse. The
wonderful *foudres* nestle between the gothic

left the landmark tooth-shaped mountain,
Pic Saint-Loup, seen from the east

arches of the aisle to this day. The property was acquired in 1838 by the Turenne family, who still own and run it. It combines its draw as a tourist attraction with active winemaking, and the retail shop and tasting rooms greet the visitor even before they are allowed to enter the abbey.

Sixty per cent of the vineyard is devoted to vins de pays, and as well as an attractive Cabernet Sauvignon★ there is a curiosity called "Les Dix Arpents de Frère Nonenque"★ of which 20% is represented by the forgotten grape here spelt Morrastel, a black berry which produces white juice; it is today part of an unusual and attractive red wine with distinct overtones of ripe crushed fruits, especially bitter cherries. Frère Nonenque was an elderly monk living in the abbey who had special responsibility for the vines. Some of his colleagues were converted to Protestantism and left. Years later they returned with soldiers and Frère Nonenque was murdered while they recaptured the estate.

The classique AOC red★★ is perhaps the most attractive of the wines here, although the top cuvée called "Cuvée de Turenne"★★ has a refreshing minerality derived from the red bauxite terroir to the north of the church.

This property is a must to visit. Not far from Pézenas or even Montpellier, it is remotely situated but well worth the detour.

B25 Philippe Rustan

LE MAS D'AIME
22 Avenue de Bédarieux
34770 Poussan
☎ 04-67-78-98-32
Ⓦ www.Lemasdaime.com C

Philippe's grandfather was called Aimé, and in homage, Philippe has named his wines after the mas he built in Aimé's memory. His father is a coopérateur, but Philippe's training saw him decide his own future as a grower and producer of micro-cuvées of high quality. After an unorthodox education, including time in Germany, he produced his first wine in 1998. Paradoxically he does not base his wines on

the Syrah grape, but on the much derided Aramon and Alicante, as well as the more acceptable Grenache. His real forte, however, is Carignan, of which he produces a superb mono-cépage wine called "La Vieille Bataille"★★★, one of the best of its kind in the South. His pure Alicante★ is perhaps the only wine from this grape to be aged in barrique, and represents his everyday quaffing wine: dark and brooding, the colour clings to the glass but the blackberry fruit on the palate is a sheer delight. Perhaps it was the Alicante grape with its deep colour which gave Keats his "purple-stained mouth". To these two grapes Philippe adds a little Grenache for his top wine "La Doyenne"★★★, which manages to be an AOC wine – just as his mono-cépage of pure Grenache does, this is called "Sainte-Cathérine"★★. There is also a Grenache vin de pays called "Les Raisins Oubliés"★★.

Philippe's seven hectares are spread quite symmetrically round the small town of Poussan on five different terroirs, each with different micro-climates. The average production of twenty-five hectolitres to the hectare produces 25,000 bottles. Vines are grown en gobelet. Some of his Carignan is fifty years old, and his Aramon is centenarian. For Philippe, the care of such vines is emotional: "They make the terroir speak like a person." Each terroir is vinified separately and the wines are all aged in barrel for between ten and twenty months. They are neither filtered or fined.

Philippe knows he is a good winemaker, but he has kept enough modesty to say that just because he produced superb wines in his first year, it does not mean to say he has "arrived": "Each year, everything starts again, you put yourself on trial once more, and you learn every day."

B27 Marlène Soria

DOMAINE PEYRE ROSE
34230 Saint-Pargoire
☎ 04-67-98-75-50 D

Madame Soria first came here in 1973 when on holiday: the local stone glowed pink and

the pink cistus was in full flower. Everything seemed pink, so she immediately thought of the name Peyre Rose: pink stone.

There was nothing here then, just a few ruins of an old hamlet, totally deserted and overgrown with plants from the garrigue. Access was barely possible except on a four-legged animal, and even today you have to travel three kilometres (1.7 miles) or so over a rough track leading out of the middle of the fire station in Saint-Pargoire. As the crow flies, the Abbaye de Valmagne lies not far to the south.

The courage and imagination which were needed to establish this, one of the top handful of vineyards in the Languedoc, is beyond the comprehension of most mortals, but Madame Soria had plenty of vision and persistence. She gradually built herself a cosy home, and little by little has established winemaking facilities perfectly suited to her own artisanal style. She even has four beautiful new oval foudres in which she is maturing her 2000 vintage.

She makes a little white wine, but scarcely for commercialisation. The reds come from about twenty-two hectares of vines: Syrah, Grenache, and Mourvèdre in two quite distinct parcels, from which she makes two quite different but equally excellent cuvées: "Clos des Cistes"★★★ and "Syrah Léone"★★★, named after the lady from whom she bought the land in question. The first of these lives up to its name, with the fresh scents of the garrigue prominent on the nose and a good acidity which ensures that it lasts well; the second has a more meaty, leathery quality. Both are extremely deep wines, given very long cuvaisons of up to three months. They require long élevage; and, if you ask Madame Soria why she has adopted a policy which means that wines are not available for sale until three and a half years after the vintage, she replies disarmingly that when she started in 1983, she simply could not find any customers, so had to keep the wine a long time. This is no longer a problem today. Cavistes and restaurants fight over her scarce bottles, despite their high price. Visitors should make an appointment – and ask for directions.

B24 Michel Moreau

TERRE-MEGERE
34660 Cournonsec ·
☎ 04-67-85-42-85 A

Near Grenoble, where Michel Moreau comes from, they have a grape called "Galopine", which is either the same as Viognier, or is a close relation, so he has adopted Viognier and is said to have been one of its pioneers in Languedoc. His better Viognier wine is thus called "Galopine"★★★: it is blended with a little lightly-oaked Chardonnay and is top class. The vines produce a mere ten hectolitres per hectare, so the wine costs rather more than the rest of his production. Another Viognier vin de pays★ is good too, and has some Clairette and Muscat in it as well as the Chardonnay.

Michel came south to work as an administrator in the Grande Ecole d'Agriculture at Montpellier, decided to stay, and acquired seven hectares of vines from which he sent the grapes to the Coopérative. He gave all that up in 1980 and acquired Terre Mégère, an old sheep-fold, in the lee of the hills; the name means "barren land" and he now has twenty-two hectares in production, most of which he reclaimed from the garrigue, but he also has some richer land down on the plain where he makes some excellent vins de pays from Merlot★★ and Cabernet★. The Merlot is vinified, unusually, by *macération carbonique*, and the Coopérative's refusal to handle this wine on that account was the cause of his leaving.

There are two AOC Coteaux du Languedoc wines: a delicious "Classique"★ from Grenache, Mourvèdre, and Cinsault, and a grander *cuvée* called "Les Dolomies"★★ which is mostly from Syrah with some Mourvèdre and/or Grenache; neither is oaked, and both are reasonably quick to mature. Michel attributes this to the adoption of *microbullage* which he believes achieves the same degree of oxygenation as wooden barrels, thus hastening maturity, but without adding the tannins of new oak.

When Moreau first established his grape production, he had a further tract of land on which he used to breed donkeys and eventually had no fewer than sixty. Sadly the pressure of his viticulture has obliged him to give up this eccentric sideline, but the donkeys still feature on his wine labels. The wines themselves are outstandingly good value for money.

other good grès growers

Alain Reder
Roucaillat, Comberousse de Fertalières, Montbazin, 34660 Cournonterral
☎ 04-67-85-05-18

pic saint-loup

The legend is that Saint Loup, returning from the Crusades, discovered that his beloved had married someone else in his absence – neither the first nor last time that such a thing has happened. He took his vows and lived a hermit on this mountain for the rest of his life.

From the west this famous landmark looks like a large, quite ordinary round hill, but once you have travelled the valley which separates the Pic from the Mountain of Hortus, the true face of the Pic is disclosed, a sharp tooth jutting out defiantly into the skyline. It has become the symbol of one of the most energetic and fashionable vineyards of the Languedoc, which has applied for its own AOC.

Already it has set stricter rules for growers using the name Pic Saint-Loup; red wines must include at least 90% of Syrah and/or Grenache and/or Mourvèdre, and the vines must be at least six years old before they qualify. Younger grapes and other grape varieties may be used for AOC Coteaux du Languedoc wines without the Saint-Loup cachet. There are over a score of independent producers, all fired to make wine of a high standard. Many of the best of them have no wine to offer because it has all been snapped up by the fashion-conscious

restaurants and *cavistes*. Excellence comes from a combination of factors: a more temperate hill-country climate, with less extreme heat and a little more rainfall; and winds from the mountains to the north which cool the vineyards at night and protect the grapes against rot and disease.

B14 Anne et André Leenhardt

CHATEAU DE CAZENEUVE
34270 Lauret
☎ 04-67-59-07-49 B/C

Until 1988, André Leenhardt's real job was as a technical consultant on aromatic plants to the Chamber of Agriculture. In that year, he discovered that Pic Saint-Loup was better for growing vines than thyme or arnica, and bought the Cazeneuve domaine, complete with all its outbuildings. Not needing the long low building opposite the *chais* he sold it on to make a successful *auberge*, which caters for a large weekend crowd of Montpellierois. The *auberge* has fifty-two shareholders and a wine list including over one hundred Languedoc names.

Before André arrived, there were indeed vines here, but nearly all were for table grapes, and only a few Syrah and Grenache vines were for making wine. André replanted it all with the usual Languedoc wine grapes, excepting Carignan. Today there are sixteen hectares in production and another four awaiting their destiny. His policy is to limit the growth of the young vines until they are really ready to go, forcing them to channel their energy into their roots, driving them deep down into the soil. A high level of organic matter is applied to the vineyards, which are all worked by hand. Only the fruit from the youngest vines is destalked and it is not submitted to *pigeage*, in fact André is not all that keen on *pigeage* especially for grapes which have been completely destalked.

André makes three red wines: "Les Terres Rouges" ★★, from young vines, given a short *cuvaison*, and raised entirely in tank, a wine to be appreciated for its suppleness and fruit. Bigger in structure is "Les Calcaires"★★★, almost black, shot through with plummy violet characters, scented with flowers and ripe cherries, and with good tannins which do, however, need a little time to soften. Bigger still is the oak-aged "Roc des Mates"★★, given a long *cuvaison* and at least fourteen months in barrels, which are renewed every four years. Not as immediately attractive as Les Calcaires, this wine nevertheless has tremendous ageing potential and should last for years.

There is also a delicious white★★, half barrel-fermented. Largely from Roussanne but also with some Grenache Blanc and Viognier; it is aged in barrel on its lees, and has considerable weight and style.

André is president of the Syndicat of Pic Saint-Loup growers.

B15 Les Frères Ravaille

ERMITAGE DU PIC SAINT-LOUP
34270 Saint-Mathieu-de-Treviers
☎ 04-67-55-20-15 B/C

The Ravaille family have owned this property since the Revolution. The grandfather of the three brothers who are today's proprietors joined the coopérative in 1951. In 1992 the brothers decided to go independent, though even today they still send some of their grapes there. The restoration of the old cellars will take some time because parts of these buildings go back to the Middle Ages. They are constructed at the southern foot of the Pic itself, and the slopes give to the wine explicit hints of the garrigue and the wild flowers which grow in the rocky terrain. The slopes offer good drainage too, a fact which, combined with the cool temperatures here, gives the wines just a little extra acidity and helps to give them long life as well as vivacity. The soil is mostly chalky clay but there are also big round pebbles much appreciated by the Syrah.

right the three Ravaille brothers take an apériif in the sun at their Pic Saint-Loup Ermitage

A little rosé is made from Cinsault grapes and a small amount of white wine from Roussanne, Viognier, and Marsanne – this last is given some oak-ageing. Ninety-five per cent of the production is red wines which have become increasingly well-known and admired in recent years, to the point where this now must rank as one of the top estates in the Pic.

The traditionally vinified "Classique"★★ is from 60% Syrah, 30% Grenache, and 10% Mourvèdre. The "Cuvée Saint-Agnès"★★★ has more Syrah and less Grenache, but the main difference is that this wine comes from better parcels of vines and is a bigger proposition altogether. The top wine is called "Guilhem Gaucelm"★★★, after the first person named in the local archives as authorized to make wine here. This is virtually all Syrah, with just enough Grenache to comply with the AOC rules which require at least two grape varieties. The two varieties are vinified separately in open *cuves* with *pigeage* twice daily. The different parcels of the vineyard from which the grapes come are also vinified separately.

The brothers Ravaille seem to share no family likeness whatsoever, but their wines do. Full and round, they sometimes suggest citrus fruits, and certainly the more familiar crushed fruits such as raspberries and blackcurrants. Although the brothers have been making their own wine for some years, one has the feeling that they are still experimenting.

B11 La Famille Causse

CHÂTEAU DE L'EUZIÈRE
34270 Fontanès
☎ 04-67-55-21-41 A/B

The Causse family can boast four generations of winemakers at this excellent property, whose name derives from *yeuse*, the local word for the evergreen oaks which make up so much of the vegetation on the garrigue. Their *chais* is in the middle of the village of Fontanès and easy to find, unlike

many other growers locally who seem determined to hide from visitors.

There are twenty-five hectares, devoted largely to the Syrah grape, but with some Grenache and Mourvèdre also planted. The small production of white wine is from Rolle, Grenache Blanc, and Roussanne and is called "Grains de Lune"★★; it is given six hours' preliminary skin contact before fermentation and is matured for seven months on its lees before bottling.

For evidence of the long tradition of viticulture here, one need look no further than the splendid old *foudres* which still do service in the *chais*. The house-style can best be described as preferring elegance and finesse to power, a harking back to the times when those qualities were more appreciated than they are today. But the wines manage to achieve surprisingly modern levels of alcohol: the "Cuvée Tourmaline"★ can pack 14% without the least difficulty. This wine can also be drunk cool, so Madame Causse recommends.

The wines have, too, a delightfully clear limpidity and brilliance, never dense or grainy in texture. They have good concentration and structure but are not over-extracted. For example the "Cuvée Almandin"★★ is mostly from low-yielding Syrah, plants which have smaller grapes than usual; and the *tête de cuvée* called "Les Escarboucles"★★★ which is marketed in burgundy-style bottles. Its oak is very gentle and unobtrusive, and the dominant notes of cherries and flowers from the garrigue are never smothered.

B17 Jean Orliac

DOMAINE DE L'HORTUS
34270 Valflaunès
☎ 04-67-55-31-20 B/C

Jean Orliac came from Toulouse where his grandfather was associated with Domaine de Ribonnet. After his degree at the Grande Ecole in Montpellier he "discovered" the valley which runs between the Pic and the Montagne d'Hortus, which at the time was

more or less abandoned, particularly at its western end. It was an area which he already knew from hang-gliding off the Pic.

Gradually he has assembled thirty-two hectares of vines, some of which are leased, but French law guarantees a leaseholder much more freedom than it allows the owner. Jean has planted Mourvèdre and Syrah on opposite sides of the valley – an unusual but wise move. Lower down there is some Grenache, and on the flat land by the stream are his white grapes, Roussanne, Viognier, Sauvignon and Chardonnay. He considers that this arrangement of the *cépages* in this terroir, and in this micro-climate is ideal, the Mourvèdre with its long growing cycle benefitting from maximum sunshine, while the Syrah, with its shorter cycle and earlier maturity, thrives in a certain amount of shade.

He makes two *cuvées* of each colour, plus a little rosé by *saignage*. The whites have to be sold as Vins de Pays du Val de Montferrand because of the choice of grape varieties, but are just as fine as the reds for all that. The basic version called "Bergerie de l'Hortus"★, is made from all four white grapes, the Sauvignon being given a preliminary cold maceration for forty-eight hours. Some of the Chardonnay is barrel-fermented but the rest, together with the other grape varieties, is vinified and raised in *cuve*. The more ambitious *cuvée*, called simply "Domaine d'Hortus"★★★, is made from two-thirds Chardonnay which is barrel-fermented, and one-third Viognier which is not. The result is exceptionally rich and the finish is long.

The reds follow a similar pattern: the "Bergerie"★★ is from younger vines, nearly all Syrah and Grenache, and is raised two-thirds in *cuve* and one-third in barrels which have seen at least two wines. The red "Domaine d'Hortus"★★★ must be one of the finest of the appellation and comes from 10–15% Grenache, and the rest equally from Syrah and Mourvèdre. This is a sumptuous Pic, rich in scents of the garrigue, very ripe fruit, and the oak is handled in masterly fashion.

B12 Jack Boutin

CHATEAU LA ROQUE
34270 Fontanès
☎ 04-67-55-34-47 **B**

Jack Boutin was as excited as his
father was alarmed when, in 1984, the
son announced his intention of buying this
property which was then badly run down.
It nevertheless had forty hectares of first
class vineyard potential, tucked away in an
amphitheatre of hillside. The vines included
an old plantation of south-facing Mourvèdre,
today Jack's pride and joy.

The estate is nowadays magnificent, its
buildings fully restored, one of them, a small
tower, housing a deep well. The vines are as
impeccably maintained as the extensive park.
The property has a long history. The French
Crown confiscated it after final victory against
the Cathars, and wine was being made here
in the eleventh century. Jack is a newcomer

to wine, although his grandfather had some
vines over at Sommières to the east. In the
vineyard he tries to be as organically correct
as possible. In the *chais* he is assisted by
a well-known oenologist, Marc Auclair.

The vines for his white wine face east,
avoiding the most extreme of the midday heat.
They are mainly Rolle and Marsanne, with a little
Grenache Blanc. There is also some Viognier
and Boutin says that the authorities do not
seem to be upset by his including a non-AOC
grape in small quantities. The white wine★★
comes in an oaked and unoaked style. The
former is given twelve hours' skin contact
before being barrel-fermented; a malolactic
fermentation follows and the wine is aged
in barrel for eight months before bottling.

A fine rosé★★ is *saigné* from 60%
Mourvèdre. The yields for this and the red
wines of the property are as low as thirty
hectolitres per hectare. A notably unusual
wine is his 90% Mourvèdre★★★, made from

above Jack Boutin relaxes in the shady avenue
leading to the Château La Roque

the vines which he bought in 1984 and which
is aged in some old *foudres* which Jack has
acquired for the purpose. There is also a more
orthodox red "Cuvée Cupa Numismae"★★.

The wines of this property have not
attracted the same media attention as some
others. That is not Jack's style, but they are
fine indeed and deserve to be better known.

B13 Françoise, Julien, et Christophe Peyrus

CLOS MARIE
route de Cazeneuve
34270 Lauret
☎ 04-67-59-06-96 **A/B**

Christophe, whose grandfather was a grower
in Cahors, married into wine in Pic Saint-Loup
where his in-laws had been members of the

coopérative for many years. Marie is his wife's grandmother, but you will be lucky to find the Clos named after her without asking for help, for the family does not seem to court publicity.

Today, Christophe looks after about fifteen hectares of prime parcels of vineyard round the village of Lauret, some on chalky clay which produce structured, tannic wines, and some on stonier ground which give a more delicate result. Christophe replanted much of the land when he arrived and today he has equal areas of Syrah and Grenache with just a *petit grain de poivre* of Mourvèdre for his Pic Saint-Loup wines. Some old Cinsault and Carignan are reserved for a wine called Métairie du Clos★.

His first vintage was in 1994 and it catapulted him into the front rank of young growers in this young cru. Having reconstituted the vineyard, he has now built a brand new *chais*, one storey of which is underground. The grapes go into the *cuve* without pumping, after being carefully destalked and lightly crushed.

Vinification is simple, Christophe being one of those who believe that a wine is made in the vineyard rather than the *chais*. However, he attaches great importance to mastering new oak techniques, renewing barrels on a five year cycle so as not to exaggerate their effects. His basic red is aged in tank and is called "Quatre Saisons"★.

Then comes "Olivette"★★, a delicate wine sometimes redolent of spices and crushed berries. Finally "Simon"★★★ whose time spent in barrel will depend on the character of the vintage. In great years he makes a fourth wine called "Glorieuses"★★★, named after the island in the Indian Ocean with which he fell in love during his earlier career as a marine.

Christophe's white wine★★★ is excellent too, and he is proud of it. Largely consisting of Roussanne grafted onto old rootstocks, with some old Clairette, it also contains Maccabeu, a grape seldom found as far north or east in Languedoc as this. With this

cocktail Christophe has managed to combine the virtues of freshness with considerable *gras*.

B16 Isabelle et Guilhem Bruguière

MAS BRUGUIERE
34270 Valflaunès
☎ 04-67-55-20-97 A/B

This property shares with Domaine de l'Hortus (q.v.) virtually the whole of the valley which leads from the vineyards of the Pic up to the col which separates the Pic from the Montagne d'Hortus. One cannot help noticing that both vineyards have followed the same policy of planting their Mourvèdre facing south on the slopes of the Montagne and their Syrah on the northward facing slopes of the Pic itself. One wonders who had the idea first – not that it matters much because both derive considerable benefit from the basic decision, whoever it was that originally took it.

Guilhem Bruguière gives the impression of being modest and quiet, but there must be something gritty about his character because it is he, perhaps more than anybody else, who has been responsible for the rapid rise of Pic Saint-Loup as a wine-growing region. The family has been making wine in the area since the times of the Revolution, but it is Guilhem who foresaw to a large extent the coming of the *cépages améliorateurs* into the special terroir and micro-climate of the Pic. His own vineyard is small, a mere twelve hectares, although there are eight more available for planting, and there is little doubt that his son Xavier has ambitions in that direction whenever the time comes.

Meanwhile Guilhem's own wines are textbook Pic Saint-Loup: an un-oaked white from Roussanne★★★, with aromas of fresh hay and spring flowers, good depth of flavour and a long finish; a big rosé★, *saigné* from Syrah and Grenache; and three reds. First, a curiously named "Cuvée Vinam de Calcadiz"★, called this after a parcel of land attached to the now ruined castle of Montferrand which straddles the ridge running eastward from the Pic. It is a quaffable light wine for drinking young and made from vines which are a little too youthful yet to qualify for the Pic label.

"L'Arbouse"★★★, named after the locally found strawberry-tree which flourishes in this garrigue country, is more complex and made from 60% Syrah and 20% each of Grenache and Mourvèdre. This wine has a bouquet which calls you back to it again and again. The top *cuvée* is called "Grenardière"★★★ and is raised in oak: it represents a quarter of the Mas Bruguière production.

These wines give the impression of being real stayers: there is nothing flashy about them and they all need time to show their best, even the white.

B18 Michel Jorcin et Rémy Duchemin

DOMAINE DE MORTIES
34270 Saint-Jean-de-Cuculles
☎ 04-67-55-11-12 B

These two brothers-in-law came to winemaking from quite different directions. Jorcin was a goat-farmer, and Duchemin a video-dealer in Paris. Both wanted a different quality of life and they found, suddenly, in 1993, an abandoned twenty-six-hectare vineyard in the lee of the Pic Saint-Loup: Domaine de Morties. At the heart of it is the exquisitely attractive *mas* which Duchemin has tastefully made into a beautiful home for modern living.

Both of them took crash courses in winemaking: Jorcin in Die and Duchemin in Switzerland. Their first task was to replace the Aramon and poor quality Cinsault grapes. They were careful to keep the Carignan which is so much at the heart of their production. This is one of the few estates in the Pic where Carignan is successful and treasured. One of their best wines is a 100% Carignan varietal★★★, sold as a vin de pays.

They kept also the old *cuves* and lined them with epoxy resin. Looking back, Duchemin now regrets that they did not plant at higher density, and they would not have bought only cloned plants. If these were mistakes, the wines are none the worse.

They profit from the appellation for white wines by making a blend★★ from Marsanne, Viognier, and the more recently planted Rolle. As for the reds, whose number may vary from year to year, it is quite possible to like them in inverse order to their price. The first AOC coteaux★★★ wine is 70% Grenache and is a wonderful expression of that grape, with just a little Syrah blended in to add spice. Rémy prefers to keep his Syrah mainly for the

"better" *cuvées*. He vinifies both this grape and the Carignan by *macération carbonique*, favouring long *cuvaisons* because he wants to make wines that will age well. The "Pic Saint-Loup"★★ name may be added to the second wine, made from equal quantities of Syrah and Grenache with just a little Mourvèdre and Carignan; this is one-third oak-aged and suggests mushrooms and game from the woods. The top wine is called "Che Sera Sera"★★ and is all Syrah, and, though aged in wood for twelve months, the oak barely shows; the wine is long, with good harmonious tannins.

other good pic saint-loup growers

Marguérite Laliam
Château Benel Laliam,
34980 Saint-Gély-du-Fesc
☎ 04-67-84-23-85

Jean-Pierre Rambier
Domaine du Haut-Lirou,
34270 St-Jean-de-Cuculle
☎ 04-67-55-38-50

GAEC de Lancyre
Château de Lancyre, 34270 Valflaunès
☎ 04-67-55-31-20

Jean-Benoît Cavalier
Château de Lascaux,
34270 Vacquières
☎ 04-67-59-00-08

Claude et Marcel Arlès
Château de Lascours,
34980 Sauteyragues
☎ 04-67-59-00-58

Olivier Bridel
Château de Lavabre, 34270 Claret
☎ 04-67-59-02-25

Christine, Jean-Louis, et Christophe Puech
Domaine Puech, 25 rue du Four,
34890 Saint-Clément-de-Rivière
☎ 04-67-84-12-31

aniane and its vin de pays

The sleepy town of Aniane has made history, twice: first when Aimé Guibert amazed the world with the creation of his Bordeaux-style wines from Daumas Gassac, and again in 2001 when the same Monsieur Guibert, in some kind of unholy alliance with the Communist mayor of Aniane and with the support of the anti-globalist José Bové, managed to preserve the woodlands around the village, which Guibert said were so precious to the local ecology, from being bought up by Robert Mondavi of California fame. Mondavi's plan was to fell the trees and plant Cabernet and other grapes with a view to making a premium wine which he hoped would sell for 500 francs a bottle. Whether this would have benefited anyone other than Mondavi is hard to say.

This battle divided the local population into two fiercely opposed camps, and victory was not declared until the result of the mayoral elections, fought virtually entirely on this one issue. The anti-Mondavi camp won the *mairie*. More significantly, the issue aroused enormous interest throughout the wine world, where the debate scarcely touched on the environmental issues. The media were more interested in Aniane's rejection of California investment. Mondavi retired hurt but with a dignity that Guibert was clever enough to praise. But then he could afford to. Mondavi has abandoned the Languedoc, having sold his other interests to the Limoux coopérative.

B35 Philippe Ellner

DOMAINE DES CONQUETES
34150 Aniane
☎ 04-67-57-35-99 B/C

The vin de pays from this property is called Guillaume des Conquêtes, but the real name of the district is "Conquettes", meaning small shells. This may be a French pun, but the wines here are no joke, as befits a Champenoise couple who had the temerity to come to the birthplace of Daumas Gassac to make wine. The Ellners have retained their interests in

Champagne, but spend all their time and energy on this vineyard just outside Aniane. They fell in love with the place when visiting friends at nearby Puechabon in 1982, and their first efforts at viticulture went to the local coopérative. After substantially replanting the vineyard, they started to make and bottle their own wines in 1996, and quickly established the kind of reputation which exempted them from the need to sell on their own doorstep. Distribution is mainly through *cavistes*.

Their sixteen hectares are dotted around, though they are trying to rationalize their holdings. For their only AOC red★★, they use Syrah, which dominates the minority Mourvèdre and Grenache. Dark in colour, there is a lot of blackcurrant. The Ellner style is for structured wines with a lot of oak-ageing, so cellarage is necessary while the tannins from the wood merge with those of the grapes.

Their one white wine★★ is sold as a vin de pays because it is made exclusively from Chardonnay and Chenin Blanc neither of which is permitted in the appellation. It is assembled before fermentation is begun, then vinified partly in wood and partly in tank. This wine is full of citrus, pineapple, and other exotic fruits and is a good example of modern Languedoc style.

The "Guillaume des Conquêtes"★★ is a blend of everything the Ellners have, both Mediterranean and Atlantic, largely Cabernet, Grenache, and Merlot. Ellner says that the Cabernet gives freshness to the blend. Good it is, and by no means a second string to the AOC red. Expect animal aromas on the nose, but plenty of red fruits on the palate.

B37 Aimé Guibert

MAS DE DAUMAS GASSAC
34150 Aniane
☎ 04-67-57-71-28
Ⓦ www.daumas-gassac.com D

Certainly this is the best-known of all Languedoc wine estates, the only one to have had a book entirely devoted to it: *Daumas Gassac; the Birth of a Grand Cru* by Alastair

MacKenzie (Seagrave Foulkes, London 1995). Identified by the famous geologist, Henri Enjalbert, in the 1970s, as having a potential for making great wine, and later by a pioneering oenologist (Emile Peynaud) as a likely site for the Cabernet Sauvignon grape, this property was bought by Aimé Guibert as a retreat from the relative rigours of the Aveyron climate, and without any idea that it would achieve international fame as a vineyard.

Guibert, a lawyer by profession, was used to dispensing advice, so it was natural that he should accept it too, however unlikely it may have seemed at the time. In the very unusual terroir of Daumas Gassac, he planted his Cabernet, with a smattering of all sorts of other grapes, and it was not long before the experts' advice had proved spot on. By the early 1980s, Daumas Gassac had made Guibert's reputation and almost single-handedly put Languedoc back on the map of quality French vineyards.

Today, Guibert leads the field from the front: no easy task when there is so much talent only too ready and able to challenge his supreme position, some of it on his own doorstep. Having started with just one sumptuous red *cuvée*★★★, followed later by a white★★★, there is now a *deuxieme vin*★★, in the Bordeaux manner, and a host of varietals to demonstrate the many grape varieties which go to make up the main wines.

Recently a 50/50 blend of Syrah and Grenache has been launched, made from grapes carefully selected from nearby growers; it is called "Sol de Landoc"★★. and is designed for much earlier drinking than the *grand vin*.

The apparently unlimited investment, the state-of-the-art equipment, and the California-style *caveau de dégustation*, are reminiscent of Mondavi, to whom Guibert has so effectively shown the door. But, despite the spin, the wines are superb after suitable bottle-ageing – ten years or more for a good vintage. Guibert's success with the Cabernet

right fig trees grow close to a vineyard, balancing the ecology and the terroir

Sauvignon grape has no doubt prompted hundreds of others to have a go with it, but none has so far beaten Daumas Gassac for its quality, so dependent on the very particular terroir – and not shared by other growers, even in the village of Aniane. Guibert's competition comes almost exclusively from those who have kept wholly or at least in part to the southern *cépages*, as has...

B36 Laurent Vaillé

LA GRANGE DES PERES
34150 Aniane
☎ 04-67-57-70-55 D

...who has added only 20% Cabernet to his holdings of Syrah and Mourvèdre. The resulting wine is thus quite different in style, though not in price, from Daumas Gassac. The whole philosophy of Laurent Vaillé is different too: he is a true artisanal grower. He is slow to reveal his secrets, but when asked the key to his success, he replies modestly: "Work".

He has done *stages* with Chave in Hermitage, the Comtes Lafon in Burgundy, and Trévallon in Provence: he says that, like a composer, you must study the works of the masters, but that does not mean that you copy them. You create your own way.

This partly poetical, partly philosophical approach is balanced by a devotion to perfection which is quite extraordinary, and which infects the whole family. The vineyard is incredibly forbidding; the vines grown almost touching the ground so that pruning or picking them is kidney- as well as back-breaking. The yields are tiny and the vineyard itself cannot measure more than seven hectares.

Vaillé makes only two wines – both ★★★. In the red, the Cabernet is balanced by roughly equal proportions of Syrah and Mourvèdre. All grapes are aged in a mixture of new and old wood, and then assembled and allowed to rest in tank before being bottled, two and a half years after the vintage. The oak

left a doyen of Montpeyroux, Aimé Commeyras, of Domaine L'Aiguelière

is, however, perfectly discreet, the wines perfectly balanced, the freshness of the Cabernet offsetting the rich fruit and spices of the Languedoc grapes. Aristocratic style and elegance are supported by firm but not overpowering structure; the wine manages to be modern without being "New World".

The white wine is nearly all Roussanne, with just a touch each of Chardonnay and Marsanne, barrel-fermented in *demi-muids* rather than *barriques*, to ensure discretion in the effect of the wood. Vaillé says too that the bigger the barrel, the more likely the wood is to be first class – important when you are using it to ferment as well as to age. This white explodes in the mouth without being in any way vulgar, and the finish is incredibly long. These are without question some of the finest wines to come out of the South.

B34 Géraldine Combes et Xavier Peyraud

MAS DES BROUSSES
34150 Puechabon
☎ 04-67-57-33-75 B

Géraldine's family have been making wine in this village near Aniane for many generations, long before the Guiberts and the Vaillés were born; the family still sends two-thirds of their production (much of it Carignan) to the Aniane coopérative. They have twenty-eight hectares of vines on chalky clay above the valley of the River Hérault. Perhaps it was the arrival of Xavier Peyraud, a member of the famous Bandol family of Domaine Tempier fame, that sparked off the idea of going independent, a process which Géraldine and Xavier will complete when they can. Meanwhile they are installed in the Combes family *cave* just next to the church in the pretty village of Puechabon, the minimum of facilities allied to a maximum of skill and passion. Their first venture into AOC Coteaux du Languedoc was in 1997, a great success which was even improved upon in 1998. These wines have a rare serenity and gentleness not often found in the South, the 1998 in particular lacking

nothing in roundness and good fruit, and showing excellent balance. Then in 1999 they ventured into the use of oak *demi-muids*, some new but mostly old. These more recent vintages confirm, even enhance the reputation of the earlier wines, the house-style still keeping to an elegance which is very satisfying and which above all avoids any bitterness or astringency. The excessive concentration and alcohol levels so beloved of the professional tasters are not found here.

The AOC wine – ★★ or possibly ★★★ (a great compliment in Aniane) – comes from Grenache and Syrah, but Xavier, in true Bandol tradition, has recently planted a little Mourvèdre. There is also a light and delicate rosé and a vin de pays★ from Cabernet and Merlot, but it is the AOC wines on which reputation will grow here.

These growers obviously have a bright future: they already export much of their production to Switzerland and Belgium.

montpeyroux

There is a buzz about the winemakers of Montpeyroux, who are almost as far from the sea as it is possible to be for people living and working in the Languedoc. Their region covers a cluster of villages – Jonquières, Saint-Saturnin, and Saint-André de Sangonis – that share a similar style of wine, and vineyards toward Octon, where the wines have a little more rusticity. The coopératives here are important, but the independent growers make an impressive roll of honour. They are proud of their terroir and aim to preserve it from amalgamation by securing it as a cru in its own right. The mountains of the Cévennes dominate the landscape, and the soil is *argilo-calcaire*.

B40 Aimé Commeyras et Pierre-Louis Tessèdre

SCEA DOMAINE L'AIGUELIERE
2 Place du Square
34150 Montpeyroux
☎ 04-67-96-61-43 B

Monsieur Commeyras, now one of the doyens of Montpeyroux, was once president of the local coopérative, where he felt that not enough attention was being given to the qualitative assessment of the different vineyards within the region. He joined forces with Pierre-Louis Tessèdre, a well-known oenologist, left the coopérative in 1983, and created what is today the Domaine L'Aiguelière. Its twenty-five hectares produce now some of the best wines in Montpeyroux. The soils are varied: some chalky clay, some *graves*, some sandstone, and some of the typical stone deposits which are to be found in the hillsides of the Hérault.

Commeyras, though older than some of his colleagues in Montpeyroux, has lost none of his enquiring spirit. He was an early fan of Syrah, and he practises more ecological principles than many others preach. He has only recently produced any white wine and then only one *cuvée*: an unoaked Viognier-Sémillon blend, "Sarments"★★, made from lightly pressed grapes, and matured on its lees. Its *encépagement* and general style are reminiscent of Gilles Perraudin's Domaine des Pierres Plantées, with a very similar blend of exoticism and just the right touch of acidity.

Otherwise, all the wines here are red; there is not even any rosé. First there is an attractive vin de pays from 70% Grenache and 30% Syrah called "Grenat"★★, which cannot be marketed as an appellation wine because some of the vines are outside the delimited area. His red "Tradition"★★ comes in oaked and unoaked form and is made from rather more Syrah than Grenache and just a touch of Mourvèdre. The wine which Commeyras regards as his top *cuvée* is called variously "Côte Dorée" or "Côte Rousse"★★★, depending on which parcels of vine provide the grapes, all of them Syrah. It enjoys over four weeks in the vats before being aged in new Tronçais or Allier wood for ten months. A bottle of this will suit well those who would otherwise be drinking New World wines – which might also cost twice as much.

B42 Sylvain Fadat

DOMAINE D'AUPILHAC
28 rue du Plô
34150 Montpeyroux
☎ 04-67-96-61-19 C

Allow plenty of time for a visit: this bubbling, passionate man will have plenty to tell you, unrehearsed, and unedited, but it will all be fascinating. He is the sort of grower who makes you wish you had a few vines of your own.

Both his grandparents had some, but his own parents not. He luckily inherited four and a half hectares of very old Carignan of which he is proud. From it he makes a wonderful *mono-cépage*★★★. Although he is obliged to sell this as a vin de pays, he gets more for it than some of his AOC wines. It ages wonderfully too. Sylvain demonstrates, as if proof were needed, that a heavy culpability rests on the shoulders of those who have been the cause of so much destruction of the Carignan stock.

Quality in a wine, that is to say the complete expression of the terroir is, according to Sylvain, the product of the vineyard, not the *chais*. The grapes must be fully ripe and properly balanced within themselves when picked, so *vendanges vertes* are essential, except curiously, for his Carignan grapes: these vines are so old, apparently, that they limit their yield automatically. Although he has an impressive range of new stainless steel tanks, and a virtually underground and therefore cool cellar for his barriques, he is sceptical about the value of any interference with the wine once it has entered the vats. His wines are never filtered or fined.

Mont Baudile is the highest local mountain, and its name is given to Sylvain's eccentric white vin de pays★★, which comes from a strange cocktail of Ugni Blanc, Grenache Blanc, and Chardonnay, and is fermented partly in *cuve*, partly in wood. This atypical wine is gutsy enough to cope with sweetbreads or poultry in sauce.

There is a red "Mont Baudile"★★ also, quaffable, a wine for every day. Grenache and Cinsault are at its base and also of his rosé★★, which Sylvain makes by direct pressing rather than *saignage*. He says that, for him, *saignage* unbalances the rest of the wines off which a rosé is drawn.

A Merlot/Cabernet blend from grapes grown at Aniane is aggressively rustic, but the two AOC reds are top class, the first★★★ has some of all five grapes and is given a maceration of up to thirty-five days in a good year, with frequent *pigeage*. It is aged for seventeen months or so in barrels which have already seen one or more vintages. The second is called "Le Clos"★★ and contains usually 40% each of Mourvèdre and Carignan, and 20% Syrah; the thirty months which it spends in barrel will earn an extra★ for oak lovers, but some may find it a bit too much.

Sylvain wants to see Montpeyroux, of which he is deputy mayor, fully promoted as a cru in its own right. He believes in the hierarchization of the best areas, and spurns the idea of a global Languedoc appellation. He believes that this would benefit only the mass-producers, the blenders, and the négociants.

B39 Alain Chabanon

DOMAINE FONT CAUDE
34150 Lagamas
☎ 04-67-57-84-64 C/D

Alain Chabanon is doing so well that there are no signposts to his domaine; he says he prefers customers not to call in case he has nothing left to sell them. Visit and taste all the same – if you can find him – because his highly personalized wines are superb.

After a formal technical education at Montpellier and then Bordeaux, he went to work with Alain Brumont in Madiran for two years. In 1987 he bought fourteen hectares in the Montpeyroux area, to which he has since added a further seven. Most recently he has installed both his home and his *chais* in a brand-new construction outside the village of

Lagamas. This has happily coincided with the expiration of his contract with the coopérative, with whom he started his career.

Alain Chabanon has the same kind of pzazz as his mentor Alain Brumont, and he knows it. From Brumont he has inherited a love of long fermentations and a penchant for sweet wines. Alain makes his – which he calls "Le Villard"★★★ – wholly from Chenin Blanc, from a miniscule yield of seven hectolitres per hectare. Normally the grapes shrivel on the vine in the hot sun, but, in a rare year when the autumn is wet, they may attract botrytis. A direct comparison of the two styles is fascinating. The grapes are barrel-fermented and aged for thirty months in oak, but here Alain Chabanon parts company with Brumont, because he uses only casks which have seen at least two vintages, so that the effect of the wood is very discreet. There is a dry Chenin too called "Trélans"★★★ which has a little Rolle in it to give an authentic Languedoc touch.

The red Montpeyroux "Tradition"★★★ is from 80% Syrah and 20% Grenache. Again the yields are low, a mere twenty-three hectolitres per hectare. The *cuvaison* is long, five weeks or more, and the Grenache is aged in tank to preserve its fruit, but the Syrah is given sixteen months in barrel and another fourteen in tank. There is no filtering or fining and the wine is kept another three months after *assemblage* before bottling.

"Les Boissières"★★★ is a mainly Grenache red from older vines, aged in tank for thirty months after five weeks' maceration. Alain's Grenache wine is hugely ripe and rich, but not too heady.

The top red called "L'Esprit de Font Caude"★★★ would be all Syrah, but Alain gives it just enough Grenache to ensure appellation status. Yields of only eighteen hectolitres per hectare, a maceration of no less than seven weeks, two years at least in barrel, and a few more months in tank ensure a hugely concentrated wine in New World style, but the oak-ageing is masterly.

Alain's grandparents were all vignerons,

above Sylvain Fadat of Domaine d'Aupilhac pours some of his delicious Carignan

but his parents were not, so he was not brought up in the world of wine. The secret of his success must lie in his incisive intelligence, passion, and sheer application. His wines are far from cheap, but how can one expect otherwise when none shows a return to their grower for at least three years after the grapes are harvested?

B41 René-Marie et Charles Giner

DOMAINE SAINT-ANDRIEU
La Dysse
34150 Montpeyroux
☎ 04-67-96-61-37 B/C

The family house and *chais*, which are at the eastern end of Montpeyroux, and which are called La Dysse, belong to Madame

Giner, but the parents of both husband and wife were vignerons in the district before them, so making wine is in the blood, for sure. Monsieur Giner usually does the honours for visitors and is a gracious host. He will fondly show you round the seventeenth century property with its labyrinthine cellars, some two storeys below ground, as if they might be the catacombs of Montpeyroux.

To the original vineyards attached to the property, the Giners added more on the higher ground up toward the hills. This provided a range of terroirs and micro-climates which have persuaded them to exploit the different characteristics of their holdings by producing no less than four reds. First a quaffing wine from Grenache, Carignan, and Syrah called "Vallongue"★, straightforward, fruity and supple on the palate; then the Tradition, as it were, called "La Séranne"★★★, from Grenache, Syrah, two different parcels each of Mourvèdre and Carignan, spicy and fruity

with animal overtones, long and well-balanced; then a Grenache and Mourvèdre blend called "Les Marnes Bleues"★, perhaps a little dry and austere, but time may soften the tannins.

Finally "L'Yeuse Noir"★★, raised in oak and based on two different parcels of Mourvèdre, very old Carignan, Grenache, and Syrah. The *cuvaisons* here are long, but the Giners look for harmony and complexity rather than power.

It is worth mentioning that Montpeyroux is not the ideal home for the Syrah grape, which can roast here in the hot summer sun. Several growers have expressed this view, so remember that, for all its virtues, it is not a universal favourite.

This could well be the most "artisanal" domaine in Montpeyroux: the Giners demonstrate that top quality can be achieved without ruinous expenditure on stainless steel and state-of-the-art technology. Hats off to them!

saint-saturnin

Saint-Saturnin and Montpeyroux adjoin each other, but here the coopérative has maintained a tight grip on local winemaking.

B43 Jean-François Vallat

DOMAINE LES THERONS
(Château Mandagot)
34150 Montpeyroux
☎ 04-67-96-64-06 A

Monsieur Vallat is based in Montpeyroux but has vines in Saint-Saturnin of which he makes the best independently-produced example★.

terrasses de larzac

Temporarily, until it is decided what other areas this name will include, it is a convenient label to describe the most northern vineyards of Languedoc, those which grow at the foot of the Larzac plateau and on either side of the motorway which descends from the Pas d'Escalette. The land here is higher, the climate cooler and wetter; winters can be quite cold.

B38 Claude Favard

DOMAINE DE GRANOUPIAC
34725 Saint-André-de-Sangonis
☎ 04-67-96-62-58 A/B

This is another family of former *coopérateurs*, originally based in Gignac. Indeed, Favard still has seven hectares of vines there. Granoupiac, just a few kilometres to the west, came up for sale in 1983 without the "big house" and Claude Favard snapped it up. One wonders whether he saw the AOC coming two years later.

  The queues of cars waiting here in the courtyard attest to the popularity of the wines with the locals. Claude no longer sells *en négoce*, but his customers do buy *en vrac*. He is one of those estimable winemakers who

left Alain Chabanon, of Domaine Font Caude, through his glasses darkly

manages to combine impeccable standards with reasonable prices.

Claude has been lured into the use of new wood by the forces of the market, and in particular by his distributor in the UK and the USA. But it is not his real love, which remains true to traditional styles made with sure technique. His white AC★★ combines Roussanne, Grenache Blanc, and Rolle in unoaked form to produce a wine which has many of the exotic characteristics of more elaborate wines at double the price. For those who like rosé wines to be pale and light, Claude's★ will do nicely, with just a touch of bitterness deriving from the Cinsault grape.

There are four reds: the regular customers' favourite which is a vin de pays called "Garance"★, and derives from Carignan, Cinsault, and Cabernet Sauvignon, excellent for everyday drinking; a pure Merlot★★ is easy too, with excellent softness and roundness but absolutely nothing flabby about it. The AOC red★★ uses all the traditional grapes bar Cinsault, the Carignan being vinified by *macération carbonique*, while the oaked version★★ is, despite Claude's protestations, perhaps their best wine of all: it is aged for one year in wood, and another year in tank.

B44 Isabelle et François de Cabissole

CHATEAU DE JONQUIERES
34725 Jonquières
☎ 04-67-96-62-58 **B**

This is a real château, and quite a gem at that. Although it is in the middle of the village, you would not know it was there but for the discreet signpost inviting you to come in and buy wine. The building dates back to the twelfth century, but was "modernized" in the seventeenth. The courtyard boasts a deliciously asymmetrical double staircase, and the large park behind the château has a charming folly: an elaborate free-standing stone gateway which leads nowhere.

There are nineteen hectares planted with vines, seven of them to the north of the château on soil which is relatively rich and much suited to Grenache Blanc. The remaining vines are a short way down the road to Montpeyroux on the south side. Wine was made here even before the phylloxera, and records show that some of it was exported to Canada in 1865. It won a silver medal in 1889 at the Hérault wine show: there is a plaque to prove it.

The de Cabissoles joined the coopérative at Montpeyroux in 1965, with the full intention of being fully modern and mechanized. Gradually, however, their philosophy changed in the direction of *culture raisonnée*. Eventually, in 1992, they bought themselves out of their contract with the coopérative and started to make and bottle their own wine.

The de Cabissoles threaten to dig up their small planting of Alicante, which is a pity because when tasted from the cask and blended with the *vin de presse* from some other *cépages*, it was rather agreeable. Their serious red wine★★★ is from equal quantities of Syrah, Grenache, and Mourvèdre with just a touch each of Cinsault and Carignan too. It has good depth and fruit, and the quality – as the de Cabissoles have gained in experience – has increased enormously. It's a wine that ages well too.

The wines are available only through specialist wine shops in the South.

B45 Jean-Pierre Jullien

MAS CAL DEMOURA
34725 Jonquières
☎ 04-67-88-61-51 **B**

The Julliens specialize in charm, and Jean-Pierre, Olivier's father, has the voice of a radio presenter and the smile of a seraphim. The two of them live within a hundred yards of each other, the father as proud of the son as the latter is grateful to his father. But they carry on independent winemaking operations – though Jean-Pierre is quick to acknowledge that here the son is the teacher and the father is the pupil. By this he means that it was Olivier who in 1993 coached him in the making of his own wine. Previously the older Julliens, growers for 400 years, had all been *coopérateurs*.

Jean-Pierre has only seven hectares, but he manages to grow all five Languedoc grape varieties and a makes a rosé★ *saigné* from Cinsault, Carignan, and Syrah. It is called Qu'esaquo?, which means in modern French *Qu'est-ce-que c'est*? His red wine★★, which has a total ageing of eighteen months, has a bit of everything, and, although Olivier has taught him how to handle oak barrels, which he does magnificently well, his one aim is to let the fruit show through and speak for itself. He cannot understand why people keep their wines for so long that the fruit dries out. "If you find the girl of your dreams, you do not put her in a drawer for twenty years", he says.

Visit Jean-Pierre for a lesson in how not to retire. Cal Demoura is Occitan for "You must stay". You will wish that you could.

B46 Olivier Jullien

MAS JULLIEN
route de Saint-André
34725 Jonquières
☎ 04-67-96-60-04 **B/C**

Olivier was only twenty when in 1985 he decided to start his own vineyard next door to that of his father, not because they did not get on – quite the reverse – but because he was able to see that his future as a grower lay in learning to make and bottle his own wine, rather than sending his grapes to the local coopérative. He also needed to learn how to reconcile his own often-conflicting ideas with the already rapidly changing scene in the Languedoc.

The conflict within Olivier has always been his pursuit of absolute quality while at the same time resisting the tag of élitism and remaining one of the lads. To this end he has always adopted an improvisatory attitude to his vineyard: the modern idea of a business plan would be abhorrent to him. He has, for example, switched back and forth on the question of new wood; sold some parcels of his land and bought others, the area under vine varying between twelve and fifteen hectares; and in recent years he has reduced the number of *cuvées* he produces to as few as possible. Today he makes one white, one rosé, and two reds. All of them are in the top flight of Languedoc wines.

Olivier was lucky to have started when he did, because in 1985 land in Jonquières was going for a song. He acquired it bit by bit, just as he had developed his *chais*. His reputation, however, was made instantly and he became an overnight star.

Olivier does not believe in convention: he creates his own. His white vin de pays★★, for example, is a strange cocktail of Terret, Carignan Blanc, and Grenache Blanc, rich and delicate at the same time. Of his two reds, "Les Etats d'Ame du Mas Jullien"★★ may be a quaffing wine but it has real distinction, while the serious red wine of the house, called "Les Depierre-les-Cailloutis"★★★, is a Languedoc best-seller, so successful that it is hard to buy any without reserving it in advance. Olivier sells half his output to private buyers, only a quarter to *cavistes* and restaurants, and the remainder of the wine goes for export.

Readers should be warned, however, that by the time they manage to visit Olivier at Mas Jullien, everything may have changed, everything, that is, except his enduring passion and energy.

B47 Guilhem Dardé

MAS DES CHIMERES
34800 Octon
☎ 04-67-96-22-70 A/B

Guilhem is as good value for money as his wines: his arboreal jet-black moustache and eyebrows, twinkling eyes, and mischievous sense of humour guarantee a memorable visit. His domaine is in the lee of the plateau of Larzac. This arid *causse*, home only to unthirsty sheep, was the scene of epic

peasant resistance to the French Government who were determined to extend their military establishment there, much to the fury of the local sheep-farmers who send their milk to nearby Roquefort for conversion into cheese. Guilhem, with his more infamous general, Bové, was a leading light in the Confédération Paysanne which quietly but effectively told the Government where it got off. There followed another campaign to prevent a moto-cross circuit and property development round Lake Salagou, just below Guilhem's village and his vines. Guilhem's personal success here earned him the mayoralty of Octon.

It is typical of Guilhem that, when he decided to leave the local coopérative in 1993, he did not ask them, but simply set up on his own. A mutually acceptable settlement followed. He used to have seventeen hectares of vines, the grapes of which he sent to another coopérative at Clermont L'Hérault, but he dug these up.

His remaining twelve hectares leave him independent. A totally free spirit; he likes to make wines within the appellation, because it makes him feel good. But as a winemaker he does not care whether his wines are vins de pays or whatever. Take his 100% Cinsault for example, which he calls "Oeillade"★★ after a plant which may or may not be the same as the unfashionable Cinsault – in the local markets grapes similar to Cinsault are enjoyed as table grapes and called "Oeillade". Whatever the truth, this wine has a delicious bouquet and flavour of bitter cherries: its charm and good acidity make a flavoury summer bottle.

Then there is his 100% "Carignan"★★, with an unusually flowery character when Guilhem vinifies it traditionally. Some of these grapes get a *macération carbonique*, and the resulting *assemblage* shows off the typical gentle bitterness of the *cépage*.

His red AC★★★ is the wine for which he is best known and it would be hard to find a better example, certainly at the price this one sells for. Tasted from the barrel, the

constituent Syrah, Grenache, and Mourvèdre make a facinating comparison: the Mourvèdre in particular showing velvety spice, the texture being nearly as singular as the flavour; or the round Grenache with its gentle suggestions, when so very young, of the pharmacy; or the Syrah, aged in old Sauvignon Blanc casks from Bordeaux, with rare overtones of good meat stock.

"Hérétique"★★ is the name given aptly to Guilhem's Merlot-Cabernet vin de pays, rather classy in its field, but a wine which may need more time to come to its best than his AOC wine. An abundance of rich fruit will no doubt see off the tannins one day.

other good larzac growers

Charles Capaud
Domaine La Croix-Chaptal,
34725 Saint-André-de-Sangonis
☎ 04-67-16-09-36

Madame Mireille Bertrand
Domaine de Malavieille, 34800 Mérifons
☎ 04-67-96-34-67

cabrières

This terroir almost adjoins Faugères to the east and enjoys the same band of schistous soil. It is surrounded by hills and dominated by the striking profile of Pic Vissou which is some 490 metres (1,600 feet) high. The coopérative dominates the production, which includes a rosé wine of which the village is very proud. There is only one independent producer, and independent is indeed the word.

B48 Guy Mathieu

DOMAINE DU TEMPLE
Les Crozes
34800 Cabrières
☎ 04-67-96-07-84 A

Mathieu is an ex-President of the local coopérative. When he started to make and bottle his own wine, he felt he should resign from this job, although he still sends a good proportion of his grapes its way.

The property has a long history involving many of the medieval great and good, as well as some downright rogues and thieves. Guy Mathieu is the archetypal peasant grower. He had the very good fortune to buy up, for next to nothing in 1990, the dilapidated estate, which had fallen on neglected times. It could quite possibly be the most isolated *mas* in the whole of Languedoc: at the end of a three-kilometre road which serves no other dwelling, although it is flanked on either side by nothing but vines. All of these, except those around the Domaine du Temple, belong to other *coopérateurs*.

Guy has twenty hectares of grapes all of which are picked by hand. They include some very peachy Viognier★, Cinsault which is used to make two rosés, one★ with Syrah added, the other with Grenache and Mourvèdre. The three reds are all extremely good value: the "Cuvée Tiveret" ★ from Syrah, Mourvèdre, and Grenache, all vines which Mathieu planted himself as soon as he had moved in; a Tradition called "Jacques de Molay"★★, from Syrah and Mourvèdre only, which has rather more matter and is altogether more serious; and an oaked version of the same★ from old vines. Guy uses only twenty-five per cent new oak, but the wood is fairly prominent and needs time for its tannins to resolve. He is assisted in the *chais* by the peripatetic Guy Bascou (see domaines Condamine l'Evêque and Gourgazaud).

After a tour of more sophisticated growers further afield, a visit to Guy Mathieu in his wonderfully tranquil setting, with a glass of his good red in the shade of the old *mas*, makes a delightful relaxation. However, be prepared for dissertations of a political incorrectness which may take the breath away.

right the irrepressible Guilhem Dardé, of Mas des Chimères, and Mayor of Octon

picpoul de pinet

This is the name given to the white wines from a quite self-contained AOC area, limited to the six communes of Castelnau-de-Guers, Florensac, Mèze, Montagnac, Pinet, and Pomérols, all lying close to the Bassin de Thau. The Bassin is a salt water lagoon devoted to the cultivation of oysters and mussels, for which this wine forms a perfect partnership.

Picpoul's particularity derives from the grape, here confusingly spelt "Piquepoul". In any event it is nothing to do with the grape bearing the same name grown in the Gers as a basis for armagnac. It is undoubtedly a traditional grape of the Languedoc, in three guises, black, "Gris" and white. Here we are concerned only with the white grape, which has a history in the South going back at least to the sixteenth century.

Picpoul de Pinet may contain no other juice than that of the Piquepoul grape which thrives on the sandy soil mixed with pebbles, sometimes with gravelly stone, to be found in this maritime location. Typically, the wine will have good acidity, but with some suavity and just a touch of bitterness on the finish. Citrus and grapefruit flavours have been noted by many. Others describe the wine as being "in the Italian style". The appellation extends a few kilometres inland, and the best wines are made from grapes grown on the slightly rising ground away from the shore. The granting of AOC status has acted as a great spur to increase quality at the expense of yield, and to upgrade the standards of vinification. "Rather flabby" may have been an apt description of these wines some years ago, but it will not do today. On the other hand, attempts by some growers to age the wine in wood seem to deny the terroir, and the partnership with shellfish.

There are altogether 650 hectares achieving appellation status, for which the permitted yield is limited to fifty hectolitres to the hectare. There are six coopératives and thirteen independent growers. One of the best-known is:

left Claude-Hélène Jourdan of Domaine Félines-Jourdan, which is close to the Bassin de Thau

B31 Marie-Hélène Jourdan

DOMAINE FELINES-JOURDAN
34140 Mèze
☎ 04-67-43-69-29 A

The domaine itself, and its *caves*, are
very close to the sea in the small hamlet
of Félines a few kilometres to the west
of Mèze; its vineyards, which go right
down to the edge of the Bassin, are mostly
devoted to vins de pays. The Jourdans
have a hundred hectares, the majority
of which is assigned to such wines, only
fifteen per cent of their total production
being of Picpoul de Pinet. As well as Félines
vines, they have plantations at Montagnac
a little further inland, where most of the
Piquepoul is grown, and at Pomérols
further west.

Piquepoul matures after the hottest
weather has passed, so it ripens over a
longer period than earlier-maturing varieties.
Grapes picked early, even if fully ripe, can
have quite a different character from those
gathered at the end of the season. Three
different samples from the *cuve* may
demonstrate this point admirably – if you
manage to visit, and taste, in the winter
before the wine is blended. The Jourdans
aspire to a fruitier style than some other
growers: a Picpoul★★ with more *gras* which
will match food other than shellfish.
Sometimes the wine has a hint of pears and
even butter, suggesting a Languedoc
equivalent to a good Côtes de Gascogne.

Of the vins de pays, the Syrah/Grenache
blend called "Les Romarins"★, a gutsy wine
with just enough tannins to balance it,
is to be preferred to the 100% Grenache.
There is also a curiosity, a Muscat★,
made from late-picked grapes and given
a discreet oaking – an exotic wine, whose
fermentation is stopped by refrigeration
rather than by additional alcohol, it is from
a very small production, but turns out as
a worthy rival to similar styles from the more
prestigious sources.

B33 SCEA C. et L. Gaujal

CUVEE LUDOVIC GAUJAL
Château de Pinet
34850 Pinet
☎ 04-67-77-02-12 A

Like Félines-Jourdan, this is a wine often
to be found in restaurants and shops along
the waterfront of the Bassin de Thau. It is very
sound Picpoul de Pinet★★ – and pushes
thirteen degrees of alcohol. There is said to be
fierce rivalry between the growers of Pinet and
those of the adjoining village of Pomérols,
each group accusing the other of illegal
practices in their winemaking. Probably there
is no truth at all in these stories, certainly here
where winemaking is of a high standard.

A tale is told, however, that is so unlikely
it must be true. Ludovic, the grandfather of
the present grower, was visited in the early
1930s by the Marquis de Lur-Saluces, the
owner of world-famous Château d'Yquem,
which at that time was going through a bad
patch. The two men valued each others'
company and passed long hours discussing
the sweet white wines of France in the relative
cool of the Languedoc twilight. The Marquis
was so pleased with his visit, he liked the
Languedoc so much, and he rated Gaujal's
wines so highly that, at the end of his stay,
he seriously proposed an incredible deal: a
straight swap of Yquem for Domaine Gaujal.
Without hesitating, Gaujal declined. Later
generations have paid more dearly for an
interest in Yquem.

B29 Roland Tarroux

MAS SAINT-LAURENT
Montmèze
34140 Mèze
☎ 04-67-43-92-30 A

Phone Roland Tarroux for an appointment
and he will tell you instantly that he is the
only winemaker in the world whose vines
grow among dinosaur eggs. And this is no
joke, because he has plenty of learned
papers from the University of Montpellier

confirming that this property was the site
of an important colony of these prehistoric
beasts at least sixty million years ago.

Monsieur Tarroux's vines are happily more
recent and rank among the best Piquepoul.
The domaine dates back to the end of
the nineteenth century, when Roland's great-
grandfather arrived in the area to look for work
– any work. He bought a small parcel of land
to build a modest house, and the property
has now expanded to thirty-two hectares of
vineyard, planted partly with Piquepoul, partly
with other *cépages* for vins de pays.

Roland works as close as he can to fully
organic practices without being a paid-up
member. He is enough of a traditionalist to
bottle his wine on the old moon of February,
after giving it a traditional fermentation. He
attributes the slightly Tuscan style of Picpoul
to his belief that the grape variety may go
back to ancient Rome or even Greece –
scarcely a long history when compared with
that of the dinosaurs. It is certainly as much
a part of Languedoc history as say Clairette
or even Terret★★, of which Roland has five
hectares from which he makes an
unfashionable but attractively dry floral wine,
which has good attack but also some
softness on the palate. All these grapes were
used, historically, by the vermouth-makers
before they discovered cheaper sources of
juice in Sicily and southern Italy.

Tarroux's Picpoul★★ is drier, has more
acidity and speaks "shellfish" louder than
some of the more Southern styles, and what
is wrong with that when the oyster beds of
the Bassin, clearly visible from Roland's
sitting-room, beckon so seductively?

Of his vins de pays, try the rosé★★
(Cinsault/Carignan/Grenache), a pretty
pale pink colour, with a bouquet of early
summer fruits, surprisingly full in the mouth
and all too easy to drink; or the Cabernet
Sauvignon/Grenache/Syrah blend★★. This
needs keeping: five years after a good vintage.

Unless Roland remembers first, ask him
before you leave for a pocketful of fossilized
dinosaur eggs to take home for the children.

B30 Albert Morin

DOMAINE MORIN-LANGARAN
34140 Mèze
☎ 04-67-43-58-01 A

The owner does not attach his name to that of his property out of conceit but because a long and dramatic lawsuit obliged him to. Even though this property goes back to the fourteenth century, Monsieur Morin has a Pagnol-like tale to tell about attempts to stop him using the name Langaran by the owners of a similarly-named property who should have known better. At the last moment, a learned lady researcher offered him evidence (shades of *Manon des Sources*) which enabled him to prove a much longer history than his rivals', relieving him of a heavy claim for damages and costs.

Indeed, the name is linked with the property since 1595, when Pierre Engarran bought it. Even he, however, had to survive twenty-five years of litigation before he was confirmed in ownership. From 1714 to 1936 it remained within one family and this period saw much renown brought to the wines. Pasteur stopped here to take away some samples, and the Empress Eugènie, who loved the Mediterranean climate, thought of buying the estate as a *maison secondaire*. The Morins bought Langaran, as it is now spelt, in 1966, though the family had long experience of being winemakers for over a hundred years before that.

Today Albert Morin makes a first-class Picpoul★★ from sixteen hectares already planted when he arrived. The wine is somewhere between Félines-Jourdan and Mas Saint-Laurent in style, making it a good all-rounder with most types of fish. Try it with red mullet grilled over charcoal.

Morin's vins de pays, for which the grapes come from a vineyard some kilometres away, include a varietal Sauvignon★ and a Chardonnay from young grapes. Roussanne is the basis of a *cuvée prestige*★★ that sees some oak. The reds include a Syrah/Cinsault blend★ made traditionally, and an oaked

assemblage of Cabernet Sauvignon and Merlot★. Before you take leave of Monsieur Morin, be sure to taste his sweet Muscat★★: he avoids the risk of the fermentation starting again by being highly meticulous about the sterility of the bottling environment.

Morin likes to sell as much of his wine as he can from the domaine: personal customers are the most loyal, so visitors are always assured of a warm welcome. He offers guided tours of the vineyards and the *caves*.

other good picpoul growers

Domaine de Farlet
34140 Mèze
(organic)
☎ 04-67-43-50-05

Robert Mur
La Grangette, route de Pomérols,
34120 Castelnau-de-Guers
(organic)
☎ 04-67-98-13-56

Lucette et Joseph Albajan
Domaine de la Mirande,
34120 Castelnau-de-Guers
☎ 04-67-98-21-52,

Fabrice Lagille
Cave l'Ormarine,
1 avenue de Picpoul,
34850 Pinet
☎ 04-67-77-03-10

Olivier Azan
Château Petit Roubié,
34850 Pinet
(organic)
☎ 04-67-77-09-28

Cave des Costières de Pomérols
Hugues de Beauvignac,
34810 Pomérols
☎ 04-67-77-01-59

SARL Domaine de Belle-Mare
34140 Mèze
☎ 04-67-43-17-68

la clape

La Clape is a maritime area dominated by a large hill rising some 215 metres (700 feet) above the Languedoc plain. It was once an island at a time when all the surrounding area to the north and west was under the sea. The waters had already receded by Roman times, and they re-established a link between their local capital, Narbonne, and the Mediterranean by diverting the river Aude to present-day Gruissan. When the Romans were driven out of Gaul, the river re-asserted its old route and the water-links to Gruissan became a series of lagoons which are today a feature of the local landscape.

It is possible that the vineyard of La Clape was the first to be created by the Romans in Languedoc. At least, its wines were considered the best of the region because it was these that were sent back to Rome, while the rest were mostly drunk on the spot. Two factors single out La Clape from the "mainland": its exceptionally dry climate with an average annual rainfall of only fifty centimetres (twenty inches), and its terroir. There are strange, misshapen outcrops of rock, infilled by garrigue, interspersed with vines where they will grow. The lack of rain is made up for, especially in August, by the frequent sea-mists which keep the vines moist and prevent them burning in the hot sun.

La Clape is the only subdivision of the Coteaux du Languedoc that may add its name to white wines as well as red. Bourboulenc is the grape most suited to the terroir and must constitute at least forty per cent of the white *encépagement*. For the reds, Grenache must contribute at least twenty per cent, Syrah, Mourvèdre, and Grenache together seventy per cent. Carignan and Cinsault may be added.

H3 La Famille Chamayrac

CHATEAU MIRE L'ETANG
11560 Fleury d'Aude
☎ 04-68-33-62-84 A

The *étang* (pond) is called Pissevache, which inspires little confidence. But have no fear: the wines are not only good but good

value too. Pierre Chamayrac bought this sixty-hectare property in 1971. Today, he has the Syrah, Mourvèdre, and Grenache with which he replanted the vineyard thirty years back. He kept the ancient stone vats in the *chais*, however, which have walls more than a metre thick and provide wonderful insulation against the torrid summer heat. Pierre is supposed to have retired, but vignerons seldom do. He and his son Philippe work in tandem.

Eight hectares or so of vines are situated on the low-lying land by the sea-shore, and here grow the grapes for some modest vins de table. The main vineyards are a little further inland on the lower slopes of the Massif.

In addition to Bourboulenc, Pierre has for his white wine★ some Roussanne which he finds more aromatic than Marsanne, and Grenache Blanc. There are two rosés: one *saigné* from Grenache and called "Gris"★, pale as its name implies; and the other rather deeper and called "Corail"★ in which Syrah and Cinsault are added to the Grenache. This is the colour of rose petals.

The red "Tradition"★★ is as fine as it is untypical, deep, smokey, and seductive. The oaked version called "Ducs de Fleury"★★ is even smokier but much more discreetly

above grapes have a decorative, as well as a commercial, role to play

oaked than the top wine called "Réserve du Château"★ in which the wood influence is surely too prominent?

Spécialités de la maison include a Muscat★★, effectively a *vendange tardive* wine, though not allowed to call itself that. From a tiny yield of eight hectolitres per hectare, this nectar is not as expensive as you might think it would be. Nor is the delicious Cartagène★★ made from very late-picked Grenache and fortified with the local eau-de-vie.

H2 Jean-Paul Rosset

CHATEAU DE NEGLY
11560 Fleury d'Aude
☎ 04-68-32-36-28 A; top wines C

Red wines are sometimes described as "table" wines, their purpose being to accompany food. When, therefore, a *maître de chais* says that he cannot imagine what food could accompany his wines, one is entitled to wonder whether he has lost his way. Such is the case with the top wines – the *micro-cuvées* – of this estate, made to California formula with long *cuvaisons*, maximum extraction, high levels of alcohol, and considerable over-oaking.

This is a pity because the basic appellation wines here and the vins de pays are good, even if one gets the impression that they are not so highly rated by their makers. The white Marsanne★, barrel-fermented with the now usual *bâtonnage*, has good acidity to balance its typical Southern "fat", while the Bourboulenc★★ is more floral and fresh. The rosé, *saigné* from Syrah and Grenache, is good mainstream stuff. The AOC red★★ is a step up in class: blended half from Grenache, half from Carignan, the latter partly vinified traditionally and partly by *macération carbonique*. It has an interesting coffee and toast character, somewhat atypical.

The proprietor is a Narbonne businessman, who has quite rightly put the winemaking ahead of the restoration of this interesting but run-down château. He acquired it in 1992 and kept the old Grenache and Carignan vines, planting Syrah, Mourvèdre, and more Grenache. The vineyards are in the charge of a son of François Pugibet (*see* Domaine de la Colombette, page 78), while the winemaker is Monsieur Cyril Chamontin. The latter does not think that Carignan does well here, but he has retrained it *en palissage*, along with the rest of the vines.

left Christophe Bousquet of Château Pech Redon, dismisses varietal wines as "made by those who have no terroir to express"

Today, quality is the result of low yields of about thirty hectolitres per hectare. Harvesting is done in small *cagettes* so as to protect the integrity of the fruit. There is a double *triage* at the vine and in the *chais*. All the grapes are destalked except the Carignan which is destined for *macération carbonique*. The huge old concrete *cuves* have been subdivided so as to allow separate vinification of each parcel and of each grape variety, so blends can be more carefully constructed. There is an air-conditioned space for the 150 barriques of which twenty per cent are renewed each year.

H1 Jacques de Saint-Exupéry

CHATEAU PECH-CELEYRAN
11110 Salles-d'Aude
☎ 04-68-33-50-04
Ⓦ www.pech-celeyran.com **A**

This peacefully beautiful estate is the doyen of the La Clape vineyards, as well as being probably the best-known. Its fame rests partly on its Toulouse-Lautrec associations; it was the painter's mother's property and the family used to come to Céleyran for their summer holidays, when teenage Henri experimented with his paints. His subjects were often his holiday-companions, the workers in the vineyards. There is an exquisite selection of these early paintings in the museum at Albi, about two-hours' drive away. Lautrec's mother, who survived him, gave the city a magnificent collection of her son's works, which now comprise what is possibly the best permanent one-man show in the world.

The château is not old. It was built very much in the style of a *maison de maître* in the nineteenth century when the present estate was split off from its much older neighbour across the main road. It was thought at the time that Pech-Céleyran got the worst of this family partition, since the soil was much less productive. Today this is a blessing.

The property came to the Saint-Exupérys by inheritance down the female line, and today looks much as it would have done in Toulouse-Lautrec's childhood. The thickly

wooded park is ethereal in the misty light of a hot summer morning, and the *chais* still holds the breathtaking collection of old giant *foudres*, no longer used, alas, for the storage of wine, but living on as an art gallery.

Today, Jacques de Saint-Exupéry looks after the vines, while his son Nicolas makes the wine and deals with the commercial side. The family has managed to achieve a fine balance between experimentation and tradition, between quality and commercial success. In its time it pioneered the planting of new *cépages* for vins de pays. These account for fifty per cent of Pech-Celeyran production because, for obscure bureaucratic reasons, only half the estate qualifies as AOC land. The white vin de pays★★ is remarkable for its fruit and freshness. It is made from Viognier, Maccabeu, and some Chardonnay which was planted as early as 1987 on old Alicante rootstocks. Its red counterpart★★, which contains Languedoc grapes as well as Merlot, Cot, and Cabernet, derives its cigar-box aroma from the last-named of these varieties, and hints of strawberries from old Carignan.

The red AC★★★ is much deeper in colour, but still has the same red fruit, with spices from Mourvèdre, and just a hint of cigars, which Nicolas attributes to the terroir. The white AC★★★ is usually from Marsanne, Roussanne, and Maccabeu and is given a light oak treatment which you might not detect if you were not told. It has rather better acidity than the vin de pays.

Pech-Céleyran does not bother with oak for its reds, not even for a recently introduced *tête de cuvée* called "La Réserve"★★★.

H4 Jean-Claude et Christophe Bousquet

CHATEAU PECH REDON
route de Gruissan
11100 Narbonne
☎ 04-68-90-41-22 **A**

Jean-Claude was a *coopérateur* at Saint-Saturnin, one of the founders and later President of the Syndicat of Languedoc

growers. His natural ambition to make his own wine could only be achieved, because of his contract with the coopérative, by selling up and moving elsewhere. At the time, Pech Redon belonged to Jean Demolombe, one of the Languedoc pioneers. Modern grape varieties had already been planted by him in the 1970s. Ill health obliged him to sell the estate, and the Bousquets seized the chance to buy a vineyard already up and running, and well-maintained.

Pech Redon means "rounded hilltop": the estate is the highest in La Clape and takes its name from the summit of the *massif*. To reach it requires a journey of three kilometres (1.7 miles) up a rough road which leads only to this vineyard. Christophe Bousquet is well fired by the passionate motivation needed to live in such solitude. Although a trained oenologist, he surprises by being more interested in his vineyards than what goes on in the *chais*. He is an absolutely convinced terroir man: the preservation of identity is for him the key to professional integrity. He is not interested in fashion, but only in what he as a grower can persuade his vines to give him. He disputes, for example, the general opinion that Carignan does not grow well at La Clape; he has no problem with it, believing it to thrive on the moisture which comes off the sea in August. The high elevation of his land is especially suited to the Bourboulenc grape because he picks much later than other local growers, and its already long vegetal cycle can here be extended until early October.

Christophe makes a little vin de pays from Chardonnay, but otherwise all his wines are AOC. The white★★ (Bourboulenc and Grenache Blanc) has wonderful freshness, which he points out is not the same thing as acidity. Christophe does little to interfere with the natural processes of vinification save that this wine he ages on its lees. He makes a little rosé★★★ too, a wine of which he is proud because he made his name with it. From the best *cuves* of Syrah and Grenache, it is drawn off within a matter of hours. Such short *saignage* makes for elegance and finesse.

The basic red appellation wine is called "Les Cades"★★★, which means juniper bush. It has lovely scents from the garrigue, and sometimes tar and minerals too beneath the fruit. The unfashionable blend is Cinsault/Carignan/Grenache, which shows that you can make a first class wine without the *cépages améliorateurs*, although, in years when the Cinsault is not successful, Christophe replaces it with Syrah. An oaked blend of Syrah and Grenache is called "L'Epervier"★★★ (sparrowhawk), but you hardly notice the wood because none of it is new.

Top of the range is "La Centaurée"★★★, named after the wild flower of which a rare sub-species is peculiar to La Clape. The wine comes from the oldest Syrah and Grenache, half aged in *cuve*, a quarter in old wood, and a quarter in wood which is either new or which has seen only one wine. This is deep, smokey, toasty, and highly garrigue-scented.

Christophe despises *vins de cépage*, which he says are so often the mainstay of people who have no terroir to express. This does not stop him making a curious hundred per cent Alicante, a variety which he claims can bear comparison with any other grapes he grows. Try it and see.

other good la clape growers

Charles Mock
Château de Capitoul, route de Gruissan,
11100 Narbonne
☎ 04-68-49-23-30

EARL Ferri-Arnaud
Domaine Ferri-Arnaud, avenue de l'Hérault,
11560 Fleury d'Aude
☎ 04-68-33-62-43

Gérard Bertrand
Domaine de l'Hospitalet,
route de Narbonne Plage, 11100 Narbonne
☎ 04-68-45-34-47

Jacques Boscary
Château Rouquette-sur-Mer,
11100 Narbonne-Plage
☎ 04-68-49-90-41

terrasses de béziers

The best wines here are grown on the plateau which divides the mouths of the rivers Orb and Aude, close to the Mediterranean coast.

B62 Marc de Bréon

DOMAINE D'ESPAGNAC
34410 Sauvian
☎ 04-67-32-17-71 A

Writing in 1816, André Jullien noted the Muscat which was grown here but has now disappeared, but even more to his liking were the red wines: "Sauvian...has in its neighbourhood the growth called Despagnac (sic), which produces dark-coloured, well-structured wines with plenty of alcohol; they are somethng like those of Collioure...".

Today it is difficult to know what to make of Espagnac. The domaine is large, eighty-four hectares, about two-thirds of which rank for AOC, and the rest vins de pays. The best grapes are grown on terraces which look toward the sea and benefit from its cooling moisture. Nearly all the production is destined for supermarkets and the like, and yet these wines, a multi-*cépage* AC★ and a Merlot varietal★, are of surprisingly good quality and value for money. But the *tête de cuvée*★★★ – prepared for an English importer – is of such differently superior standard that it is a wonder they do not aim for the quality market. They have the terroir and the ability, but somehow the confidence and drive is yet to be found.

Espagnac is very hard to locate. It is marked on the Michelin maps, but the neighbourhood is criss-crossed by a confusion of minor roads, tracks, and worse. When you eventually arrive, it is attractive in an untidy sort of way, like somewhere out of a nineteenth-century etching. The huge round stones underfoot attest immediately to the difficult nature of the terroir. There is nothing remarkable about the grape varieties grown, but the wines are carefully made and should be followed in the hope that the potential of the property and its winemakers will soon be fully realized.

B32 Guy Rambier et Jacques Tournant

VIGNOBLES MONTFREUX DE FAGES
(Château Font des Prieurs et Domaine Haut de Bel Air)
route de Mèze
34340 Marseillan
☎ 04-67-77-59-17
Ⓦ www.montfreux-de-fages.com A

This is a partnership between Guy Rambier, vigneron, and Jacques Tournant, wine-loving businessman and nature-lover. There are two quite separate properties: eleven hectares of the AOC Château, near Gabian, north of Pézenas, and thirty-nine (including four of Piquepoul), at the domaine, a stone's throw from the Bassin de Thau. Apart from the Picpoul, all the latter wines are vins de pays. Both estates are run on wholly organic lines.

The AOC Château grapes are vinified in unlined cement; Guy says that an unlined tank can breathe more easily. The vinification, all done at Marseillan, is entirely by *macération carbonique*, even for the Grenache, something rare. The unoaked wine★★ has pleasant notes of tobacco and *pain grillé*. The oaked version★★ is well-handled.

Of the vins de pays, there is a "Sauvignon de Minuit"★★, grown inland at Gabian and harvested after dark. The Sauvignon makes a fresh, spring-like wine with a slightly smokey nose. There is a "Chardonnay de Minuit"★ too, grown at Marseillan. And an attractive blend called "Mariage en Blanc"★★ from Roussanne, Marsanne, Chardonnay, and Sauvignon.

Of the red vins de pays, the Cabernet/Merlot/Grenache blend★ bottled under the Domaine label rather recalls a Côtes de Malepère: agreeably forward and easy, lacking a bit of acidity perhaps, but Rambier is trying to get permission to plant a little Petit Verdot to remedy this. There is an oaked version, but the use of wood at this domaine is still experimental and may take a year or two for them to master.

This is a good property for the price-conscious, though there are better Picpouls to be had.

B64 Jacques et Any Gauch

DOMAINE DU NOUVEAU MONDE
34350 Vendres
☎ 04-67-37-33-68 vdp A; AOC B

This domaine is almost on the beach at
Vendres, but the owners also have some
AOC land on the Terrasses de Béziers which
Jacques one day hopes will be designated
a *cru* in its own right; he heads the campaign
which is trying to achieve this.

His father-in-law bought the property in
1956 and Jacques took it over in 1983. He
dug up some of the vineyards near the sea
so as to transfer the planting rights to the
AOC land, where he now has the usual
Syrah, Grenache, and Mourvèdre, the last-
named being particularly happy in its quasi-
maritime situation. Jacques reserves it for his

top wine. His "Tradition"★★ has a twenty-five-
day *cuvaison* followed by two years' ageing
in epoxy-lined cement, while an oaked
version★★ enjoys twelve to fifteen months in
barrels which have already been used once.
Both are excellent, bright ruby in colour, with
good legs, crushed fruit aromas, and a very
Rhône-ish character – better than many wines
from the area.

Vins de pays include a Chardonnay★: pale,
delicate, but, in trying not to be Burgundian, a
little lacking in personality. To be preferred is a
delicious "Chasan"★★, in which Chardonnay's
parentage is a strong influence, stronger in fact
than in the Chardonnay varietal.

The red vin de pays is the usual Cabernet
and Merlot blend★, deep in colour, with good
roundness from the Merlot grape. While the
wine is not too tannic, it is not facile either.

above local council elections, *à la* Languedocienne

There is an oaked *cuvée*★★ of this, which
is even better, one third of the wine being
given a gentle dose of not too new wood.

Do not forget the Gris de Gris★, a very
pale onion-skin style of pinkish wine with
excellent acidity, perfume, and length.

B63 Georges et Jacques Damitio, Clem et Christopher Thomas, et François Serres

CHATEAU LE THOU
34410 Sauvian
☎ 04-67-32-16-42 B

Excellence has marked the careers of this
unlikely partnership, and the same excellence
shows in its wines. François Serres, chosen by

La Revenue Vinicole Internationale as oenologist of the year 1998, earned his spurs at Château Rayas in Châteauneuf-du-Pape. Clem Thomas was captain of the Welsh Rugby Team, perhaps longer ago than he cares to remember – a passion which his son Christopher has inherited. Georges Damitio was a fanatical gymnast – though his son, Jacques, is more intellectually inclined as a lawyer in Paris.

His sister Bernadette is general manager, while an outside shareholder, Gilles Betthaeuser, qualified as a shareholder through his devotion to sport. Completing this formidable team is the *régisseur*, Thierry Ajac, at the property since 1990, and who has been responsible for the gradual improvement of the estate.

This new team took over only in April 2001, but has lost no time in putting this property back on the map of quality Languedoc. The previous years, despite the devotion and hard work of Ajac, had seen a lack of change due to the inevitable indecision arising from family inheritance problems. Today it is all Go.

Built on the ruins of a Roman Villa, the present buildings, which go back in part to the fourteenth and fifteenth centuries, benefited from a Roman aqueduct which provided water to the city of Béziers. The name "Thou" comes from the Languedoc word "*tao*" meaning a water-pipe. The old piping to the domaine is still there and in use.

The vineyards are on the terraces which divide the mouths of the rivers Orb and Aude, enjoying a typical chalk and clay soil. Nineteen of the twenty-four hectares rank for AOC Coteaux du Languedoc, the other five for vins de pays. "Georges et Clem"★★★ derives from 70% Syrah and 30% Grenache, while the property's second wine★★ sometimes has a little Carignan too.

Cuvaisons are for thirty and twenty-one days respectively, and the top wine is raised in oak for six months. The hallmarks of both

left Catherine Roque, of Domaine de Clovallon, is an architect turned vigneronne

are rich ripe red fruits, with plenty of pepper and spice from the Syrah grape. Neither wine is filtered. The Merlot★★ vin de pays is a charmer, dark in colour, and unexpectedly firm on the palate.

pézenas, béziers, and côtes de thongue vins de pays

Lord Clive of India, having dug himself a black hole in Calcutta, had to extricate himself, so he came to Pézenas in France, where he introduced mince pies to the French. Today *les petites pâtes de Pézenas* make the fortune of the town. Only in part though, because Pézenas is also a densely planted centre for Languedoc wines, especially vins de pays. Nearby is the valley of the River Thongue, where growers have managed to discover an identity amounting to a terroir of their own, with a forward-looking Syndicat of motivated vignerons.

B56 Prosper et Louis-Marie Teisserenc, Charles Duby, et Guillaume de Foxière

DOMAINE DE L'ARJOLLE
34480 Pouzolles
☎ 04-67-24-81-18 B

It would be hard to find a jollier bunch of vignerons than the extended Teisserenc family, but then with eighty hectares to tend, including twenty-five in the nearby village of Margon, they need all hands on deck to cope with a very considerable enterprise. There is no warmer welcome in the Languedoc, and their generosity is legendary. You will be asked to stay if you show the slightest inclination, but at the least you will be given a hugely generous tasting of the considerable range of wines which they produce.

Back in 1974, Louis-Marie, dubbed "the bearded wonder of the Languedoc", joined forces with his banker brother Prosper to recreate what had been the family domaine for hundreds of years. But, being non-traditionalists, they chose to plant the "foreign" grape varieties like Cabernet

Sauvignon (today they have ten hectares), Merlot of the same area, half as much of Cabernet Franc, eight hectares of Muscat, seven of Sauvignon, and a little each of Viognier, Gamay, Syrah, and... er, Zinfandel.

The *cépages* are chosen according to their aptitude to terroir, and cultivated to suit their styles, whether *en palissage*, or by Guyot *simple* or *double*, or even after the shape of the lyre, as with the Viognier and Muscat.

Here, every member of the family has their appointed role. Charles Duby, brother-in-law of the Teisserenc brothers, is in the vineyard; nephew Guilhem looks after the equipment; while Roland, Prosper's son, works with his father on the vines. The womenfolk of the family look after everyone at lunchtime, including all the employees, and any visitors who happen to be on hand.

There is now a magnificent new *cave de stockage*, bringing together the operations formerly scattered round the countryside, but the vinification remains traditional in the old buildings close by.

With their sense of adventure, the range of wines here remains enormous, and ever-changing, so detailed comment is likely to become obsolete fairly quickly. But it seems unlikely that such marvels as the Cabernet/Merlot blend called simply "Cuvée de l'Arjolle"★★ will be quickly superseded, nor the "Cabernet de l'Arjolle"★★★, a blend of the two Cabernets in true Médoc style, a wine which needs many years to come into its own; nor yet again the "Muscat en Vendanges Tardives"★★★ that keeps a vivacity and freshness to offset its luxurious sugar. Whatever you taste here is bound to be good and the value for money is terrific.

C1 Catherine Roque

DOMAINE DE CLOVALLON
34600 Bédarieux
☎ 04-67-95-19-71 B/C

Dynamic Catherine likes to give the impression that she approached the planting of her vineyard as if it were a herbaceous

border: it amused her to have just three-and-a-half hectares of vines in those early days. However, the bug quickly got her, and today her sparkling eyes betray an unexcelled devotion and fanaticism for her new *métier*.

Catherine bought her old mill in 1989. Bédarieux, considered too cold and northerly for the traditional Languedoc grapes, was not favoured by the authorities as an area of appellation, so all of Catherine's wines are of vin de pays status, a fact which does not worry her one little bit.

As if to say an ironic thank you to the authorities, she set about planting grape varieties calculated to shock them: Pinot Noir, which she is at pains to point out has a long local history according to her own researches in the archives of Toulouse; Chardonnay, Viognier, Clairette, and even some Aramon, all of them varieties that are well suited to her north-facing slopes.

Architect by profession, and painter in the little spare time that her grapes allow her, Catherine has evolved a style which leans to elegance, and what she calls "purity" of expression. Even if her choice of grapes reflects her love of wines from other French regions, she is not trying to imitate but to create. Thus, her Chardonnay★★ is fresh, rather than fat or buttery; it is flowery and delicate, and very modestly does not seek to exceed twelve-and-a-half degrees of alcohol. Her "Clairette du Languedoc"★★★, an original and outstanding expression of a much maligned grape, has just the required touch of gentle bitterness which, for Catherine, defines the essential character of Clairette.

But perhaps the best of all her white wines is the blend that she makes from all her white grapes together, which even includes a little Riesling and Petit Manseng, and which she calls "Les Aurièges"★★★: a wine with the kind of bite and acidity that Southern producers often try to kindle, but equally often they fail to achieve.

Her reds include a Pinot Noir★★ which recalls Sancerre rather than Burgundy, and her Syrah★★ is peppery and spicy on the nose, with strong flavours of cinnamon and cloves.

Catherine has acquired a few hectares in Faugères, which lie a little way from her original vineyards, just over the hills to the south. Her vines here are on the highest ground of the appellation. She is still getting used to the Faugères schist, so temporarily labels the wine as "Mas d'Alezon Coteaux du Languedoc"★★.

The *assemblage* is, for once, traditional. The yields are less than half the norm for Faugères, and the *cuvaison* twice as long, followed by two years in wood. This wine could turn out to be Catherine's star red.

B58 Rémi et Isabelle Ducellier

LES CHEMINS DE BASSAC
34480 Puimisson
☎ 04-67-36-09-67 B

What do you do when you suddenly find that you have inherited eighty hectares of vines in the Languedoc – especially if you are a couple of history teachers far away in the north of France? A rhetorical question, of course, in a wine book: in this case, our two heroes gave up their profession, and came south to start a new career, managing to bring with them their love of opera, the cello, and their talents as painters, which last they deploy on their attractive and unusual labels.

Sensibly, they decided that eighty hectares were many too many, and anyway the grape varieties planted left much to be desired. So they started from scratch and dug up all the old vines, including, alas, some old Carignan; but then all beginners make mistakes.

The Ducelliers are organic producers. They replanted just under fifteen of the eighty hectares: three hectares or so each of Grenache and Mourvèdre, one-and-a-half each of Syrah, Cabernet, and Pinot Noir, and two each of Roussanne and Viognier. The old *cave* was brought back into use, and 1992 saw their first vintage. Being – at least for the

moment – limited to making vins de pays, pending possible admission to AOC status, they have been adventurous in their *assemblages*, which change from year to year. Although their basic red called "Pierre Elie"★★★ is usually half Syrah, half Grenache, sometimes it may have some Mourvèdre, Cabernet or even Pinot. The wine called "Cap de l'Homme"★★★ may in one year be a Mourvèdre/Grenache blend, given a long maceration – typically thirty days or more – and raised partly in new barrels and older *foudres*; otherwise it may be 40% Syrah, 40% Cabernet, and 20% Grenache. Whatever the *assemblage*, success seems inevitable. These are big wines, and will almost certainly repay some years ageing in cellar; they should be opened well in advance of consumption.

The rosé★★ more than repays drinking on its own: *saigné* from Syrah and Mourvèdre, or perhaps sometimes pure Grenache (a rare way of making rosé), it can be the colour of smoked rainbow trout, lively, and powerful. The white from Roussanne and Viognier★★ is not oaked.

B59 François et Vincent Pugibet

DOMAINE DE LA COLOMBETTE
Ancienne route de Bédarieux
34500 Béziers
☎ 04-67-31-05-53 mostly A, some C

François' paternal grandfather created this frost-free domaine at the beginning of the last century. François' father then preferred to employ a manager to look after the estate. It was only in 1968, when François took over, that serious attention was given to replanting and nurturing the vineyards. His first success was in 1985 with his Chardonnay; since then, he has been joined by his son Vincent as his partner. Visitors cannot fail to notice the close bonding between father and son; they obviously think and feel as one.

François is difficult to interrupt when in full flow, unless it be by Vincent, when the duologue will take on the style of versicle and

response, the one dovetailing perfectly into the other without break. Allow plenty of time, therefore, for your visit, especially since your hosts will be supremely generous in offering their wines to taste.

The vines are wholly outside the appellation, so all the wines are vins de pays. The vines which François planted all those years ago are now in their prime, the Syrah, Grenache, and Chardonnay all being over thirty years old.

François does not necessarily bow to received wisdom. He is less interested in low yields, for example, than in high density planting, at up to 8,000 vines per hectare. Only small containers are used for the vinification: barrels for the Chardonnay, the rest of the wine in tank. *Cuvaisons* are surprisingly short for the reds – as little as two weeks.

There is no wine here which deserves less than ★★★: the delicate Sauvignon Blanc, for example, with its elderflower and hedgerow scents instead of the more usual gooseberries and cat's pee; the dry Muscat is clean and elegant with none of the bitterness on the palate sometimes found with this grape; the discreetly oaked Chardonnay, like low-fat butter, is an original expression of this hackneyed grape; the unusually light Syrah with its flavours of freshly crushed fruits; the Grenache, loaded with blackcurrants and blackberries; the rather more austere CabernetSauvignon, which François confesses is not his favourite grape; the Pinot Noir made in small barrels, with both father and son taking turns at *pigeage*, and which spends two years in old wood. Most astonishing of all is the 100% Lladoner Pelut – the cousin of Grenache with the funny name – with less blackcurrant than the Grenache but more fat and length.

There are plenty of affordable wines from this property, and they are of the highest quality; even the star Lladoner Pelut and the Pinot Noir are worth double the price that is asked for them.

B55 Guy et Guilhem Bascou

DOMAINE LA CONDAMINE L'EVEQUE
34120 Nézignan-l'Evêque
☎ 04-67-98-27-61 A

Guy is an important figure in Languedoc: formerly head of the oenology department at Montpellier Lycée, he is both oenological consultant and managing director at Château de Gourgazaud in the Minervois (q.v.), as well as being consultant to many other growers. These external activities mean that his son Guilhem is left with most of the duties at home, where there are forty hectares, in addition to the ten hectares of Picpoul at Pomérols, and another ten down on the plain. The division of duties may be a good idea if it keeps father and son out of each other's way, but one cannot help feeling that it would be no bad thing if Guy had a little more time for his own back yard.

Not that Guilhem is anything but a good winemaker: the wines of La Condamine are good, if not of Gourgazaud quality. There is, incidentally, a curious similarity between the grapes grown here and at Gourgazaud. There are no Grenache, Cinsault, or Carignan vines at either. "Foreign" varieties are represented by Cabernet and Merlot, and, for white wines, Sauvignon, Viognier, and Chardonnay.

The wines here are good for early drinking. An unoaked Viognier★, for example, has good apricot-and-peaches style, but is restrained by the grapes from younger vines which are mixed with those from the older plants. A varietal Mourvèdre★ has all the spices of the grape, but is quite soft and easy, sometimes with a slightly farmyard finish. Attractive, too, is a Cabernet/Merlot blend called simply "No 4"★★: unoaked and quaffable. A Merlot varietal is appropriately sweet and round without pushing the alcohol level too far. The pure Syrah★★ may be the best of all the reds.

One of the main attractions of these very decent wines is their value for money.

right François Pugibet, of Domaine de La Colombette: produces affordable vins de pays of the highest quality

B57 Jacques et Françoise Boyer

DOMAINE LA CROIX-BELLE
34480 Puissalicon
☎ 04-67-36-27-23 **A**

Jacques Boyer was for many years the president of the Syndicat of growers in the Côtes de Thongue, before passing on the *baguette* to the Teisserencs. This bears out the passion and fidelity for his local *pays*, and for the domaine which has been in the family for hundreds of years. This, too, is a large estate, with seventy hectares under vine and no fewer than fifteen different grape varieties. Thus all sorts of wines are made here, but they divide conveniently into categories.

First there are the *vins de cépage*: Sauvignon, Chardonnay, Merlot, Cabernet, and Muscat Sec. Then the *assemblages* which are of all three colours. The "Prestige" range is again a collection of *assemblages*, comprising some of the best wines the Boyers make. Finally, there are the few wines which are raised in wood: the Chardonnay, which is fermented as well as aged in barrel, and some of the best

cuvées of red wine. Apart from the last-named, all the wines are matured in *cuve*, the whites on their lees. Among these must be mentioned "Le Champ de Lys"★★, a Grenache Blanc, Viognier, Sauvignon blend, and the so-called "No. 7"★★, containing, as its name implies, no fewer than seven different *cépages*, including Carignan Blanc and Chasan as well as the more obvious varieties.

Madame Boyer is cross if you pass over her rosé called "Les Champs des Grillons"★★, so don't, because it is very good, raised in two wonderful old *foudres*. Excellent, too, are the red "Champ du Coq"★ – a commercial style wine with class – and the red "No. 7"★★: extraordinarily soft and round, with very ripe fruit, and of an amazingly deep colour.

B50 Jean-Pierre Vanel

DOMAINE LA CROIX-VANEL
34720 Caux
☎ 04-67-09-32-39 **B**

Jean-Pierre Vanel used to have a restaurant in Sète, so is not new to the appreciation of

above fragments of fossilized dinosaur eggs found in the soil at Mas Saint Laurent

good wine, even if his first vintage was as recent as 1998. The *cave* is in the middle of the village of Caux, but the vineyard is two kilometres (1.1 miles) away on *argilo-calcaire* soil of the Quaternary era. Vanel has no Mourvèdre, otherwise he has the usual red grapes, including two different parcels of Grenache. The Syrah and some of the old Carignan is vinified by *macération carbonique*, otherwise the grapes are destalked and crushed in the usual way. *Cuvaisons* are long, up to a month or more, and in small *cuves* so that each parcel and grape variety can be vinified and monitored separately. The size also facilitates the *pigeage*.

Jean-Pierre makes a rare 100% Cinsault called "Clos des Glycines"★, with an attractive eucalyptus nose and plenty of red fruits and garrigue character. The middle red is an *assemblage* and called "Clos Fine Amor"★. Its greater complexity does not necessarily make it more interesting than the

Cinsault *mono-cépage*. Vanel has not hitherto used new wood, but from 2000 onward his top wine, "Clos Mélanie"★★, will have just a touch of it. A nice rosé goes under the bizarre name of "Mimile Zonza"★, while there is, also, a *moelleux* from Grenache Blanc called appropriately enough "Ma Non Troppo"★★ – an unusual style to find these days but it must be typical of those the Languedoc used to make in the days before the region discovered dry white wines.

Despite – or perhaps because of – the unusual range of these wines, more than eighty per cent are exported.

B53 H. F. Bouchard et Fils

DOMAINE DESHENRYS
3 rue de Fraisse
342900 Alignan-du-Vent
☎ 04-67-24-91-67
Ⓦ www.vignoblesbouchard.com B

Nicolas, the son of the house, is the fifth generation to make wine here. His ancestor Ferdinand was already winning medals in Turin in 1911, so there is no shortage of experience at this substantial vineyard of sixty hectares, fifty of which are in production. The family also has an interest in another property called Abbaye Sylva Plan in Faugères (q.v.) which adds a further thirty-one hectares to the portfolio. Faugères is not all that far distant from Alignan as the crow flies.

There is a small production of AOC Coteaux du Languedoc from Syrah and Grenache, lightly oaked. This is top quality★★, combining some finesse with good Southern style. But most of the wine is produced as Vin de Pays des Côtes de Thongue in the form of varietals, all of which are attractive and well-made in their different ways★★: whites from Sauvignon, Viognier, and Chardonnay, all given skin contact and the Chardonnay recurring in an oaked version; a dry Muscat and a blend of Sauvignon, Roussanne, Viognier, Petit Manseng, and Muscat. There is a rosé, *saigné* from all the Languedoc grape varieties and from Cabernet

Sauvignon too, and three red varietals from Carignan, Merlot, and Cabernet, all given relatively short *cuvaisons* of eight to ten days. To round off the range, there is a sweet Muscat★, pale in colour, but rich in character; said to be able to accommodate chocolate.

The policy at Deshenrys is to concentrate further on *assemblages*, with fewer single varietal wines made in the future.

B49 Cécile et Bernard Belhasen

DOMAINE FONTEDICTO
(formerly Domaine Fontarèche)
34720 Caux
☎ 04-67-98-40-22 B

This must be the only *cave* in the Languedoc to have background music by Pergolesi. In the foreground, Monsieur Belhasen will hold forth on his philosophy of life in general and viticulture in particular, both of which are ultra-organic. He has been in the Languedoc for twenty-four years, but he and his wife content themselves with just five hectares of vines, all *dans un seul tenant*, which affords them the advantage of not being "infected" by non-organic influences, such as the seepage of chemical fertilisers and the spread of noxious sprays. The vineyard is 150 metres (500 feet) above the Languedoc plain, and is on the top of a north-facing slope which ensures even greater well-being for its micro-environment.

Bernard relishes life in the uncluttered atmosphere of the Languedoc garrigue. Working with his hands, as closely to nature as possible, with only his wife and a proud white mare to help him, he is able to respect utterly what he produces. He believes that those who have the misfortune to live in towns are subconsciously missing out, which is why they are never content, and the young there cause so much trouble.

His terroir is very chalky and the vines are protected by high outcrops of volcanic rock. He does not speak of monoculture, because for him viticulture extends beyond the growing of vines to the care of the whole of the natural environment, particularly the trees

and the wild plants. This leads him to deplore the official policy of *remembrement* – the gathering together of parcels of land under one ownership with the consequent destruction of hedges and woodland.

The practical application of these ideas certainly produces at least one very remarkable wine: a white, entirely from Terret vines★★★ which are over fifty years old. The yield from them is tiny, a mere eight to ten hectolitres per hectare, but their juice is pure gold in colour and the wine has plenty of *gras*. It is completely dry and the finish is seemingly never-ending. In some years, he manages to make a mere 600 bottles. He does not believe in *vendanges vertes*: for him this practice interrupts the development of the vine, and a really severe pruning when the plant is dormant should be enough to enable the vine to grow naturally and without being ground to a halt.

Fontedicto also has red wines from Carignan, Syrah, and Grenache, and an atypical rosé mostly from Aramon★★ aged in barrique. "Pirouette"★★ is a light red based on Carignan with just a little Grenache and Syrah, and "Les Coulisses"★ is a rather sturdier wine from the same grapes. But it is the Terret which will linger long in the memory, while your ideas about viticulture may never be the same again after a visit here.

B54 Bernard Coste

DOMAINE MONT ROSE
Tourbes
34120 Pézenas
☎ 04-67-98-63-33
Ⓦ www.domaine-montrose.com A

This is a good-value, reliable, and mainstream property which does not hit the high spots but which nevertheless fills a useful gap in terms of reasonably-priced everyday drinking. All the wines are Vins de Pays des Côtes de Thongue, because none of the vines is within an area of AOC.

The operation is substantial, covering fifty-five hectares. It lies just off the main Route

Nationale 9 to the west of Valros. Monsieur Coste, whose family has been living in the area since the seventeenth century, also runs a camping and sort of leisure centre on the site, which he is trying to segregate a little from the winemaking operation. Considerable improvements at obviously great cost are underway to modernize the *cave* and the equipment, all of which is perfectly satisfactory but hardly state-of-the-art.

One of Monsieur Coste's ancestors, Henri, developed the vineyards at the end of the nineteenth century. He was a vintner in Sète and founded what has now become one of the biggest local banks. Today, Michel Le Goael is the full-time winemaker in charge of the commercial side of the operation.

All the red Mediterranean grapes are planted, except Mourvèdre; Rolle, Grenache Blanc, and Viognier represent the local white *cépages*. Bordeaux contributes Cabernet Sauvignon, Merlot, and white Sauvignon Blanc; Burgundy some Chardonnay.

The Rolle is featured in a blend with the other white grapes, making a dry wine called "Les Lézards"★, and, more interestingly, in a pure 100% *moelleux* version★★ from *vendanges tardives*. Varietals from Sauvignon and Chardonnay are good, but the top-priced white, "Cuvée Salamandre"★, is a mix of all the grapes bar Sauvignon and is aged in wood.

Syrah is sometimes blended with Merlot, sometimes with Cabernet, but the resulting red, Les Lézards, is topped by the red "Salamandre"★ which is half Syrah, 35% Cabernet, and 15% Merlot. There are rosés too at very fair prices.

D7 Jean Pétaivy

**DOMAINE DE NAIRAN AND
DOMAINE DE MALLEMORT**
34620 Puisserguier
☎ 04-67-93-74-20 A

The Nairan estate, with thirty hectares currently under vine, came to Monsieur Pétaivy by inheritance from his mother's side of the family; Mallemort, with its sixty-five hectares, is a paternal heritage. They more or less adjoin. To taste and buy, you visit the latter and its steeply mansarded gothic château, its discreetly tumbledown outbuildings, creaky parquet, and brooding trees. Monsieur Pétaivy may invite you to join him for a tasting in his dining-room, under an old paraffin chandelier whose twelve candleholders are converted to electricity – so as not to detract, perhaps, from the bouquet of the excellent Pétaivy wines.

At a guess, you might place Jean Pétaivy as a classic example of the local landed gentry, someone who might farm out his vineyards as being either of no great interest or too much trouble. But you would be wrong, because he has in his time played an important role in the Languedoc revival, particularly in the establishment of the vins de pays of which he is such an excellent producer. He is also a former President of the Caves Particulières of the Hérault and of the Syndicat of the growers in Languedoc-Roussillon. He worked with his father to rebuild the vineyards of both family estates, which today are managed and marketed quite separately under their own banners. He was a pioneer planter of the two Cabernets, Merlot, Sauvignon, and Chardonnay, and one of the early practitioners of low temperature fermentation of white wines in the region. He is still pioneering: one of his best wines being a 100% Chasan★★, a beautiful crisp, bone-dry white with good acidity and a natural to accompany oysters.

He makes nothing but the *vins de cépage* which he pioneered. New wood is reserved exclusively for his Cabernet Sauvignon★; otherwise he prefers to use his old *foudres*, especially for his other red wines. His white and pink wines are all raised in stainless steel or concrete vats.

Monsieur Pétaivy will soon be ready to hand on his vineyards to his two grandsons if they show anything like his own passion for the job. After all the good work he has put in, one hopes that there will eventually be a successful and smooth transition.

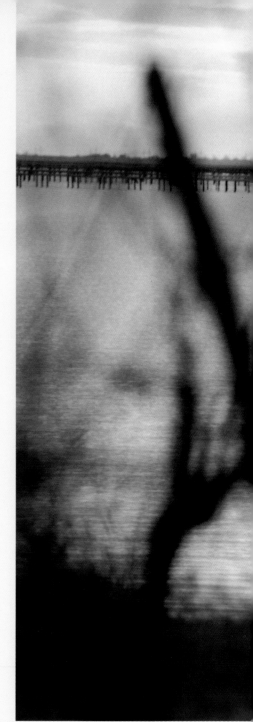

B61 Jérôme Ferracci

DOMAINE PERDIGUIER
34370 Maraussan
☎ 04-67-90-37-44 B

Jean Perdiguier was the Treasury representative of King Charles V in Languedoc, and in 1375 he was rewarded with the gift of the Bastide called En Auger, on the right bank of the River Orb. Nearby, he built himself the château which today bears

his name, but the bastide has disappeared. Perdiguier was obviously liked more by the King than by the locals – tax-paying has never been a favourite pastime in Languedoc. He did not last very long in his château: he met his end in Montpellier, murdered by angry enemies.

There have been many changes here down the years: the sixteenth and seventeenth centuries saw the decline of the fortified style of châteaux, which gradually were converted to more gentle domestic use. At Perdiguier, recent restoration works have revealed some delightful frescoes in the spiral stone staircase of the southern tower, depicting rustic goings-on in a style which might be described as pre-Poussin.

At the Revolution, the property was sold off and went into a period of decline. Today, the Ferracci family has fifty years of ownership behind it. The present generation has undertaken its restoration

above flamingoes search for fish in the Bassin de Thau, near Picpoul de Pinet

and made it a delightful home. One wing has been adapted for receptions, where you can invite 150 or more guests, on condition that you offer them the wine of the château.

This last will be of no pain to the guests because the wine here is outstandingly good. There are twenty-one hectares or so in production, all of which are marketed as

vins de pays des Coteaux d'Ensérune. The vineyards have been in course of improvement and replanting since 1982, and the Ferraccis bottled their first wines made under their own flag as recently as 1998. They have now virtually realized their intention to assemble all their parcels of vines *dans un seul tenant* round the château.

The terroir is very mixed in character, largely dictated by the way the River Orb has, over the centuries, deposited its alluvial soil and stones. Big round pebbles are mixed with clay and chalk and a deal of gravelly stone and sand, but even within a few yards in the same parcel, you can find up to three or more different soil characteristics.

The grape varieties are largely Merlot and Cabernet Sauvignon, though there are some Syrah and Pinot Noir vines too. Chardonnay is the only white grape planted. The grapes are all trained *en cordon royat*, and *culture*

raisonnée is the order of the day. The weeds are allowed to grow freely in the winter, and are dug up in the spring to make the only compost the Ferraccis allow.

Of the three red wines, the Merlot★ varietal, aged in *cuve*, is a good everyday drinking wine; the Domaine de Perdiguier★★ is a half-Cabernet Sauvignon, half-Merlot blend, and the superb Cuvée En Auger★★★ is 80% Cabernet and 20% Merlot – one of the relatively rare successes of this blend in the South. Both reds are raised in barrels which have already seen one or two wines. There is a rosé★, *saigné* from Merlot and Syrah, which is also brought up in wood.

The quality at Perdiguier is bound to be on the increase as the replanted vines start to mature and produce, so the potential here is virtually unlimited – as is the determination of Jérome Feracci to make the best possible quality wines.

B51 Jean-Claude Le Brun et Chantal Lecouty

LE PRIEURE DE SAINT-JEAN-DE-BEBIAN
Route de Nizas
34120 Pézenas
☎ **04-67-98-13-60**
ⓦ **www.Bebian.com D**

The Romans were here before the monks took over in the eleventh century, and certainly before Maurice Roux bought in 1954. In 1975 Roux' grandson Alain took over the running of the estate and acquired a formidable international reputation for its wines. Le Prieuré and Mas de Daumas Gassac were spoken of for some years as *hors concours* as far as Southern France was concerned. Roux (the grandson) planted Syrah, Grenache, and

Mourvèdre, but kept the old Carignan and Cinsault and added the traditional Rhône whites. His envied reputation was earned despite, or perhaps because of, his unsophisticated approach to vinification. All that mattered to him were low yields and very ripe fruit. He did not even have any oak barrels.

Le-Brun and Lecouty have a more "correct" approach. Their careers until the early 1990s had been in journalism, and they were joint editors of the influential French wine magazine *La Revue du Vin de France*. Chantal says that if anyone had asked her at that time if she thought she might ever became a winemaker, she would have been horrified. But someone must have made them both an offer they could not refuse, because they sold out and had to find a new career in their early retirement.

Their dream was to buy Le Prieuré, but it was not available even though Roux had lost interest in his vineyard. Jean-Claude and Chantal were instead about to settle for second-best somewhere down the road, and were on the brink of signing the papers when that owner died. Simultaneously it seemed that Roux had changed his mind. Contracts for Le Prieuré were completed the next day.

Such a romantic story was bound to prefigure a renaissance in the fortunes of Le Prieuré. The elegant property has now been exquisitely restored down to the last door-panel, and one day the owners hope to do the same for the pretty Romanesque chapel which visitors pass on their way to the front gates.

The wines have fully regained their former reputation. Today they have more finesse and elegance than in Roux's day: his aim had been power and richness. Jean-Claude and Chantal have not, however, foregone any of the Mediterranean style which always differentiated these wines from those of Daumas Gassac.

They make one first wine and one second wine, after the Bordeaux pattern; the latter is called "La Chapelle de Bébian"★★ and is a useful home for some of the old-fashioned grapes such as Carignan. The first wine★★★ is quite simply one of the top handful in the whole Languedoc.

Jean-Claude and Chantal are developing their first white wine★★★ which has so far proved almost as successful as their reds; it may contain Clairette, some young and low-yielding Roussanne, Piquepoul, and Terret, and is a good boost for the reputation of white Languedoc grapes which critics have been only too keen to deride. Pale in colour, this wine has a strongly scented nose with an enchanting aroma of white peaches. The acidity is finely judged.

Those who say that these wines are expensive should understand they are no more so than many inferior wines from Bordeaux, Burgundy, Australia, and California. Category D perhaps, but worth every euro.

B60 Cécile et Gustave Viennet

DOMAINE DE RAISSAC
route de Murviel
34500 Béziers
☎ 04-67-28-15-61
Ⓦ www.raissac.com A

Brother and sister, the young Viennets, the sixth generation of growers here, have quickly taken to running this large business with its 108 hectares just a few kilometres out of Béziers. The domaine itself goes back to the seventeenth century when it was called "Le Puech Cocut", meaning Cuckoo Hill, both of which names are used in the large range of wines produced here. The real Château of Raissac is some little way to the east and today houses an interesting museum of ceramics. The two properties came into the same ownership only in 1828.

There is a great diversity of different terroirs: vines on a lower level enjoying alluvial soil washed down by the rivers, while higher up there are the usual large round pebbles, and elsewhere a chalky clay soil rich in marine fossils. The cellars are in the wings of the château, while the ageing of the wines takes place in almost completely subterranean rock. There is no concealing the frankly commercial nature of this operation, but the quality is consistently good, even in the wines which are made for, and to the specification of supermarkets.

The Viennets will not, however, put the domaine label on any bottles whose vinification and *assemblage* have not been under their sole control. Amongst the latter are good varietals from Viognier and Chardonnay★, a rosé from Cabernet, and reds from Merlot★★ and Cabernet Sauvignon. The top of range wine is sold under the name of "Gustave Fayet", an ancestor of the present Viennets.

The white★ is from the best parcels of Chardonnay, each vinified separately, partly in wood and partly in tank, so as to produce an impression of very light oxidization.

The red★★ is typically from 80% Merlot and 20% Cabernet Sauvignon, vinified traditionally in *cuve* and then aged twelve months in wood.

other good vins de pays growers

Karl Mauguin et Basile Saint-Germain
Domaine les Aurelles,
26 Avenue Fontès, 34720 Caux
☎ 04-67-98-46-21

Amand Durand
Domaine Durand-Camillo,
44 Boulevard du Puits Allier, 34720 Caux
☎ 04-67-98-44-26

Ursula et Eric Jérusalem
Hermitage de Combas,
34290 Servian
☎ 04-67-39-28-91

Gilles Martin
Domaine de Nizas, (same ownership as Clos du Val, California), 34720 Caux
☎ 04-67-90-17-92

Gilbert Lépine
Domaine du Parc, 34120 Pézenas (organic)
☎ 04-67-77-42-97

clairette du languedoc

The unblended Clairette grape survives in two small pockets of the Languedoc: at Bellegarde near Nîmes (see Costières de Nîmes) and on some limestone soil to the north of Pézenas, where it has this little appellation all to itself. Otherwise it hangs on as a supporting variety, e.g. in Limoux and Châteauneuf-du-Pape.

Clairette has a history going back to Roman times. Pliny was among its fans, so was King Louis XI of France. The makers of vermouth discovered the virtues of its high alcoholic propensity and low acidity, and almost monopolized its production until they found cheaper alternatives in Italy. Unfortunately, the qualities Noilly-Prat and others admired are not those required in a modern table wine: the juice simply did not keep unless blended with other varieties with greater acidity. Furthermore, Clairette is difficult to grow because it is liable to *coulure* and rot. It was once said that Clairette needs to be drunk almost before bottling, but its survival is due to improved methods of vinification.

At best, Clairette is delightfully fruity, a character enhanced by hand-harvesting, total destalking, and gentle vinification at controlled temperatures. Some of the vines here are very old indeed, producing a pale straw-coloured wine with a powerful nose of flowers and citrus fruits, and a wide range of aromas on the palate. In the best years some of the wines are even oaked, so there must be some confidence in their keeping potential.

The coopérative at Adissan has revived the former style of sweet Clairette, a honey-and-peach kind of wine which can acquire the *rancio* taste found in some vins doux naturels (q.v.). This is doubtless the style of wine which the ancients liked: they called it "Clératz" to differentiate it from the dry style called "Picquardentz". This region is enjoying a modest revival with four coopératives and nine independent growers claiming the appellation over some eighty-eight hectares.

As befits a wine with such a long tradition, the appellation itself dates back a long way to 1948. The Coopérative at Adissan goes back further still to 1928, and has been one of the motors in the rediscovery of Clairette. Around two-thirds of the members are now growing Clairette, and between 1990 and 1999, they increased production from 2,000 bottles a year to nearly 70,000. The looseness of the appellation statutes has permitted enthusiasts for the wine to explore new methods of vinification, and these have largely contributed to the increase in quality and stabiity of the wines.

The historical ubiquity of the clairette grape is demonstrated by the inclusion of a small part of the appellation some way to the north of the main area. This forms a small strip of land in the vicinity of Saint-André de Sangonis. Catherine Roque at Bédarieux is outside the Clairette appellation but is permitted to include an outstanding example of Clairette among her portfolio of otherwise non-appellation wines (see page 77). The attractive and refreshing bitterness of the grape reminds her of oranges rather than the more usual almonds.

Until recently commentators have been somewhat snooty about Clairette, both as a grape and as a *mono-cépage* wine. Already the improvement in quality in recent years is helping to re-establish it as more than just a local and historical curiosity.

---

special features of clairette du languedoc

the wines white only; grown exclusively from the Clairette grape.

AOC area 8 communes to the north of Pézenas on terraces overlooking the river Hérault 30 kilometres (16.2 miles) or so from the sea.

the soil a mixture of quartz pebbles, chalk, and sandy clay, with some schist as well.

notable producer

B52 Jean-Louis Randon

CHATEAU SAINT-ANDRE
34120 Pézenas
☎ 04-67-98-33-46 B

This extremely attractive *mas*, the principal part of which dates back to the seventeenth century, lies just off the road from Pézenas to Nizas, almost opposite Le Prieuré de Saint-Jean-de-Bébian. You need to know this because otherwise you may never find Monsieur Randon, which would be a pity because he makes one of the most traditional, and at the same time original, white wines of Languedoc.

On the highest ground of the domaine, some 150 metres (500 feet) above sea-level, he grows his Clairette grapes from which he makes "Les Frigolas" ★★★ (the name coming from an Occitan word meaning wild thyme). The surrounding vegetation is low garrigue. The geology is unusual: the topsoil is pebbly

to the point that no earth is visible; underneath, a thick bed of chalk is covered with a layer of basalt discharged as lava from a former volcano a short way away – and, happily, long extinct. The soil is thus rich in iron, phosphates, magnesium, and other elements which give this wine a liveliness and freshness not always yielded by the grape variety in this area.

There are five hectares of Clairette, some of the vines being forty years old. Harvesting is by hand, the grapes are pressed whole, fermented long and at low temperatures, and aged on their lees in stainless steel. The wine has good weight, a bouquet of wild herbs, and a slight hint of almonds on the palate; there is a gentle bitterness on the aftertaste which is most refreshing and reflects the particular terroir.

The Randons also make an attractive Viognier ★ in exactly the same way as their Clairette; it is lighter in style than usual and manages to have the same kind of vivacity as the Clairette. Randon does not use any barriques for his white wines, but he is

above in Languedoc even the makers of wrought-iron gates cannot resist the grape

contemplating experimenting in this direction with his red AOC Coteaux du Languedoc, a perfectly attractive wine but more orthodox and less adventurous than the whites.

other good clairette growers

Monsieur Pacaud
Domaine de Cambous,
34725 Saint-André-de-Sangonis
☎ 04-67-16-09-36

Bernard Jany
Château la Condamine-Bertrand,
34120 Saint-Lézignan-la-Cèbe
☎ 04-67-25-27-96

★★Cave Coopérative la
Clairette d'Adissan
34230 Adissan
☎ 04-67-25-01-07

(*See also* Catherine Roque, Domaine de Clovallon, page 77.)

faugères

Between the main range of the Cévennes and their last flourish, the Montagne Noire, lies the granite plateau called the Natural Park of Upper Languedoc, a cool oasis of oak and chestnut, laced with refreshing mountain streams. This high ground is separated from the historic city of Béziers to the south by the AOC Faugères.

There are thirty-seven or so private producers and three coopératives in the region of Faugères, and in 1999 they produced 84,000 hectolitres of red and rosé wine.

The landscape is particularly beautiful, often offering views to the towns of Béziers and Pézenas on the plain and to the sea. On rare clear days, Mont Canigou in the Pyrenees rises above the misty humidity of the flat lands between. Looking northward, the mountains form an indigo backdrop

to the green vines, the terracotta pantiles, and the glowing yellow ochre of the buildings. And where the vines won't grow there is the scent of the wild flowers and plants of the garrigue. With every step you take here you will crush thyme, and to right and left of you there will be shrubs of bushes, rosemary, and wild mint.

This appellation illustrates well the contrast between vineyards which are all contained within one parcel of land, often planted round the house and *chais* of the owner, and called "*dans un seul tenant*", and the others where parcels of land in the same ownership are dotted round the countryside. Diversity has its advantages: a grower can benefit from vineyards in different terroirs, and he can sometimes hedge the risk of hail which tends to strike very locally so that one area of vines may be hit but others will not be. The snag is the extra time and cost involved in working the different parcels of land and moving men and equipment from one to the other. From the 1960s onward, some growers have tended to plant in terraced rows following the contours of the land, which the vines exaggerate with sensuous curves. These terraces both ease the passage of machinery and they also help to limit soil erosion.

The soil is entirely schist – or many might know it as shale – a hard but brittle slate-like material, which flakes like pastry and can even break vertically, producing what the French call *frites*. It recurs in Saint-Chinian, parts of Minervois, Corbières, and Roussillon. Schist takes three forms in this region: large slates which they call "*dalles*", on which hardly anything grows and the vine can yield only tiny quantities of fruit; another less mean kind sometimes called "*grésaux*" because of

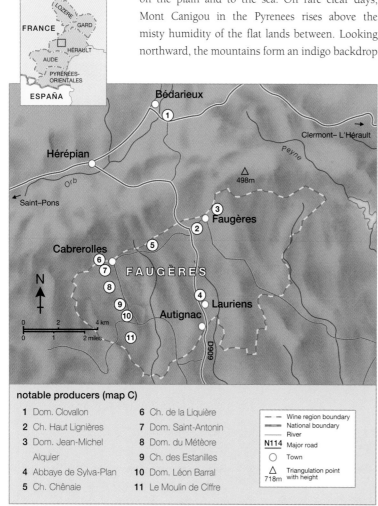

notable producers (map C)

1 Dom. Clovallon
2 Ch. Haut Lignières
3 Dom. Jean-Michel Alquier
4 Abbaye de Sylva-Plan
5 Ch. Chênaie
6 Ch. de la Liquière
7 Dom. Saint-Antonin
8 Dom. du Métèore
9 Ch. des Estanilles
10 Dom. Léon Barral
11 Le Moulin de Ciffre

- – – Wine region boundary
- ▬▬ National boundary
- —— River
- N114 Major road
- ○ Town
- △ 718m Triangulation point with height

its more sandstony texture; and the friable, very brittle, fragile type which you can break in your fingers, and which produces the *frites*.

A band of this schist marks the separation between the mountains and the beginning of the plain. All Faugères is on it. It was a result of pressure and heat caused by the upheavals of the mountain systems of Europe 500 million years ago. In Faugères the schist layer can be anything from three to ten kilometres (1.6 to 5.4 miles) wide. Sometimes it is blueish in colour, when the tougher pieces are especially good for making roofing-slates called *ardoises*; otherwise it can be reddish if it has a high iron content, but usually the colour is more muted, shades of chestnut, green, and beige predominating. Its great feature for the vine-grower is that it forces the vine-roots deep into the ground where they can search for moisture. The schist retains and reflects back the heat of the sun too, so that the locals have a saying that *"les raisins mûrissent la nuit"* (the grapes ripen in the night).

Faugères differs from many winemaking areas of Languedoc in that its history shows no connection whatever with the Church. Until the beginning of this century, it was known mainly for its eau-de-vie, which was called Fine de Faugères. For this, only white wine was required, and so the area was predominantly given over to white grapes such as Terret, Carignan Blanc, and Muscat. Red wine production is here a relatively recent innovation, dating from the post-phylloxera period and even later, and it was based on the feeble but high yielding Aramon grape. The coming of the main line rail links to the north must have been a great impetus to local production: the romantically forlorn and disused railway station at Laurens features an oversized doorway through which the old *foudres* would have been loaded onto the trains bound for Paris. Immediately adjoining are the premises of former négociants, now vanished.

The local growers are reviving the former production of eau-de-vie made from the wine of their white grapes. There is at the moment no appellation for white Faugères, though an application has been made by the Syndicat of local producers. Such processes tend to take a very long time. Bernard Vidal (*see* page 96), who is responsible for conducting the negotiations, is also behind the move to get more and more growers to adopt a *culture raisonnée*. Subscribers to this plan are those entitled to use a logo depicting three towers (Les Trois Tours). He wants supporters of this project to have the right to publish the fact with a special supplementary label on the bottle. The plan has got off to a solid if slow start. Many growers, conservative by nature, feel that they are being invited to subscribe to yet another system of control. Bernard rejects and denies this approach, seeing the need for flexibility above all things in winemaking.

The red wines of Faugères are generally round, balanced, and full-bodied. They are said to suggest blackcurrants, raspberries, and a little vanilla even when not oaked. Two-thirds of the production is sold in bottle and only one-third *en vrac*; sixteen per cent is exported, of which Belgium takes about half. About one half of all production finds its way to hypermarkets and supermarkets, and one-third to restaurants, hotels, cafés, and specialist wine shops.

In the opinion of many, Faugères holds the most promise of all the appellations in the Languedoc; the wines are the product of such recent and rapid development that their full potential is yet to be realized. This is partly because the average age of the vignerons is only thirty-five. Another feature is the compulsory ultra-short pruning of the vines. Some growers favour training the surplus vegetation *en échalas*, a method that involves tying the greenery to the main stem of the plant once the *vendange verte* has been carried out.

---

special features of faugères

the wines red and rosé only from grapes grown in communes of Autignac, Cabrerolles, Caussiniojouls, Faugères, Fos, Laurens, and Roquessels, north of Béziers. White wines sold as Côteaux du Languedoc or vins de pays.

grapes varieties Carignan limited to 40%, Cinsault 20%; Syrah and Mourvèdre together a minimum of 15%; Mourvèdre a minimum 5%, Grenache (including Lladoner) min 20%. By 2005 Syrah, Grenache, and Mourvèdre must be at least 50% of total AOC planting.

vine age vines must be at least 4 years old and planted at a density of at least 4,000 plants per hectare by 2003.

the soil exclusively schist.

above schist defines the terroir everywhere in this appellation

above, right the vines at Faugères sometimes follow the contours of the hills – here seen in the full colours of autumn

right times change; the wines made in Faugères no longer travel by rail and the station is derelict

notable producers

C4 H. F. Bouchard et Fils

ABBAYE DE SYLVA-PLAN
34480 Laurens
☎ 04-67-90-28-96
Ⓦ www.vignoblesbouchard.com **B**

A partnership between the Bouchards of
Côtes de Thongue (q.v.) and Cédric Guy has
resulted in this thirty-one-hectare domaine at
Faugères suddenly attracting a deal of public
attention. The first vintage was in 1998 and
was called "La Closeraie". It was a highly
successful début★★. From a mixed terroir
of schist, marble, and clay, the Syrah and
Carignan were vinified by *macération
carbonique,* the Mourvèdre and Grenache
traditionally, with long *cuvaisons* in all cases.
The bouquet unveils cherries, sweet spices,
and some chocolate. Full and fleshy on the
palate with fine tannins; cherries and spice
return on the long after-taste.

The first effort at an *élevage* partly in
new barrels came in 1999, the results with
dense, deep colour, a smokey nose, and
well-mastered oaking★★. The wine is titled
"Songe de l'Abbaye".

C3 Jean-Michel Alquier

DOMAINE JEAN-MICHEL ALQUIER
4 route de Pézènes-les-Mines
34600 Faugères
☎ 04-67-23-07-89 **B**

The vineyards were established in 1872. They
were first planted by Jean-Michel's great-
grandfather. His son married a lady with urban
rather than rural tastes, so they went to live in
Paris, where they built on her connections to
establish a market for the wine produced
back at Faugères. A manager was engaged
to run the vineyard during their absence.

During the Second World War, Jean-
Michel's grandfather was taken prisoner and
returned from Germany in very poor health,
dying soon afterward. This left Jean-Michel's
father, Gilbert, in charge. Gilbert had the
foresight to anticipate the popularity of Syrah
and Mourvèdre, and restructured the
vineyards with these varieties to the exclusion
of all other reds. For the whites he planted
Viognier and Marsanne, as well as the more
usual Grenache Blanc. He was also the first
Faugères grower to bottle his own wines: he
was able to exploit Parisian contacts to sell
them in this format.

On Gilbert's death the vineyard was split
between his two sons. Today Jean-Michel
and his brother Frédéric each have thirteen
hectares in the hills above the road east out
of Faugères. The vines are at some 150
metres (500 feet) above sea level, and the
grapes therefore tend to ripen a fortnight or
so later than those of other growers on the
lower ground toward the sea. The views over
the Languedoc plain are splendid.

The Alquier wines are all of top quality,
some would say the best of the appellation.
They are all given some ageing in oak, but so
masterly is the handling of the wood that you
would hardly notice it in the wine. The
outstanding white Côteaux du Languedoc★★
a blend of Marsanne-Viognier-Grenache has
the customary apricots and peaches on the
palate being enriched, according to Jean-
Michel, by quinces and exotic fruits. The red
"Tradition"★★ is fine too, but the top *cuvée*
called "Les Bastides"★★★ is superb, improving
with complexity after a few years in bottle.

C10 Didier Barral

DOMAINE LEON BARRAL
Lenthéric
34480 Cabrerolles
☎ 04-67-90-29-13 **B/C**

The youth of the growers in Faugères is
exemplified by Didier Barral, a questioning and
rebellious young man ready to challenge the
assumptions inherited from his father who was
a *coopérateur*. Having decided at an early age
that he was going to make his own wine rather
than sell to the coopérative, he took himself off
to study winemaking in Montpellier and then
did a *stage* in the Côtes du Rhône. Needing
a *cave* of his own, he bought one which
belonged to a grower who had become a
coopérateur and so no longer needed it.

Didier now has twenty-five hectares, on
which a little of everything grows. Somewhere
out on the revolutionary wing of the organic
growers, he questions even some of their
tenets which he claims they have adopted
for financial and marketing reasons rather
than from conviction. Didier also points out
that they get special government subventions
for their organic pains, and condemns the
sanction which they give to the use of
Bordeaux mixture as a spray, which they
say is natural but which he says still damages
the soil. Nor will he have anything to do with
industrial yeasts, believing that it kills the
natural ones and affects the flavour of wine.

To Didier, everything starts from the soil
which must be made as healthy as possible.
He welcomes the mix of vineyard and
garrigue in Faugères because the garrigue
shelters flora and fauna which are naturally
beneficial to the terroir. His next concern is
for the basic plant and the way it is grafted
onto its disease-free rootstock. He insists
on the kind of graft which is called *greffe
anglaise*, consisting of a kind of double notch
which does not allow any separating of the
plant from the rootstock at all, thus
concentrating the surge of the *sève* (sap)
to the grapes and foliage above. He rejects
the traditional grafting technique believing the
sap causes a bulbous formation at the joint.

Didier attaches a deal more importance
to the vineyard than the *chais*. He claims that
his vinification is of the simplest kind, though
the results make that hard to believe. He
uses the traditional methods of *égrappage*
and fermentation, *pigeage* by hand and not
by machine. Long macerations are followed
by ageing in wood, and the *assemblage*
follows eighteen months or so later. He
scorns the modern bottling plant, deploring
the use of filters and pumps which interfere
with the natural qualities of the wine. "All you
need is a north wind and an old moon."

The first thing to strike one *chez* Barral is the sheer depth of colour, body, and the immense structure of these wines, invariably ★★★. From the cask, even the Cinsault at 15 degrees is a revelation, rivalling in power many another grower's Grenache, with mountains of fresh fruit, damsons, and bitter cherries, but not at all soupy. The Carignan again was massively deep and concentrated when tasted from the cask, and the Grenache loaded with sweet rich fruit and, curiously, more approachable than the two wines which preceded it. The Syrah from the wood was more typical of the appellation, but Barral does not share everyone else's love affair with this grape; he believes that all varieties are of equal importance. It is what you do with them in the blending room which counts. He does not conceal his love for the Mourvèdre,

however, and barrel samples should develop magnificently indeed, with a long life ahead.

Barral is now a successful and fashionable grower, despite his reputation as an *enfant terrible*, or perhaps because of it. But he has not always had it his own way. The day before his very first vintage, in 1993, hail swept through his vineyard with such ferocity that he lost almost all of his first year's crop. He says it was like having a serious injury: you are never quite the same afterward, just rather a changed person. The wine-lover should feel much the same way after a visit here.

C5 André Chabbert et Fils

CHATEAU CHENAIE
34600 Caussiniojouls
☎ **04-67-23-17-73 A/C**

above at La Linquière, the art of sign-writing lags behind the times

André Chabbert still retains a keen interest in what goes on at this outstanding property, because a true vigneron never retires. His sons Eric and Cyril have, however, effectively taken over the reins. The family has been in the picturesquely situated village of Caussiniojouls for six generations, winemakers since before the days of phylloxera. Their roots go even deeper than those of their vines and they show abundantly if you are fortunate enough to be given a guided tour by Eric. He seems to recognize every vine and every piece of schist almost as members of his family, his passion for his terroir pouring out in floods as he explains the different slopes of the vineyard, their exposure to wind and sun, the effect of

C9 Michel, Monique, et Sophie Louison

CHATEAU DES ESTANILLES
Lenthéric
34480 Cabrerolles
☎ 04-67-90-29-25 A/C

Michel Louison lives just across the road from Didier Barral, but there could hardly be a bigger contrast between two growers. The first thing that must strike you at Estanilles is the Iberio-Tuscan complex which Louison has created to house family, winemaking, stocks, personnel, and two wire-haired terriers. No expense has been spared in making a cool, air-conditioned tasting room with white-tiled floor, and *crachoirs* with running water. Off this leads the *chais* with endless rows of gleaming stainless steel *cuves*, and beyond that the stockholding area, all air-conditioned and as squeaky clean as a brand new hospital. This is the fruit of Michel's success as a winemaker.

Michel manages to retain the grudging approval of the traditionalists as well as the *avant-garde*, while adopting the best techniques from both. In his time he has been famous as a rebel, and is still not willing to rest on his laurels. He uses only caterpillar tractors in the vineyards so as to reduce disturbance of the soil to a minimum. He was one of the first to pioneer high density plantations of up to 6,000 plants per hectare, following the contours of the land; the adoption of Syrah and Mourvèdre at previously unknown altitudes; and the production of a varietal Syrah wine, previously forbidden in the Côteaux du Languedoc.

On the other hand, his red "Tradition"★★ is deliciously simple and uncomplex, quaffable, with notes of liquorice, peppers, and tobacco. "The Cuvée Prestige"★★★, from Syrah, Mourvèdre, and Grenache is raised partly in oak, partly not. It is bottled eighteen months after the vintage to allow a

hail and bad weather on individual plants, and the different characteristics of the grape varieties he grows. An accompanied tour of the vineyards in his four-wheel drive is an education. For him Château Chênaie is out there in the sun and not in the office.

All the vinification is traditional: with *égrappage*, no *macération carbonique*. His delicious wines include a white Côteaux du Languedoc★, which Eric says is from Roussanne (although the apricot flavour of the wine might suggest Viognier to some), and which makes a mouthwatering prelude to his rosé, for which he reserves his Cinsault from

very, very old vines. There are three reds, a pattern which seems general in Faugères: the "Tradition"★★ has ripe fruits and spice, and sometimes a slightly prickly finish which makes the wine fresh and excellent for early drinking; the more serious "Les Douves"★★ from 70% Syrah, 20% Mourvèdre, and 10% Grenache, a fashionable mixture which produces a style typical of good modern Faugères; and finally an oaked wine called "Loublivia"★ in which Eric uses a good dose of old Carignan to lighten the 80% Mourvèdre content. These wines do not come as cheap as some, but the quality is in balance with the price.

long *élevage*. The oak is not prominent in this wine, but with his 100% Syrah you have to be a real fanatic for new wood, unless you have the patience to wait ten or fifteen years.

Unusually, the grapes from Grenache, Carignan, and Cinsault are vinified traditionally but together, only the Syrah and Mourvèdre being made on their own. Macerations are long – up to forty days in the case of the Syrah – with frequent *remontages*. The white Côteaux du Languedoc★ is relatively orthodox, but it is matured on its lees, 25% of it in oak. The "Prestige Rosé"★★ is another of Louison's specialities: 100% Mourvèdre and oak-aged. It is also expensive but still good value.

C2 Elké Kreutzfeldt

CHATEAU HAUT LIGNIERES
lieu-dit Bel-Air
34600 Faugères
☎ 04-67-95-38-27 A/B

Frédéric Naem and his sister-in-law, Madame Kreutzfeldt, have installed their tasting rooms and at least part of their *chais* on the northern outskirts of Faugères village, a shrewd move because their fifteen hectares of vines are buried deep in the countryside at Caussiniojouls, where they would attract little passing trade. The vineyard includes a high proportion (45%) of Syrah, and Cinsault too (22%), which are put to good use in the excellent rosé★, which sells very well at the door especially in summer. Do not be deceived by its apparent lightness both of colour and flavour. It packs a good thirteen degrees of alcohol.

Although they have only been in Faugères since 1994, these growers have quickly established a reputation for balancing finesse and power in their wines, which age well, having a silky charm and delicacy as well as depth of flavour and length of finish. All the grapes are picked by hand, even though they vinify their Carignan traditionally rather than by *macération carbonique*. Of their three reds, the "Tradition"★★ is very attractive when young, good with, say, chicken, having a

bouquet of fresh crushed red fruits. There is some substance to the wine on the palate, its tannins being soft and velvety.

A second red, "Romy"★, is typically 50% Syrah which is given some oak-ageing, the other varieties – Mourvèdre and Grenache – being raised in *cuve*. It is bottled eighteen months after vintage and needs to be kept. It has a more complex nose than the "Tradition", with scents of the garrigue, a touch of tar, and smoke. There is a flavour of Morello cherries and the finish is long and peppery.

The third red, "Carmina Butis"★, is raised wholly in new wood after *assemblage*, though the taste of oak is not at all aggressive and is well balanced by the ultra-ripe sweet fruit. This is what French commentators call a *sudiste* wine: it is very chewy, even a little soupy in texture, needing several years in cellar to show its best.

A well-run commercial property, but one that is certainly not prepared to compromise on *typicité*.

C8 Geneviève Libes et Ginette Coste

DOMAINE DU METEORE
34480 Cabrerolles
☎ 04-67-90-21-12 A

There are two factors to note here, apart from the quality of the wines: the extraordinarily good value for money, and the large hole made in the vineyard by a meteor countless years ago.

Madame Libes recounts how the family had been puzzled for a long time by the circular, depressed patch in the middle of a parcel of garrigue, in which their vines seemed to grow so well. In 1950 a geological reconnaissance plane had identified this piece of vineyard as a potentially interesting subject for study and they sent along an expert to investigate. Soon the place was crawling with geologists, and it is now established that this was indeed the place where a meteor had landed in prehistory. Ever since, this unique feature has been an attraction to visitors and wine lovers.

The family first made its own wine in 1978 and since then has managed to establish a presence throughout the South. The quality of the wines is matched only by a generosity of price hard to equal. The red "Tradition"★★ must be one of the bargains of the appellation, made from equal quantities of Syrah, Mourvèdre, Carignan, and Grenache. The Carignan is made by *macération carbonique*, the other varieties usually being vinified together but not necessarily. There is an oaked red★★ based on 70% Syrah, but the wood is not aggressive.

Their rosé★ is mostly Grenache with Cinsault and a little Mourvèdre which they say suits their higher ground particularly well.

They made their first white in 1995, a Côteaux du Languedoc from equal quantities of Marsanne and Roussanne. Today they also make a vin de pays from Viognier★★, but they are not interested in experimenting with either Chardonnay or Sauvignon. The Viognier wine is particularly delicious, lighter than most, fresh and fruity, and steering clear of the perfume-cabinet. Some of the grapes are left long enough on the vine to make a dessert wine called "Balade d'Automne"★★.

C11 Jacques et Bernadette Lésineau

LE MOULIN DE CIFFRE
34480 Autignac
☎ 04-67-90-11-45 B/C

Ilt is a far cry from Château Haut-Gardère in the suburbs of Bordeaux, which the Lésineaus sold in 1998 to move to this idyllic spot at the junction of three appellations (Saint-Chinian, Côteaux du Languedoc, and Faugères). A long country road takes you from just south of Autignac into the intimate valley of the Taurou, and, as you approach the old mill, the views to the mountains across unbroken vineyard and garrigue are breathtaking. There were once two old mills here, but neither has been seen working in living memory. Today, the site is marked by an extremely attractive house, with a tower reminiscent of a lighthouse, the wood painted a cerulean blue, and the rendering of the stonework a primrose yellow.

There was little that the Lésinaus did not know about winemaking when they arrived. Though grape varieties such as Mourvèdre, and the long, hot summer days of the Languedoc must have taken some getting used to. At this vinous crossroads, there is a combination of the schist of Faugères, some of the same coral as is to be found at Coujan in Saint-Chinian – which is just across the valley – and some more normal *argilo-calcaire*.

As well as the quintet of Languedocian red grapes, the Lésinaus have some Cabernet, which they blend with Syrah to make an attractive, sturdy vin de pays★, and a little Viognier, their only white grape, from which they make a barrel-fermented *mono-cépage*★.

But it is the AOC reds which have attracted so much admiration. The first Faugères★★, from 40% Carignan, 30% Grenache, 20% Syrah, and 10% Mourvèdre, is partly aged in oak and partly in tank, while the "Cuvée Eole"★★★ is wholly raised in wood. Both have a splendid structure, considerable density, and length of finish. They are for keeping. The sole Saint-Chinian★★ is aged in *cuve*, but that is not a sign of lesser stature: with its fresh crushed fruits and sometimes prunes on the bouquet and the palate, it is well integrated, its good structure supported by fine tannins, and thus it has a good long keeping potential.

The Côteaux du Languedoc★ is lighter in style, supple and fruity, a good match for grilled meats, while the two vins de pays and an attactive rosé★ play their supporting roles well.

This is a property with enormous promise.

C7 Frédéric Albaret

DOMAINE SAINT-ANTONIN
La Liquière
34480 Cabrerolles
☎ 04-67-90-13-24 **B**

Montpellier is home to many oenology students, and Albaret was born there. But he says that he was not cut out for academic study and stayed long enough only to pick up the rudiments of technique. He discovered La Liquière – one of the remoter outposts of the Faugères appellation – in 1994, at the age of thirty-two. He managed to acquire, bit by bit, a total of twenty hectares, of which seventeen are now grape-producing. He had to scrounge around everywhere in the village to find somewhere to instal his plant and barrels but he has at last managed to get his whole operation under one roof, including a beautiful old-fashioned horizontal hydraulic press dating from the 1950s which he still uses devotedly.

Frédéric is full of paradoxes. He believes that wine is made above all to give pleasure, rather than intellectual satisfaction. He scoffs at small *micro-cuvées*, and hates all kinds of wine-snobbery. On the other hand, the whole of his crop is hand-picked, *cuvaisons* may last up to a month, there is no filtration or fining, often no sulphuring, and his passionate aim is to perfect the use of his new barrels so that you do not realize they have been used.

He makes only red wine, and only two *cuvées* at that, and they manage to bring together the strands of his philosophy. The "Tradition"★★ is a blend from Grenache, Carignan, and some Syrah and is not oaked. Frédéric believes you should always judge a winemaker by his "Tradition" wine, and this one is certainly top-flight. His "Prestige" wine is called "Magnous"★★, mostly Syrah with some Mourvèdre and Carignan, raised in oak which varies from the brand new, to older barrels which have seen up to four wines.

These wines manage to reconcile the authentic Faugères style with the stamp of a thinking and innovative winemaker; we shall hear a lot more of him.

C6 Bernard, Claudie et Sophie Vidal

CHATEAU DE LA LIQUIERE
34480 Cabrerolles
☎ 04-67-90-29-20
ⓦ **www.faugeres.com/liquiere A**

The Vidal family can trace itself back to the seventeenth century in the hamlet of La Liquière. Bernard's mother still lives in the château which was rebuilt following its sacking during the Revolution. He himself is President of the local Syndicat of growers and his father was the first to hold that office, a difficult one for an independent producer who has to promote quality in the appellation as a whole: the interests of the members of the three coopératives for whom the vine is just one of several crops are sometimes in sharp conflict.

Flexibility is the key to his own approach to vinification. For him the *raison d'être* of an AOC is the preservation of local custom, rather than rigid decree. He does not fuss about the proportions of each grape variety going into an *assemblage*, a process which he regards as improvisatory rather than formulaic, carried out by family committee. As usual, there are three styles of red: "Les Amandiers"★★ is the name given to his basic wine, which is light, round and very quaffable, with a bouquet of red fruits and pepper. The "Vieilles Vignes"★★★ is for once accurately named, being made exclusively from old vines going back forty to a hundred years, including some ancient Carignan. The fruity, spicy character of this wine is emphasized by the *macération carbonique* method of vinification. The real keeper is called "Cistus"★★ after the wild flowers which grow on the garrigue.

The rosé, for which Bernard reserves his Cinsault, is also called "Les Amandiers", as is the white Côteaux du Languedoc★ – which, in addition to Grenache Blanc, has some old Terret grapes in it. The range is completed by a white called "Schistes Blanc"★★, vinified but not aged in oak, given frequent *bâtonnage* during the winter following the vintage.

Bernard makes no wines outside AOC, except an experimental *moelleux* only recently come on stream. He does not generally hold with unblended vins de pays or *vins de cépage*. He believes that you should choose the grapes to suit the terroir, not the other way round, the way the flying winemakers operate. He also hates "Parkerization", which he regards as the quick route to globalization of over-oaked heavy-weight styles alien to Languedoc. The wines of this popular property are to be widely found in restaurants of the region.

other good faugères growers

Frédéric Alquier
Domaine G Alquier, 34600 Faugères
☎ 04-67-95-15-21

Mesdames Pellisier
Domaine du Colombié,
34480 Laurens
☎ 04-67-75-60-44

Olivier Andrieu
Clos Fantine,
La Grange de la Liquière,
34480 Cabrerolles
☎ 04-67-90-20-89

Jacques Pons
Domaine de Fraisse, 34480 Autignac
☎ 04-67-90-23-40

Messieurs Fardel, Lubac, et Pujol
Château de Grézan,
34480 Laurens
☎ 04-67-90-27-46

Jean-Luc Saur
Château Haut-Fabrègues, Lenthéric,
34480 Cabrerolles
☎ 04-67-90-21-37

Alain et Luc Ollier
Domaine Ollier-Taillefer,
34320 Fos
☎ 04-67-90-24-59

Pierre Bénézech et fils
Domaine de la Reynardière,
7 cours Jean Moulin,
34480 St-Géniez-de-Fontedit
☎ 04-67-36-25-75

(*See also* Catherine Roque, Domaine de Clovallon, page 77.)

right Bernard Vidal of Château de La Liquière extols the virtues of Faugères

saint-chinian

There is no obvious frontier between Faugères and Saint-Chinian. There is some continuity of style in the wines too. Some growers say that there is a greater range to be found in the wines grown within either region than any difference between the regions themselves.

Some also say that Faugères produces rounder, fleshier wines, and Saint-Chinian puts out a steelier, more beefy style.

Certainly the vineyards and their landscapes are different. The difference in character between the hill-vineyards in the north of Saint-Chinian and those on the land going down toward the Languedoc plain to the south is also striking, as are the views looking north toward the mountains of the Cévennes which form a stern backdrop to the sometimes rugged vineyards in the upper valley of the River Orb.

The area and its principal town are named after a monk called Anian who settled there in the ninth century and is credited with having founded the vineyards. He and his fellow *réligieux* spent their lives cutting back the dense undergrowth, driving out the wild boars and the wolves; with the latter they succeeded, but the boars remain a constant threat in the vineyards, even today. The monks then planted crops including the vine.

Anian was canonized two centuries after his death, becoming Saint Anian. In the local language, the word "Saint" is pronouned "Sainch" so with the passage of time he was remembered as Sainch-Inian. The monastery that he founded was, like many others in the region, destroyed during the wars of religion in the Middle Ages. However, the Abbey of Fontcaude still stands and has given its name to a local vin de pays.

The coming of the railways in the 1860s put Saint-Chinian on the viticultural map. Paris and the north of France then became substantial customers. The big Paris hospitals prescribed the wines of Saint-Chinian for patients as part of their cure, though whether this was because of the inherent properties of the wine or because the water of Paris was foul is not quite clear. Was it this, that in modern times, inspired Marc Valette of Domaine Canet-Valette, during his early years as a grower, to scrape a living selling vins de table to the local hospitals?

Only part of Saint-Chinian lies on the vein of schist. The ground south of the River Vernazobre, at the point where it flows into the River Orb, has a

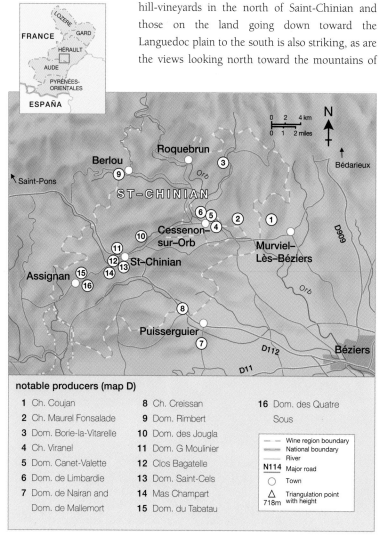

notable producers (map D)

1 Ch. Coujan	**8** Ch. Creissan	**16** Dom. des Quatre Sous
2 Ch. Maurel Fonsalade	**9** Dom. Rimbert	
3 Dom. Borie-la-Vitarelle	**10** Dom. des Jougla	
4 Ch. Viranel	**11** Dom. G Moulinier	
5 Dom. Canet-Valette	**12** Clos Bagatelle	
6 Dom. de Limbardie	**13** Dom. Saint-Cels	
7 Dom. de Nairan and Dom. de Mallemort	**14** Mas Champart	
	15 Dom. du Tabatau	

Map legend:
- — — Wine region boundary
- National boundary
- River
- N114 Major road
- ○ Town
- △ 718m Triangulation point with height

quite different geology – a subsoil of chalk formed out of the fossils left in prehistoric times by the receding sea, is covered with a gravelly clayish chalk topsoil that was washed down from inland. This sharp difference in terroir, and the fact that the height of the vineyards above the sea varies from as much as 300 metres (1,000 feet) in the north to ninety metres (300 feet) in the south, explains why there are said to be two different styles of wine in Saint-Chinian. Many growers, however, enjoy both types of soil, and there is often an overlap. There is, furthermore, a good deal of sandstone and gravelly ground.

In principle, the wines made from vines grown on the schist, though dark in colour, have a minerally character, with some acidity, a delicate bouquet, occasional smokiness, sometimes *torréfaction* (coffee roasting); often with liquorice and scents of the garrigue. The tannins resolve themselves early, leaving the wine with a velvety texture.

The wines from further south, on the *argilo-calcaire* soils, have a livelier colour which makes them very elegant to look at: they have a bouquet of fresh fruit (blackcurrants, raspberries, and cherries), and a firm structure which calls for ageing, more often than not in new wood.

Such generalizations are not wholly reliable, and in any event the styles tend to cross over when growers make two different wines from the same vineyard – for example, one which has a fairly short maceration and is intended to be drunk within two or three years of the vintage, and another with macerations of up to three weeks or even longer, which are wines for long keeping.

Despite the rules of the appellation, the old Carignan vines here are highly valued, especially on the higher ground; as everywhere, the Cinsault is the basis of most rosés.

It is surprising that, in an appellation with so many private growers, more than half the wine is still sold *en vrac*. However, the percentage of sales direct from the producer (forty-five per cent) is impressive and continues to increase, as does the volume exported.

Saint-Chinian is an attractive region irrespective of the qualities of its wines. The mountains to the north are an important feature of the landscape, as well as of the local folklore. The mountain which

the geographers originally christened La Carouse is called by the locals "Cebenna", a feminine form of the word Cévenne. The name is in honour of a daughter of the Titans, persecuted by Zeus, and said to have chosen this mountain as her last resting place. To some, the mountain in silhouette suggests the form of a sleeping woman.

The proximity of the mountains gives extra protection to this countryside from the north wind, and a particularly clear atmosphere. In this micro-climate mimosa grows wild and orange trees need no special winter protection in the sheltered village of Roquebrun. Orange trees are also hardy in Saint-Chinian itself. The *arbousier*, or so-called strawberry tree, offers its yellow flowers and red fruits simultaneously in the autumn, and many species of cistus adorn the hillsides in spring. Some villages are medieval jewels, surprisingly well-preserved given their situation, so close to modern Béziers.

What the French call *typicité* describes the style of wines made by those growers who began the Languedoc Renaissance. While benefiting from the use of the best practices in vineyard and cellar, the wines sought after by these pioneers remain steadfastly traditional.

For other growers in Saint-Chinian, *typicité* was only ever a halfway-house style. They aim to make wines with greater concentration, extraction, and sometimes higher levels of alcohol than the older school: wines which are aimed at the great restaurants of France rather than the tables of the bourgeoisie. They tend to attract the attention of the wine magazines of the world and those who bestow medals.

pages 100/1 religious rituals still pay an important part of the life cycle of those living in Saint-Chinian. On the feast day of the vignerons' patron saint, Mass is said in on of the local *chais*

special features of saint-chinian

the wines red and rosé only. Whites marketed as Coteaux du Languedoc or as vins de pays. VDQS granted in 1951. AOC since 1982.

AOC area covers 20 communes in Hérault: Assignan, Babeau-Bouldoux, Berlou, Causses-et-Veyran, Cazedarnes, Cébazan, Cessenon, Creissan, Cruzy, Ferrières-Poussarou, Murviel-lès-Béziers, Pierrerue, Prades-sur-Vernazobre, Puisserguier, Quarante, Roquebrun, Saint-Chinian, Saint-Nazaire-de-Ladarez, Vieussan, Villespassans.

grape varieties Grenache (including Lladoner Pelut), Syrah, and Mourvèdre, must together constitute at least 60% of AOC vineyards.

growers 84 independents, 17 coopératives.

the soil schist to the north, *argilo-calcaire* and some sandstone elsewhere.

notable producers

D12 La Famille Simon

CLOS BAGATELLE
La Cave des 4 Vents
34360 Saint-Chinian
☎ 04-67-93-61-63 A/B

The Simons can trace their ownership of this property back to 1623. Henry Simon, who presided over it for many years, died in 1998, but the estate is in the capable hands of his son and daughter, Luc and Christine.

They have thirty-nine hectares surrounding the family house just to the west of the town of Saint-Chinian. There are also another seven near the hamlet of Donnadieu, tucked away in the hills toward the Minervois. Here, on noticeably higher ground, the vines are on very poor schist which suits very well the old and severely pruned Carignan, vinified by

macération carbonique and given a long *cuvaison* of twenty-eight days. The wine, called "Cuvée Camille"★★, has notes of liquorice on the bouquet and is a deep rich garnet in colour. It is aged in old *foudres* of which the family has a fine collection, and which are overhauled by a traditional *tonnelier* every three years.

The main vineyard at Saint-Chinian itself yields a rosé and three reds. The *assemblage* of the pink wine is made even before the vinification. The red "Tradition"★★ is based on Carignan (60%) vinified classically. The "Sélection"★★ has Syrah and Mourvèdre but still plenty of Carignan. The Simons like putting a few white grapes in with their reds, a practice which the authorities do not seem to frown on, even if the whites concerned are Viognier (with the Syrah) and Muscat (with the Mourvèdre). The top wine is dedicated to the the late Henry and is called "La Gloire de Mon Père"★★★, adding a touch of Marcel Pagnol

above Marc Valette of Domaine Canet-Valette framed in the arch of his chais

to the *assemblage* which is half Syrah (partly vinified by *macération carbonique*), one-third Mourvèdre, which grows well here, and the rest Grenache. The malolactic fermentation takes place in new wood, where each *cépage* is aged separately for fifteen months before final *assemblage*. Rabbit flamed in armagnac or a fillet of venison with wild mushrooms are recommended dishes to serve with this special wine.

For lovers of varietal wines, there are examples from Chardonnay, Merlot, and Syrah. The young generation here would dearly like to plant some Tannat and some Sangiovese, if and when the rules would allow them to. The Simons also have vineyards at Saint-Jean-du-Minervois producing a delicious vin doux naturel★★ under the name "Bagatelle".

D3 Cathy et Jean-François Izarn

DOMAINE BORIE-LA-VITARELE
Chemin de la Vernède
34490 Saint-Nazaire-de-Ladarez
☎ 04-67-89-50-43 B

"Artisans vignerons" is a perfect description of this committed and talented couple. Starting as tenants with a bare three hectares, they now have twelve hectares of their own which they have replanted, and are developing a further five hectares on the schist. Their vines are in the commune of Causses-et-Veyran, some on arid chalk, others in pebbly ground bequeathed by a now vanished stream.

Jean-François describes his Mediterranean wines as "the pleasure of the sun in the glass". They are concentrated and, like their maker, well-built, generous, and full-bodied; yields are kept to below thirty hectolitres to the hectare. Winemaking is meticulous, long macerations up to forty days, frequent *pigeage*, and very careful attention to oak-ageing. The malolactic fermentations are allowed to take place in barrel, but only some of the wood is new, and harsh tannins are carefully avoided. The wines are neither filtered or fined.

No white wine is made here. The grape varieties are restricted to Syrah, Mourvèdre, and Grenache for the appellation wines, and there is also an important proportion of vins de pays based on Cabernet Sauvignon and Merlot, the one blended with Syrah★★, the other with Grenache★★.

Of their AOC wines, one is bottled as Coteaux du Languedoc★★, and though it is 80% Syrah and will last well, it is also agreeable when young because it is quite supple. The AOC Saint-Chinian★★★ is aged in oak, but is never too woody, nor soupy, as some other wines aspiring to this style tend to be. The rich blackberry-like fruits are allowed fully to express themselves, and the Syrah adds its usual *pain grillé* aromas.

Outside the appellations, Jean-François and Cathy make a rather startlingly delicious rosé★★★, *saigné* from a mixture of Merlot and Grenache, and vinified in barrel.

Supply of these wines is short. One place you can be sure to taste them is at the *ferme-auberge* which Jean-François and Cathy run from the old family stable, converted into a rustic dining room. Jean-François, whose father was himself a restaurateur, does the cooking. A glass of home-made *cartagène* will be your apéritif, and the house eau-de-vie de prune your digestif. A visit to Borie-la-Vitarèle is a complete gastronomic experience.

D5 Marc Valette

DOMAINE CANET-VALETTE
route de Causses-et-Veyran
34460 Cessenon-sur-Orb
☎ 04-67-89-37-50 B/C

The problem you may have with Marc Valette is to know whether or not to share the high opinion he has of himself. There is absolutely no doubting his commitment; he says that he makes the wines he wants to make, and if nobody wants to buy them he will find another *métier*. Nor can you question his outstanding skill: his vineyards are tended to perfection and the wines made with consummate attention to detail. It is also true that, in the glass, all these qualities come together in an amazing expression of the vigneron's skill. He must be regarded as the leader of the avant-garde in Saint-Chinian.

But the question remains as to what you expect of a bottle of wine. If you want a bottle to quaff with friends over a meal, not necessarily a gastronomic event but an occasion when a well-made but not overpowering wine is called for, Marc Valette's wine will clearly not fit the bill. But if you want just one glass of the very best, the most powerful, the most alcoholic, the most structured wine, either to drink on its own or as an accompaniment to equally flavourful cuisine, then Marc's will be unbeatable.

Marc makes no pretence but that he is after the highest alcoholic level he can attain, the maximum extraction – *cuvaisons* of a hundred days are the order of the day – the real blockbuster style, in fact vinous monsters, and he achieves his object perfectly.

Graduating via the coopérative, life was hard at the beginning; he carried out a long-term planting programme, ultimately completed in 1992. He now has eighteen hectares almost in one holding round the *chais*. Yields are fiercely limited, the vines are given three *tris*.

In the *chais* everything works by gravity. It is doubtful whether Marc possesses a pump. There are no *remontages*, the wine being fermented in *cuves* no taller than Marc himself, so as to permit him personally to carry out *pigeage* without danger to himself.

There are just two red wines; no rosé or, as yet, any white wines. The first, hardly a "Tradition", is called "1001 Nights"★★★, aged partly in *cuve* and partly in oak. The second wine is called "Maghani"★★★ – apparently the Persian for "Wine of the Magi" – and raised wholly in oak. Marc Valette's unexpected trump card is his masterly use of the barrel.

Like them or not, these wines are astonishing; the snag is that they are hardly obtainable, such is the speed with which Marc's reputation has grown.

D14 Isabelle et Mathieu Champart

MAS CHAMPART
Bramefan, route de Villespassans
34360 Saint-Chinian
☎ 04-67-38-20-09 A/B

The wines here belong to no particular school. They rely on their own kind of classicism to set them apart from others of the appellation.

Mathieu, a northerner, used to come to Saint-Chinian on holiday. It was here that he met Isabelle, a Parisian also on holiday. If they were to settle in the Languedoc, they had to become vignerons, even though at the time they had no taste for wine. Beginning with eight hectares and a run down house with neither electricity nor water, they started from scratch. For many years they sold their grapes to the coopérative. Meanwhile they gradually rearranged their landholdings until they had assembled sixteen hectares around their home. At last, in 1995, the Champarts were able to build a magnificent completely equipped new *chais*, a well-deserved reward for their years of hard work and sacrifice.

Their first vintage was 1988. They have since established a formidable reputation. Their wines, all traditionally vinified, follow no particular fashion but need time to develop. Aromatic subtlety and silky tannins are their hallmarks.

Their white Côteaux du Languedoc★★, a quite big and fat wine, has enough acidity (even a slight taste of *pierre de fusil*) to retain a kind of Northern style. There are three reds: the "Tradition"★★, still quite tannic in its third year, with a bouquet of cloves and coriander, good Syrah in the mouth and a finish which should lengthen nicely; an intermediate wine called "Causse du Bousquet"★★★ which has a good dose of Mourvèdre and a quarter of which is raised in partly new, partly old oak – a very firmly structured wine, with a bouquet of blackberrries and exotic perfumes, and needing four or five years at least after the vintage to show well; finally, the *tête de cuvée*, called "Clos de la Simonette"★★★, with up to 70% low-yielding Mourvèdre, given more than four weeks' maceration, and raised wholly in wood for eighteen months. This is the closest the house-style gets to the Young Turks.

There is also an attractive and very good-value vin de pays from Cabernet Franc★, but hardly in the class of the AOC wines which are such excellent value.

D1 François Guy

CHATEAU COUJAN
34490 Murviel-lès-Béziers
☎ 04-67-37-80-00
Ⓦ www.logassist.fr/coujan B

This remote estate was formerly a fief of the château of Murviel, its nearest neighbour four kilometres (2.2 miles) away; one of the

châtelaines was called Gabrielle Spinola. She took rent from Coujan in the form of a large cask of its best wine, and still collected this even after she went to live in Italy. Gabrielle Spinola's name lives on in the title of one of the Coujan *cuvées*.

The Guy family also keep peacocks, but their boxer dogs find them very tasty, so the birds keep out of sight in the trees. What visitors will see instead is the Romanesque chapel in the grounds of the château which contains some remarkable mosaics dating from the period of Roman occupation – Coujan was the site of an important Roman villa. The restoration of the chapel is a passion second only to the vine in François' life.

The vineyard lies on a unique substratum of coral. There are nearly a hundred hectares of vines. The *caveau de dégustation* is to scale and contains what must be one of the finest collections of giant *foudres* in France, some of them still used for the malolactic fermentation of the red wines. They make a magnificent setting for a tasting.

Florence, François' daughter, is in charge front-of-house. Her father was one of the pioneers in experimenting with non-traditional grape varieties. The vins de pays by no means play second fiddle to the AOC wines here and are of exceptional interest.

The whites are given a *macération pelliculaire*. The Sauvignon★★ ages unusually well, avoiding too much acidity and displaying lovely soft fruit as well as a silky texture. The younger vintages are more typical of the grape, lighter, even delicate. They are allowed to remain on their lees for six weeks before bottling. Then there is a 100% Rolle★ – a grape which also features in Coujan's AOC white★★ along with Grenache Blanc and Clairette, making a wine which is full of fruit and sunshine, with hints of melons and peaches. The rosé★ is made largely from Mourvèdre, a grape which does not surrender its colour easily, so at Coujan they add a little Grenache and Cinsault. The first red might be the Pinot★★ which has a real burgundy taste, while remaining light and distinctly quaffable.

The Guy family are also proud of their Merlot/Cabernet blend★★. François claims to have been the first to plant these varieties in the Hérault. At any rate he was making wine from them in 1974 – still a surprisingly lively bottle and probably in much better health than most clarets surviving from that year.

There are two AOC reds: Gabrielle Spinola's, which is the house's "Tradition"★★, made from all the usual grapes except Carignan, of which Coujan has none; it is as delicious as their second red, a lightly oaked Syrah/Mourvèdre blend called "Bois Joli"★★, with distinct messages of *pain grillé* and red fruits.

D8 Bernard Reveillas

CHATEAU CREISSAN
3 chemin du Moulin d'Abram
34370 Creissan
☎ 04-67-93-84-80 A

Bernard Reveillas is a round, genial, outgoing fellow with a warm welcome and a lively sense of humour. The word "château" is hardly apt to describe the outside of his comfortable, large modern villa on the outskirts of the village, but it fits well the baronial interior where guests are received in truly noble style. Two well-brought-up children look promising recruits to winemaking, and elegant Madame Reveillas may well be on hand in a chic, Parisian outfit to offer you a glass of the delicious sweet house Muscat.

Bernard's great grandfather was a winemaker, an independent producer who resisted the blandishments of the local coopérative. It was Bernard's father – when Bernard was still a young man – who started to make radical improvements to the vineyard. He was an early planter of Grenache and Syrah grapes, while at the same time continuing such traditions as his sweet Muscat and a *cartagène*.

Bernard still makes both, and delicious they are. So is the sweet rosé★★ that he makes by *saignage* from late-picked Grenache. Bernard has twenty-nine hectares

in production and a further eleven in hand for future development. Half the vines are in the appellation area which ends almost at the bottom of his garden, and the other half are used to make either Coteaux du Languedoc, or vins de pays under the name of Coteaux de Fontcaude. The last-named are marketed as "Domaine des Hautes Lasses", the use of the word "château" being forbidden in the world of vins de pays.

All the wines that Bernard makes today are for keeping, perhaps longer than those of most other properties. He practises his own version of *culture raisonnée*. He makes his own fertilisers from vegetable refuse and horse manure. He harvests, however, by machine, where the slopes permit.

Syrah and Grenache are the basis of both his Saint-Chinian★★★ and his Coteaux du Languedoc★★★ wines. For his red vin de pays he blends Cabernet Sauvignon with a little Merlot and Carignan. Since white

Saint-Chinian does not exist, his white wine is a Coteaux du Languedoc Blanc★★ made from the Grenache Blanc and Vermentino varieties which he vinifies together.

Vinifications are traditional and long – up to thirty days for the best *cuvées* and never less than twenty-five. The wines of Creissan can be confidently recommended. One of Bernard's customers has been buying them for fifty years, another for forty. That surely speaks for itself.

D10 Alain Jougla

DOMAINE DES JOUGLA
34360 Prades-sur-Vernazobre
☎ **04-67-38-06-02 A**

The small village of Prades has some 200 inhabitants only, most devoted to vine-growing in one way or another.

Situated in the valley of the River Vernazobre, it is on the frontier of the two

above a view across the hills near Berlou reveals the rolling terrain in the valley of the Orb

terroirs, schist and *argilo-calcaire*, and the Domaine des Jougla enjoys both types of soil. Alain and his wife Jocelyne are the most welcoming of hosts. Their family has been making wine from its forty hectares of vines over many generations. The present buildings date from 1900 but have been entirely modernized, though the old *foudres* have thankfully been kept.

This is a *typicité* house, but by no means stick-in-the-mud; benchmark Saint-Chinian in fact. Spend a little time in the tasting room and you will find that most of the Jougla customers are relieved to find that Alain is not trying to achieve fifteen degrees of alcohol, that he is not over-oaking the wines, or aspiring to membership of the avant-garde. Rather, they have come to buy wines which flatter rather than kill food, such as the

delicious white Coteaux du Languedoc Blanc★★, from Grenache Blanc and Bourboulenc, with its fresh fruity character and good acidity; or the varietal Viognier★★, very discreet and not parading too many of its peacock feathers; or the deeply coloured rosé★, with its distinctive strawberry and raspberry character.

There are three reds, the first of which is, for a change, not called "Tradition", but "Classique"★ – "Tradition"★ being the name reserved for the second of the trio. If these two wines represent the conventional side of Saint-Chinian, the top of the range "Signée" ★★ clearly deserves its flagship status; mostly Syrah and Grenache with some Carignan too, this is a wine wholly from the schist and from old vines too. New oak is used over a three year cycle and is not at all obtrusive, though the silky tannins need at least five years from the date of most vintages.

Not all the "new wave" of Saint-Chinian would contemplate selling wine *en vrac* to customers bringing their *bidons* to the *cave*. But the Jouglas have a loyal following among locals and faithful holidaymakers and are not ready to let them down.

D2 Philippe et Thérèse Maurel

CHATEAU MAUREL FONSALADE
34490 Causses-et-Veyran
☎ **04-67-89-57-90 B**

Madame Maurel receives visitors and customers with a gracious Old World charm, while her son Philippe is in charge of the vineyards and the *chais*. "*Fonsalade*" means in the local patois "salt spring". The water from the *fontaine* in the tasting room is indeed salty, strictly for washing glasses and not drinking.

The gentler landscape at this frontier with Faugères is a perfect setting for the equally gentle atmosphere of this charming estate. The soil here is not schist, but there is practically everything else besides; large pebbles on clay, gravelly slate, and sandstone. The preponderance of clay-based ground gives the wines power and substance.

There is no white Maurel Fonsalade, but the rosé★★ is extraordinary. While three kilometres (1.7 miles) down the road Michel Louison makes his rosé from 100% Mourvèdre raised in oak, the Maurels' top rosé is 100% Syrah, and also raised in oak. Syrah always

makes a very deep-coloured rosé and this is no exception; it has a brilliant almost ruby-red colour, more like a clairet than a rosé, redcurrants and spices on the bouquet overlaying and almost smothering the vanilla scent of the new oak. The wine is chewy and lively on the palate; the finish long and fruity.

The red "Tradition"★★ is a model of its kind – enhanced by the addition of wine from the better *cuvées* before being bottled. The range of flavours on the palate may include tobacco as well as the more usual red fruits and the herbs of the garrigue. The next red up the scale is called "Cuvée Frédéric"★★★ and is named in honour of Madame's son who was tragically killed at a young age in an avalanche. It is a fitting memorial, a beautifully smooth, lightly oaked wine from Grenache and Syrah; deep and rich, with aromas of cherry, citrus fruits and flowers, and good concentration on the palate.

The top *cuvée* is called simply "Fonsalade"★★, and adds a little Mourvèdre to the oldest Syrah and Grenache vines on the estate. A long maceration of five weeks is followed by a year spent in new oak; the wine is then put back into the tank to age further before being fined (not filtered) and bottled.

C11 Jacques et Bernadette Lésineau

LE MOULIN DE CIFFRE
34480 Autignac
☎ **04-67-90-11-45**
(*See* **Faugères, page 95.**)

D11 R. L. Moulinier

DOMAINE G. MOULINIER
34360 Saint-Chinian
☎ **04-67-38-23-18 B/C**

The Moulinier family are moderately avant-garde. Guy Moulinier now has twenty-one hectares. At first a *coopérateur*, he persuaded neighbours to allow him to use their *chais*. In 1994 he made his first wine in his own premises. He had the good fortune that Robert Parker happened to pass that way and tasted his wine. The Mouliniers have never looked back. A bigger and better *cave* has just been completed.

The vineyard is dotted around the area in many parcels, and between them they enjoy all types of terroir. Only the "modern" grape varieties, Syrah, Mourvèdre, and Grenache, are grown. All picking is by hand and it is done in small baskets which are only half-filled so that the speed of feeding them into the *égrappoir* does not cause a bottleneck in the system. The Syrah vines are given two *tris* and the Mourvèdre three. The grapes are given long maceration, with frequent *délestages*.

Guy's son, Pascal, is in charge of the vinification having spent a year studying the techniques in Burgundy. He is keen to put to good use the different characteristics of the different terroirs, which he vinifies separately. During the early risk-taking years Guy opened a wine shop in Saint-Chinian called "Espace Vin", which today takes up a deal of his time because he has become the most important local *caviste*, stocking the wines of other areas, and even single malt whiskies, as well as the wines of Saint-Chinian.

The Mouliniers make only red wine and there are usually three *cuvées*: the "Tradition"★★, something of a misnomer, because it is recognizably of the same style as its two very modern older brothers, "Les Sigillaires"★★★, macerated for three to five weeks, its 50% Syrah raised in oak, renewed every three years, and "Les Terrasses Grillées"★★★, 70% Syrah and the balance equally from Mourvèdre and Grenache, all of which are aged in oak.

At a blind tasting of world-wide Syrah wines, Les Terrasses Grillées was judged second, ahead of Guigal's La Turque 1995 and Penfold's Grange 1986. The company it enjoyed is an indication of the Moulinier style: wines of deep, rich colour, sweet ripe fruit, blackberries and blackcurrant on a velvety chocolatey base – wines which cry out for food, but of which one glass or so would be as much as the tastebuds could cope with.

D9 Jean-Marie Rimbert

DOMAINE RIMBERT
4 avenue des Mimosas
34360 Berlou
☎ 04-67-89-73-98 B

The Latin *ver luporum* means literally "springtime of the wolves" and is the derivation of the name Berlou, a commune on the right bank of the River Orb. The ground is 100% schist. Jean-Marie Rimbert, a raven-haired native of Provence, first came here in the mid-1990s to pick the grapes while on holiday. He decided to stay, and in 1996 bought up a few vines in very poor condition from a former *coopérateur* and made his first wine from very old Carignan and Syrah vines. It was a remarkable début. Today, Jean-Marie has established a reputation as one of the leading young winemakers of the appellation.

The vineyard now consists of twenty hectares, of which no less than 40% are devoted to Carignan. All the Rimbert wines are based on this grape, and there is a 100% Carignan wine "Le Chant de Marjolaine" ★★★, astonishingly deep in colour and richness.

The first of the two reds made by *assemblage* is described by Jean-Marie as "*le plaisir et la gourmandise par excellence*" and it bears the name "Les Travers de Marceau"★★. From tiny yields of less than thirty hectolitres to the hectare, Carignan still dominates but leaves room for other varieties. Bottled during the spring following the vintage, the wine has lovely fruit, is easy to drink, and is ideal for wine bars and for outdoor eating.

The top wine, called "Mas au Schiste"★★★, is a more serious affair altogether, the formula, proclaimed on its barrel revealing "34% Carignan, 29% Syrah, 21% Grenache, 16% Cinsault, *et un bon tiers de passion*". Blackcurrant dominates the bouquet of this wine, and is a hallmark of the house style. The perfumes of the garrigue which waft in through the door of the *chais* are there in the wine too, about a third of which is aged in barrique, the remainder in *cuve*, evidence that Jean-Marie is not keen to drown the fruitiness of his wine in new oak. This wine is complex and no doubt keeps well, though it can also be drunk relatively young.

Jean-Marie makes only a little rosé★, but a great deal more of a white Coteaux du Languedoc which he calls "Le Rimberlou"★★★, a rich fat wine largely based on Marsanne. It has the distinction of a thoroughbred.

D13 Etienne Rouanet

DOMAINE SAINT-CELS
34360 Saint-Chinian
☎ 04-67-38-13-32 A/B

Close to Clos Bagatelle is this seventy-hectare domaine, mostly on high gound round the Chapelle de Notre Dame which dominates the town of Saint-Chinian. There are also some parcels near Murviel-lès-Béziers. Etienne has some Mourvèdre there which gives spice and character to his top *cuvée* called "Grand Bourgas"★★. There are two other reds from the vines at Saint-Chinian itself which are grown on mixed terroirs of schist, *argilo-calcaire*, and sandstone: a "Tradition"★, which is lightish in style but very drinkable and easy to enjoy, and the "Cuvée Elégance"★★, which has more complexity and gets just a touch of oak – a wine with good structure and friendly tannins. Etienne has been making the wine here for ten years and the results are value-for-money Saint-Chinians of the "*typicité*" school.

D15 Bruno et Jean-Paul Gracia

DOMAINE DU TABATAU
34360 Assignan
☎ 04-67-38-19-60 B

Bruno says of himself: "Our domaine was officially created on Christmas Eve 1997 when my application to be classified as a 'young farmer' was accepted."

"The name 'Tabatau' is a tribute to my grandparents and my family. In patois, it means the child of the 'tabataire', the village tobacconist. My grandfather was the tabataire; he had to abandon his vineyard after being seriously wounded at Verdun, like a number of the countrymen round here. For his services to his country he was granted the Bureau de Tabac concession at Salvetat sur-Agout, north of here in the mountains."

"Thirty-five years have passed, twenty since I finished my studies...."

In 1989 I was plunged into the deep end: after an amazing apprenticeship with Monsieur Guibert, I was put in charge of the vines at Mas de Daumas Gassac. My new venture here in Assignan is on argilo-calcaire soil between 250 and 300 metres (800 and 1,000 feet) above sea-level with a dry Mediterranean climate, swept in winter by the cold, violent winds coming down from the Montagne Noire."

"When I arrived, the grapes were those usually associated with the lowliest vins de table... many of the vines being between eighty and one hundred years old. I will keep all of them. In 1998 I planted a little Chardonnay and the following year I acquired another two hectares with some Syrah, Grenache, and a little more Carignan; I have planted a little more Syrah too, some Mourvèdre, and a little Grenache Blanc. Just recently I have put in some Roussanne and Vermentino."

"Some of my harvest is vinified at the Saint-Chinian coopérative because I do not yet have the facilities to do all of it myself. What I do make here is vinified traditionally, and I use round concrete cuves some of them open, for the red grapes. The fruit is previously destalked thanks to a machine which I acquired from Madame Horat at La Grange des Quatre Sous (see page 111). I like long cuvaisons (three to five weeks) and I myself do the pigeage by hand. Some of the wine is aged in not quite new oak."

"The reds are fined with egg white but not filtered. My rosé is made by saignage, and I made my first whites in 2000." Bruno's self-effacing charm, his sense of fun, and the twinkle in his eye conceal the enormous leap from the sophistication of Daumas Gassac to this simplest of enterprises in a lost corner of the hills of Saint-Chinian. In 2001 he was joined by his brother, a soldier turned oenologist. An interim report while Bruno – an excellent catch for Saint-Chinian – settles in: first, there's a Syrah/Grenche/Carignan blend (the last two grapes predominating), which he calls "Tabataire"★★★, its malolactic fermentation is in wood, then half of it is aged for a year in a mixture of new and old barrels. Next, there is a wine for earlier drinking, called "Camprigou"★★, made from Carignan, Cinsault, Grenache, and Aramon; this last ia grape of which Bruno is not ashamed. His rosé★★ contains a little Aramon too. "If you prune it hard and ensure low yields, it will serve well," he says. What would they say to that at Daumas Gassac?

D4 Danielle et Gérard Bergasse-Milhé

CHATEAU VIRANEL
34460 Cessenon
☎ 04-90-55-85-82 A

Gérard Bergasse is hard to beat for a warm welcome, with his open, generous smile and value-for-money wines. He can trace his family's ownership of Viranel, either by inheritance or marriage, back to the sixteenth century, though not as far as the Romans – even so, Gérard is currently excavating the site of a Roman villa under the trees in his garden. The present house, with its fresco of Bacchus, anticipates the Art Nouveau period.

There are three distinct types of terrain: Cabernet (for vins de pays) and Mourvèdre are planted on the alluvial terraces close to the River Orb; Syrah, Carignan, and some Grenache on the mixture of marls and chalk around and just above the château; and Grenache (red and white) on the highest ground where some of the soil is quite acid. The vines are on average thirty-years old.

Gérard's main focus is the restaurant trade, so, to add weight to the wine, the harvest is carried out rather later than in most vineyards; acidity is thereby reduced, making the wines drinkable earlier than might otherwise be the case. To avoid astringency, the grapes go into the cuve whole, by gravity, and without pumping, thereby eliminating as far as possible the goût du rafle in the must. Remontages are avoided as far as possible in the belief that they encourage a vegetal taste; instead, the wine is given three or four délestages during the vinification. To give the "Tradition" wine extra body, 20% is, unusually, aged in wood.

The wines are, however, far from being blockbusters; Gérard believes that wine intended for consumption with food must have weight, but not enough to disguise the chef's efforts. Sommeliers will, Gérard says, tend to choose wines which show off good cooking rather than compete with it. This explains why Gérard is so devoted to the Grenache grape. He even makes a red vendanges tardives from it – from such miniscule yields that he does not sell it widely. He calls this wine "Folie d'Automne", and thinks it is a style made by only one other estate in the Languedoc – Domaine Henry at Saint-Georges-d'Orques.

His excellent rosé★★ is 40% Grenache. His white Coteaux du Languedoc★★ is 100% Grenache Blanc: displaying floral aromas, and a full, harmonious palate.

The red Tradition★★ has a little Mourvèdre – the liquorice and prune bouquet is striking, in the mouth the wine is food-flattering. The oaked wine★★ of the property is two-thirds Syrah, one-third Grenache, purple and powerful, needing time to mature.

other good saint-chinian growers

Domaine Carrière-Audier
34390 Vieussan
☎ 04-67-97-71-74

Jean-Pierre Sireyjol
Château de Castigno and Château du

Planas, 34360 Villespassans
☎ 04-67-38-05-50

Monsieur et Madame Miquel
Château Cazal-Viel,
34460 Cessenon-sur-Orb
☎ 04-67-89-63-15

Robert Eden
Domaine de Combebelle, 34360 Villespassans
☎ 04-68-38-26-88

Michel Gleizes
Domaine La Croix Sainte-Eulalie,
avenue de Saint-Chinian, Combejean,
34360 Pierrerue
☎ 04-67-38-08-51

Line Cauquil
Domaine Deslines, Donnadieu,
34360 Babeau-Bouldoux
☎ 04-67-38-19-95

EARL Château La Dournie
Château la Dournie, 34360 Saint-Chinian
☎ 04-67-38-19-43

Nadia et Cyril Bourgne
Domaine La Madura,
34360 Saint-Chinian
☎ 04-67-38-17-85

Joseph et Emilienne Lacugue
Château Milhau-Lacugue,
34620 Puisserguier
☎ 04-67-30-75-38

Thierry Navarre
Domaine Navarre, avenue de Balaussan,
34460 Roquebrun
☎ 04-67-89-53-58

SNC Vignobles Roger
Château du Prieuré des Mourgues,
34360 Pierrerue
☎ 04-67-38-18-19 or 04-68-42-23-23

Jean-Claude Rouanet
Domaine Rouanet,
34360 Babeau-Bouldoux
☎ 04-67-38-04-72

right Bruno Gracia, of Domaine du Tabatau at
Assignan; ex Mas de Daumas Gassac

Rémy Soulié

Domaine des Soulié,

rue des Figuiers, 34360 Assignan

☎ 04-67-38-11-78

Les Vins de Roquebrun

avenue des Orangers, 34460 Roquebrun

☎ 04-67-89-64-35

Cave Les Coteaux du Rieu Berlou

34360 Berlou

☎ 04-67-89-58-58

Cave les Vignerons de Saint-Chinian

route de Sorteilho, 34360 Saint-Chinian

☎ 04-67-38-28-48

vins de pays

D16 Hildegard Horat

LA GRANGE DES QUATRE SOUS
34360 Assignan
☎ **04-67-38-06-41 B**

The village of Assignan, on a plateau high in
the hills above Saint-Chinian, seems to be
favoured by unconventional winemakers.
This charming spot was cited in the will of
Garsinde, Countess of Toulouse, in the tenth
century, so Madame Horat has named one
of her wines after the Countess.

She bought her tumbledown property –
named by her appropriately – as a holiday
home in 1975. She thinks it may originally
have been a base for the Knights Templar.

A lover and restorer of ancient buildings
she has identified some artefacts which she
thinks establish this link. She became a
vigneron almost by accident when she bought
an hectare of vines from a Spaniard who had
decided to give up growing grapes. Now
there are eight hectares altogether, a holding
which she has built up bit by bit over the years.

Madame is Swiss, with good friends
back home, and she had no difficulty in
selling them her first tentative wine made
in 1983. This success prompted her to plant

left on higher ground, below the Cévennes, other
crops are grown as well as grapes

some more vines, and she chose the two
Cabernets, Merlot, Syrah, Mourvèdre – a
surprise to find this variety on such high
ground – and Cot... this last-named putting
her beyond the pale of the AOC authorities.
Madame Horat likes Cot, and is not fussed
that she is obliged to make wines without
the benefit of appellation. Moreover, she looks
forward to the day when she might be allowed
to plant some Swiss *cépages*.

Madame has not signed up to biodynamic
obligations, but she practises the precepts as
far as possible. All her wines are bottled on
the falling moon. She makes a delightful rosé★
from Cinsault, Syrah, and Mourvèdre, and two
white wines as well as her reds. A delicious
Viognier/Marsanne★★ blend, combining the
romantic Southern fruit of the first with the
more substantial backbone of the second,
has nothing flabby about it: a good touch of
acidity points the floral roundness of the fruit
flavours. There is also a Chardonnay★ varietal.
Both whites are barrel-fermented.

Her first red is called "Les Serrottes"★★
and is her unconventional Syrah/Cot blend,
given twenty-five days' maceration with *pigeage*,
and aged in *foudres* and *demi-muids*. The
"Countess Garsinde's"★★ wine is more
conventional: Mourvèdre, Syrah, and Grenache,
also given long *cuvaison* and raised in
Bordeaux barrels for a year. Finally, there
is a mix of the two Cabernets called
"Lo Molin"★.

D6 Henri Boukandoura

DOMAINE DE LIMBARDIE
Grangeneuve
34460 Cessenon
☎ **04-67-89-61-42 A**

Henri, born in North Africa and a Breton by
adoption, never intended to be a winemaker
until a holiday friend rang him one day from
the Languedoc and persuaded him to take on
thirty hectares of run-down farm near Murviel
just north of Béziers.

His first vintage was in 1987, a year that
suffered from downpour conditions, but from

nightmarish circumstances Henri managed to
make wine which was not at all bad for
a beginner and was lucky to secure an
immediate market in the UK.

Today he has twenty hectares of vines.
Being accustomed to growing only vins de
pays, he is not tempted to adopt the AOC
Saint-Chinian to which he is now entitled
having moved to a splendid house and
chais just outside Cessenon.

Tall, gaunt, and ascetic-looking, Henri
presents an image opposite to that of the
fairy-tale vigneron, but he has enough
enthusiasm, passion, and charm to match
ten of them. With the aid of the engaging
Madeleine (who claims no function beyond
that of taster) he makes a visit to this
domaine pure delight, reinforced by the
quality of his wines.

Henri's range is sensibly limited to two
reds and a rosé, but how good they are! The
rosé★★, *saigné* from Syrah and Grenache, is
mainly for regular visitors and for summer
drinking, aromatic and very dry, perfect for a
lunch shaded from the hot Languedoc sun.

The red "classique"★★ is a Merlot
Cabernet blend in which some of the *vin de
presse* is added in years which need beefing
up. This is a delicious value-for-money wine,
easy, and instantly likeable. The prestige
wine is perversely called "Tradition" ★★★
and is pure oak-aged Merlot, but the wood
is merely hinted at.

The 1998 was particularly successful,
needing some years to come round. The
1999 and 2000 are equally promising. To
give some idea of the quality, the 1994
version came fourth ahead of Pétrus in an
all-world Merlot tasting in Switzerland.

Plans for the future include a Syrah
varietal★★★ made by *macération
carbonique*, just coming on stream. The
fragrant fruit is matched by silky tannins,
the whole very delicately oaked in five-year-
old barrels. There is just the touch of acidity
needed to assure long life. It is no wonder
that this grower could sell his output six
times over.

minervois

Minerva was the Roman goddess of wisdom, an inspiration for the invading legions to bring their native vines from Italy and create vineyards in the "Narbonnensis", their new colony. Minerva continues to lend her name to this present day wine-growing area north of the River Aude and between Carcassonne and Narbonne.

When the Romans had gone, the vineyards were cherished and further developed by the Church, which also evangelized the hinterland to the north of the plain and took the vine into the foothills of the Black Mountain.

The town of Minerve itself was the scene of one of the most terrible episodes in the so-called crusade against the Cathars. One hundred and forty Cathars, walled up in the fortress of Minerve, and who refused to recant their heresy were put to the sword by the Crusaders. Today, a crumbling ruin glows red in the spectacular sunsets of the region as a bloody reminder of the bigotry and intolerance of the medieval Establishment.

Even though wisdom seemed to have abandoned the region in the Middle Ages, the vines thrived, and during the heyday of the nineteenth century, they extended downward from the hilly interior as far as the Canal du Midi, which today forms the southern boundary of the modern appellation.

The Minervois vineyard may be imagined as an amphitheatre on a vast scale: the canal as the stage, Carcassonne and Narbonne the wings, while the auditorium rises in terraces to the north. Rivers running south from the Black Mountain are the stairways which connect upper and lower levels, dividing the vineyard into a mosaic of varied terroirs, and producing a patchwork of wine styles. Sometimes the terrain is made up of polished pebbles like those to be found in dried-up river beds, or of sandstone, schist, chalk, or even white marble. This is a subtle landscape of gentle, rolling contours, though the arid vineyards in the north can reach a more dramatic height of 450 metres (1,500 feet) above sea-level.

There are variations, too, in climate within this fairly compact region. Here, conversation does not start with the question, "Lovely weather, isn't it?", but rather: "Which way is the wind blowing?" Le Marin is humid and usually brings rain; from the northwest Le Cers is cooler and drier. Breezes coming off the Black Mountain help to determine the northern limits of viticulture, where only the most sheltered sites are cultivated, in pockets of red soil nestling between the rocks or sometimes in pure chalk.

The further inland, the humidifying influence of the sea lessens, and the climate becomes more arid.

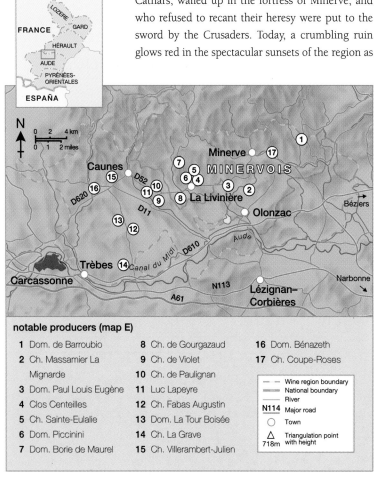

notable producers (map E)

1 Dom. de Barroubio	8 Ch. de Gourgazaud	16 Dom. Bénazeth
2 Ch. Massamier La Mignarde	9 Ch. de Violet	17 Ch. Coupe-Roses
3 Dom. Paul Louis Eugène	10 Ch. de Paulignan	
4 Clos Centeilles	11 Luc Lapeyre	
5 Ch. Sainte-Eulalie	12 Ch. Fabas Augustin	
6 Dom. Piccinini	13 Dom. La Tour Boisée	
7 Dom. Borie de Maurel	14 Ch. La Grave	
	15 Ch. Villerambert-Julien	

- - - Wine region boundary
——— National boundary
——— River
N114 Major road
○ Town
△ Triangulation point
718m with height

Between Trausse and Olonzac the rainfall is exceptionally low. Further west there are Atlantic influences. The combination of variations in soil type and micro-climate will determine which grapes grow where, and even the way the vines are trained. There are about 180 independent growers, of whom 120 or so bottle and market their own wines. Others sell *en vrac* to the trade. Minervois is made in all three colours but the whites represent a mere two or three per cent of the total AOC production. These vary from fresh, lively, and floral, to a rounder style when oaked, with hints of exotic fruits. Many growers, exploiting grape varieties which are banned from the appellation wines, make excellent white vins de pays from Chardonnay and, increasingly, Viognier. These tend to a fuller and fatter style.

At the heart of the appellation twenty private growers and four coopératives have developed the sub-appellation called "Minervois La Livinière", for making red wines which they believe have greater complexity, quality, and ageing potential; aromas of blackcurrant, herbs from the garrigue, black olives and, in maturity, leather, are characteristics which are claimed for the La Livinière growths. There is an elaborate self-regulating system of analysis and tasting before a wine may use the Livinière name.

At present only about 150 hectares produce grapes for La Livinière wine, but most growers produce mainstream Minervois as well, reserving the superior appellation for their premium wines. Big and soft on the palate, usually more or less oaked, these fleshy wines can be elegantly tannic, needing five and more years to soften.

The good name that Minervois enjoyed in the nineteenth century managed to survive the crises which followed phylloxera: with the exception of Corbières, Minervois was for many years the only named wine area in the Languedoc of which many people had heard. In modern times it has more than kept pace with the improvement in other Languedoc vineyards. As the permitted yield has fallen from sixty-two hectolitres per hectare in 1987 to forty-one in 1998, quality has increased. In 1985 only thirty per cent of the production was bottled; by 1999 the proportion had risen to seventy-six per cent. As the region has developed its tourism, wine-growers have been able to increase their sales "at the door" by a third, and the number of producers bottling their own wine has increased from forty-five in 1985, to 130 in 1999. Great strides have been taken to expand the market beyond traditional outlets. Fifty per cent of all sales are now to hypermarkets and supermarkets, only six per cent going to restaurants, and nineteen per cent to export. The UK is the best export market.

The style of Minervois varies a great deal. At their best the wines can show an elegance and finesse not always to be found elsewhere in the South. To those who say the region has peaked and that there is now little room for improvement, others reply that the future for the region lies in greater and greater concentration on Syrah and Mourvèdre, the so-called *cépages améliorateurs*. Another school believes in the importance of retaining the old Languedoc grapes, and even bringing back and replanting some which have been altogether abandoned.

White wines are a very small part of Minervois production, although they may enjoy AOC status if from the right grapes and from AOC quality land. There is a move toward a new appellation for sweet wines under the name "Minervois Noble"; this is a style which is traditional to Languedoc and was the only kind of white wine made here before the fashion for dry whites took over.

Tucked away in the northeast corner of the appellation, in the chilly uplands separating the Minervois from Saint-Chinian, is the tiny appellation called Saint-Jean-de-Minervois, which focuses mostly on vins doux naturels made from the Muscat grape. These are described in the chapter on vins doux naturels (*see* pages 174–181).

---

special features of minervois

AOC area covers 45 communes in the north-east Aude and 16 in north-west Hérault.

grape varieties reds: Grenache (including Ladoner Pelut), Syrah, and Mourvèdre must represent a minimum of 60%; Carignan a maximum 40%; Cinsault, Black Picpoul, Terret, and Aspiran are also permitted. whites: mainly Marsanne, Roussanne, and Vermentino. Picpoul, Clairette, Terret, and Muscat together may not exceed 20%, and Muscat is limited to 10%.

Minervois La Livinière confined to 6 communes: Azillanet, Azille, Cesseras, Félines, La Livinière, and Siran. Syrah and Mourvèdre must make up at least 40% of the vineyard.

vine age minimum 4 years old.

the soil chalk and pebbles on lower ground; sandstone and granite higher up.

above left young vines reach from the chalk terroir in the hills near Minerve

below left where grapes will grow, no parcel of land is wasted

above tiled roofs and ancient stone walls are typical of the medieval village of Minerve

notable producers

E1 Raymond Miquel

DOMAINE DE BARROUBIO
34360 Saint-Jean-de-Minervois
☎ 04-67-38-14-06 A
(*See also* Muscat de Saint-Jean, page 179.)

Raymond Miquel has some twenty-five
hectares planted under the Saint-Jean
appellation, and a further few hectares as
mainstream Minervois for his red wine. The
latter should not be overlooked just because
Raymond is a Muscat specialist; from an
assemblage of 40% Carignan, 30% Grenache,
and 30% Syrah, he makes a delicious light
quaffable wine★★, ideal with *charcuterie* or
perhaps with barbecue food. He is also
experimenting with an oaked wine, a
departure for a domaine which has so
far eschewed new wood.

E16 Frank Bénazeth

DOMAINE BENAZETH
8 Chemin de Bel Mati
11160 Villeneuve-Minervois
☎ 04-68-26-13-64 A

Anonymous, and behind a large red door
as you drive down the main street into
Villeneuve, are the headquarters of Frank
Bénazeth who has fifteen hectares of vines
in the nearby commune of Villégly as well as
seventeen in various parcels in his own village.
The production is entirely of red and rosé
wines, made largely from Syrah and Carignan,
with some Grenache and a little Cinsault. The
technical specifications of the wines suggest
nothing exceptional: the wines are made and
matured traditionally, and a special *cuvée* is
raised in new oak for twelve months.

In bottle, the results★★ are splendid:
indeed they have propelled this domaine to
the top of the appellation, stocked by many
international department stores. Their gold
medal in Paris should ensure their continued
place in the market.

E7 Michel Escande

DOMAINE BORIE DE MAUREL
34210 Félines-Minervois
☎ 04-68-91-63-92 C

In the years since his first vintage in 1989,
the eccentric Michel Escande has won the
adulation of the media and the nickname
"Sorcerer of Félines"; not bad for a self-taught
boatman, his earlier years having being spent
on board ship rather than in a wine-cellar. His
chais is on a hillside on the edge of the village
of Félines, but you will not be admitted
entrance: it is said that not even his wife
Sylvie is allowed in. You are, however, more
than welcome in the tasting-room.

Michel's three top wines are all single
varietals, and he makes a vin de pays, too,
which is exclusively from Cabernet
Sauvignon. On the other hand, the white and
rosé wines are both blends, as are two of the
new, less expensive reds.

His rosé★, an unusual blend of Syrah and
Marsanne, is for fairly early drinking, but all his
other wines need five years at least, more in
the case of the top reds. Even the dry white
"Aude"★ (90% Marsanne, 10% Muscat) needs
time because it is matured on its lees. The
reds, however, have made Michel's name; all
different and, in ascending order of price:

"Esprit d'Automne"★ (40% Syrah, 30%
each Grenache and Carignan). Made by
macération carbonique and given five months
in *cuve*. Michel thinks this wine captures the
spirit of harvest-time, and it certainly suggests
mushrooms in the glass. "La Féline"★★ (70%
Syrah, 20% Grenache, 10% Carignan). From
here on, everything needs ten or more years
according to Michel. This wine is vinified
traditionally and given sixteen months' ageing,
70% in *cuve* and 30% in new wood. A powerful
structure is set off by black peppercorns on
the finish. "Belle de Nuit"★★(★) (100%
Grenache). Again, a traditional vinification;
six months in *cuve*, no wood. Strong
blackcurrant and blackberry aromas.

"Maxime"★★ (100% Mourvèdre). Similarly
traditionally made but with an even longer

élevage of twelve months. Deep, peppery,
and spicy, again with blackberries.

"Syllal"★★★ (100% Syrah by *macération
carbonique*). Sixteen months in *cuve*.
Fabulous wine with green peppers very
prominent. Some animal and gamey flavours,
bitter chocolate, and roasted coffee.

Michel has also started to make a pure
Carignan. Cask samples look promising.

E4 Patricia et Daniel Boyer-Domergue

CLOS CENTEILLES
34210 Siran
☎ 04-68-91-52-18 B

Professor Domergue is the archpriest of
the lost grapes of Languedoc. As a combined
wine-scholar-cum-winemaker – he looks more
like the first than the second – he is at pains
to point out that the Grenache and Carignan
grapes are relative newcomers to the
Languedoc, and they owe their success
to the phylloxera crisis of the late nineteenth
century, when so much replanting had to be
carried out. On the other hand, the Syrah and
Mourvèdre grapes, and, above all, the old
Cinsault, were already established in the
Languedoc well before that disaster. Indeed,
it was Cinsault on which the success of the
Languedoc as a wine region in the seventeenth
and eighteenth centuries was based.

Daniel regrets bitterly that Cinsault has
fallen so low in the opinion of so-called
experts. In his view, true Languedoc style
is not represented by the huge, black and
over-oaked wines so beloved of medal-givers.

At this stage, enter Patricia, with her
diploma in viticulture and hands-on
experience working in Saint-Chinian. In vain
they searched together for a new vineyard
and *chais* until by chance, in 1990, urgently
needing somewhere to live and make wine
because Daniel had been obliged to quit
his former holding, a potential English buyer
walked away from his intended purchase
of Clos Centeilles, which was then an
abandoned and ruined property. There were

already ten hectares of Cinsault, Carignan, and Grenache as well as the possibility of making some 1990 from Daniel's former vines. But with all the work of their move, harvesting the old vines, and with Daniel still teaching, they hardly dared to taste the wine they had made. When the dust had settled in March, they were amazed at the results from the old Cinsault.

This experience started them off on their battle to re-establish the Cinsault grape. Today they make two wines almost exclusively from it. "Campagne de Centeilles"★★ (which has a little Syrah added for body) is given six weeks' maceration in huge old *foudres*, and the *chapeau* is broken up and re-submerged four times a day. The other wine, "Capitelle de Centeilles"★★★, is pure Cinsault from vines more sheltered from the wind and thus give grapes which are richer, more complex, and riper. It is otherwise made in the same way.

Daniel uses his Syrah and Mourvèdre to make a more orthodox Minervois called "Clos Centeilles"★★★, though the addition of 30% Grenache is apparently an inconsistency in the ideology. This wine is highly complex and

needs at least five years in the cellar. The paradox *chez* Domergue is with the Carignan variety. They have nothing good to say about it, cursing it as the worst grape in the world. How then do they manage to make such a delicious wine from it? "Le Carignanissime" ★★ is 100% Carignan, and while not pretending to the status of the other red wines from the domaine, it is fragrant, fruity, light, and has good acidity.

Neither vinification or the ageing of wines is traditional here. Some of the *cuvaisons* are enormously long, up to two months, and experiments have been made with longer still. No new oak is used. With their emphasis on finesse and elegance, the Domergues are a good antidote to soupy winemaking styles.

E17 Françoise et Pascal Frissant

CHATEAU COUPE-ROSES
34210 La Caunette
☎ **04-68-91-21-95 A**

The vines grow at a height of 350 metres (1,000 feet) above sea-level, and are for the

above some of the 45,000 trees planted to shade the Canal du Midi

most part on schist. At La Caunette they are some way up into the fastness of the Black Mountain and the climate is much cooler than it is at, say, La Livinière. The vines used for their white wines face north or northwest, an exposure which emphasizes the uniqueness of this terroir. It also ensures good acidity for the first of them, a vin de pays★ from a cocktail of grapes, some of which are not admitted into the appellation, Viognier for example. The more ambitious white★★ is almost entirely from Roussanne, a small proportion of which is aged in barrel. The Frissants also make a delicious orangey-pink rosé.

But the red wines represent the bulk of production. First, a delicious Carignan-based, lightish red named "La Bastide"★★ of the style which the French call a *vin des copains* (to be drunk with friends). The red "Tradition" is called "Les Plots"★★★ and is 60% Syrah, 25% Grenache, and 15% Carignan, a fine mainstream version of what a Minervois should be: brilliant in the glass, perfumed on the nose, and long and persistent on the palate. The oaked red, Cuvée Orience★★, is nearly all Syrah and is aged in wood for thirteen months. Deep purple in colour when young, the oak showing slightly on the nose, but with a warm, generous structure in the mouth, this is a wine to keep for five years or so after the vintage.

E12 Roland Augustin

CHATEAU FABAS AUGUSTIN
11800 Laure-Minervois
☎ 04-68-78-17-82 B/C

Roland is no country vigneron: he is the commercial director of Moët & Chandon no less, seeking a little diversification away from his main patch, although he still retains a small parcel of vines in Champagne. He was lured by the charms of the Minervois, not the least of which is the price of a vineyard compared, say, with the Rhône Valley.

Roland bought Château Fabas in 1995, urged on by his two sons Loie and Yanne. The property was once attached to a priory called Saint-Genest de Fabas. Severed from the Church it became a fortified farm, whose two round towers still flank the central building. The name derives from the Languedoc word "*fava*" – or *fève* (broad bean) in modern French. Roland is finishing the work of restructuring begun by his vendor. He is an innovator himself. He dreams of planting Nebbiolo. A fanatic for the harvesting-machine, he is experimenting with a programmable version which can distinguish between ripe and unripe grapes in every *cépage*.

Another passion is new wood. Already half of his production is oaked. He uses some American oak (which gives a much stronger flavour than the French) for a supermarket wine called Fabas-Prioulières.

The sixty hectares currently under vine are conventionally planted, though there is no Cinsault. Forty-seven hectares are AOC, and a further forty are available for future expansion. Roland is keen on the Vermentino grape, which he thinks is well suited to oak-ageing. His "Cuvée Virginie"★ is half Vermentino and half Maccabeu. The wine is aged on its lees and bottled unfiltered. He also makes an unoaked version★ with a high 80% Vermentino.

The red wines at Fabas are outstanding. Lovers of oak will go for the "Cuvée Réserve"★★ (Syrah and Grenache raised *en barrique*), the "Cuvée Alexandre"★★ (named after a grandson of the previous owner) and made from equal quantities of Syrah and Mourvèdre, and the top of the range wine "Seigneur de Fabas"★★ from 80% Syrah, 10% Mourvèdre, and 10% Carignan, which is given its malolactic fermentation in wood with regular *bâtonnage* on the lees. Lovers of unoaked Minervois may prefer the "Tradition"★★★. Another wine from 100% Carignan, made by *macération carbonique*, is delicious for drinking young★★★ when its fresh fruit and spicy character make it particularly quaffable.

E8 Famille Piquet

CHATEAU DE GOURGAZAUD
34210 La Livinière
☎ 04-68-78-10-02 A

Roger Piquet, once head of the big négociants Chantovent, had his company buy this château and its vineyards in 1973 with a view to planting an experimental vineyard. He was ahead of his time, however; the world was not yet ready for Languedoc. So Piquet took the project over personally and started to create what is today one of the largest and best vineyards of the appellation.

Ever inventive, Piquet also started a range of vins de pays, planting Viognier, which makes the star white wine of the house★★, and is much more interesting than the ubiquitous Chardonnay and Sauvignon varietals.

There are also vins de pays from Cabernet and Syrah, but it is above all the red Minervois AOC wines on which the reputation of this property rests. In their respective grades, all three are worthy of ★★ and even ★★★ depending on whether you like your wines oaked or not. All Gourgazaud wines are excellent value for money. The reds are all made from the same proportions of Syrah (80%) and Mourvèdre (20%) apart from the small amount of Carignan in the "Classique" ★★deep in colour and full-bodied, with hints of farmyard and the forest-floor, and on the palate has supple, fresh, young red fruits.

"Cuvée Mathilde"★★★, named after Roger Piquet's granddaughter, is essentially similar but from older vines, and from grapes grown on better parcels of land; it is also given rather longer in the *cuves*. The "Réserve" ★★(★) is the "top" wine and, again, is from the same mix of grapes. Nine months in Libournais oak barrels gives this red strong aromas of vanilla and dark fruits, with some *torréfaction*. Definitely a wine to cellar, it is the only one the château sells under the "La Livinière" appellation.

It is notable that Gourgazaud has no Grenache vines, the standby of so many local producers. ("Too much alcohol and too little flavour!" say the family.)

Today, responsibility for the vineyard rests with Guy Bascou, the owner of Domaine Condamine l'Evêque at Nézignan-l'Evêque, who has become managing director of this winemaking operation. Roger Piquet could have chosen no better steward. Perhaps Bascou is so able that Piquet feels he can let go the reins a bit and concentrate on his beloved golf? Could it be that yesterday's revolutionary is becoming today's conservative? Surely thirty years ago he would have been at the head of the Minervois Noble movement (*see* Château La Grave below)? Perhaps he might also have reconsidered the merits of the old Grenache, Cinsault, and Carignan grapes he had dug up?

Visitors to Gourgazaud should allow time to admire the pretty Provençal-style château, one of the architectural show-places of the region, restored to its present beauty in 1832. Incidentally, the word "*gourg*" means, in old French, "cesspit" or "stagnant pool", a fact not mentioned in the château brochures!

E14 Jean-Pierre et Josiane Orosquette

CHATEAU LA GRAVE
11800 Badens
☎ 04-68-79-16-00 B

When the Orosquettes bought, at the end of the 1970s, this little respected property, they found some old Maccabeu vines which are still the base of their excellent whites. Gradually Jean-Pierre and Josiane planted better dark grapes and in 1982 started to bottle and market their own wines. They were joined by their son Jean-François.

Jean-Pierre is a fanatical terroir man: "*Pour élaborer de bons vins, il faut être bon vigneron, mais sans bon terroir, il n'y a pas de bons vins*". La Grave enjoys an exceptionally dry micro-climate; the constant wind reduces the risk of disease to the vines, and thus the amount of chemical treatment.

At La Grave there are forty-eight hectares making AOC, and half as much vins de pays and vins de table. The production of white wine is unusually high at 10% of the total. The soil is mostly "*graves*". Fermentation is almost exclusively in concrete, though a small amount of sweet wine from late-picked shrivelled grapes is fermented and raised in new oak.

All the white wines are given a preliminary *macération pelliculaire*. The unoaked dry wine called "Expression"★★★ has a lovely floral character with some *agrumes* (grapefruit), the oaked "Privilège"★★★ has much more fat and would be good with poultry or veal dishes. The ultra-sweet wine is called "Confidence"★★, and again comes from Maccabeu and Grenache: the 1996 was picked on November 16th, very late for harvesting this far south. It can have a slightly maderized nose, but it is gloriously rich and clean on the palate: sweet but not cloying with layers of exotic fruits and a gentle touch of acidity. Josiane explains that this is the style of wine which is hoped to establish "Minervois Noble".

In addition to the red "Tradition"★★ there is a very attractive red for early drinking called "Tristan et Julien"★★, named after the Orosquettes' grandsons. It is made from equal quantities of Syrah, Grenache, and old-vine Carignan. The colour is rich ruby with violet tints, the nose is complex, with cherries and blackberries, flowers, and a bit of *sous-bois* ("forest floor"). To taste, the tannins are soft, full, balanced, and there is a little natural vanilla on the finish.

The Orosquettes' range is completed by an assortment of varietal wines which make an attractive collection of light vins de pays, and by a *cartagène*★★ of which they are very proud, and which they reserve for their favourite and most loyal clients. It is based on Merlot and Grenache juice and the added alcohol is *fine de Languedoc*,

The family will give visitors a welcome as warm as their broad Southern smiles.

E11 Luc Lapeyre

(LUC LAPEYRE)
11160 Trausse-Minervois
☎ 04-68-78-35-67 A

"L'Arbousier" is a restaurant in the canal-side village of Homps, very popular with vignerons. The *patronne*'s excellent list of wines features

below a contrast in methods: old and new vats at Château Massamier La Mignarde

alongside names like Fabas, Piccinini, La Tour Boisée, and Villerambert-Julien, the red wine of Luc Lapeyre. She is surely right in putting it in the same illustrious class. It is called L'Amourier★★★.

Luc's wine is otherwise hard to find. So is his *chais*, or rather his "*laboratoire*" as he prefers to call it. He has only recently managed to branch out on his own, breaking free from the local coopérative which did not want to let him go. He still has the problem of raising the necessary finance to set up as a full-scale winemaker. Meanwhile, his reputation has flourished followwng the award of several important medals for his wines.

From the 1998 vintage onward Luc started very gently to raise some of his tiny production of L'Amourier in once-used burgundy *barriques*, and recent vintages suggest a tendency to over-oak. He also makes a small amount of white wine which he markets under the name of "La Nuit Blanche"★, with an agreeable flavour of Muscat showing through, but not in the same class as the red.

The *laboratoire* is rudimentary: a few *cuves* of varying materials, barriques and, by way of storage-cum-office, two huge battered vats with their front ends removed, containing a bewildering mixture of bottles, some unlabelled, others empty, winemakers' tools, tax-records, correspondence files, and wine glasses. At the back of this chaos he might find a bottle of his Chardonnay 1994 vin de pays, dark gold in colour, a wine of which many a producer in the Côte de Beaune would have been justifiably proud; and then perhaps a cask-sample of a rich new red, made up mostly of *vin de presse* from Syrah, Carignan, Cinsault, and Grenache (complex, dark, chewy, and tannic, loaded with the ripest fruit). Another *cuvée* might be of pure Syrah with a wonderful peppery nose and some animal and gamey notes.

Luc has now won through, and is fast on his way to becoming one of the leading

left Jean-Antoine Tallavignes of Château de Paulignan

Minervois producers. He is an ebullient and entertaining host; he could be mistaken for one of his own barrels, were it not for the raven-black hair, eyes, and beard which top his rugby-player's frame. A winemaker to watch.

E2 Jacques Vénès

CHATEAU MASSAMIER LA MIGNARDE
11700 Pépieux
☎ 04-68-91-40-74
ⓦ www.massamier-la-mignarde.com **B**

Massamier was obviously a very powerful estate in its day, modernized – if that is the word – in the eighteenth century by a Monsieur Mignarde. Sadly, the buildings, especially the roofs, were badly damaged by the torrential rains in the last few days of the old millennium, and the whole estate has taken on a rather tumbledown charm. The park, however, is delightful, with a typically English ha-ha.

Frantz Vénès, the son of the house, is in charge of the winemaking here and shows enormous keenness. He gives you the feeling that standards have looked up sharply since he took an interest, and this is certainly the impression given by the wines.

There are fifty hectares, all on *argilo-calcaire* soil. A little rosé is made from Cinsault, Syrah, and Grenache, but the reds are the wines to go for here. The "Tradition" ★★ in particular is one of the best of its grade in the region; Frantz believes in bottling late, so tasting samples will be well-matured. The *assemblage* may contain as much as 60% Carignan (made by *macération carbonique*), with roughly equal quantities of Syrah and Grenache. The "Cuvée Aubin"★★★, one step up, is similar but a good deal tougher and calls for more ageing. It has a little more Syrah, a touch of Mourvèdre, and correspondingly less Carignan.

The first year in which Frantz made a "Cuvée La Livinière" was 1998. It was given some oak ageing and showed promise right from the start.

The surprise of the visit could well be Frantz' 100% Carignan★★★: a big,

surprisingly deep wine, with wonderful bitter cherries on the nose and palate. A real joy. *Pace* Boyer-Domergue (*see* page 116), could we be on the threshold of a Carignan revival? There is, too, a pure Cinsault★★★, a worthy counterpart to Domergue's.

E10 Jean-Antoine Tallavignes

CHATEAU DE PAULIGNAN
11160 Trausse-Minervois
☎ 04-68-78-31-02 **A**

The Tallavignes family came to Languedoc as Jewish refugees from Spain in the fifteenth century. Their splendid château, with its towers around a central courtyard and now offering *chambres d'hôte*, attests to their importance in the region. One of the fountains in the town of Caunes-Minervois was endowed by them.

Today, Jean-Antoine has twenty hectares of vines, but the château itself belongs to his first cousin. Their mutual grandfather was an incorrigible gambler who lost all his money and more besides. The château had to be sold to pay off his debts. Several years later, Jean-Antoine's cousin managed to buy the château back. The family had always retained the vines, however, and Jean-Antoine's father was a pioneer in rebuilding Minervois' reputation. Michel Escande and Daniel Domergue (*see* pages 116–117) both trained with Tallavignes *père*, and another pupil, Maurice Piccinini, thinks a statue should be raised in his memory. Jean-Antoine clearly had a hard act to follow.

His vineyards are on either side of the road which runs along the top of a ridge from Trausse to Félines. The soil to the west is red and a mixture of clay and chalk, while that to the east is sometimes pebbly and elsewhere a curious clay-like sand. Jean-Antoine is a hands-on vigneron, determined enough to clear up, single-handed, the damage of the fearful floods of December 1999, labouring alone to put back where they came from hundreds of tons of eroded soil.

A sixth of the vineyard area is given over to white grapes, an unusually high proportion for

the district, mostly Roussanne and Marsanne, with a little Muscat. They are given a preliminary maceration of twenty-four to forty-eight hours.

The rosé is unusual. Jean-Antoine starts with a quantity of his white juice to which he adds red Grenache grapes. When the right colour has been obtained, usually after twenty-four to forty-eight hours, the juice is drained off the grapes and fermented at a controlled temperature of twenty degrees. This wine is marketed under the name "Cuvée Trapellune"★.

There is only one red *cuvée*, which is sold to supermarkets under the label Cuvée Tallavignes. Half Syrah, and one quarter each Grenache and Mourvèdre, the wine is traditionally made with a long *cuvaison* of fifteen to twenty-one days. The *vin de presse* is added back for the last few days. The wine is then transferred to old wood and is finished off for a few months in new oak.

The Paulignan red Tradition★★ is a wine for keeping; a four-year-old wine proved far from ready on tasting, though it showed an attractively perfumed nose with some tobacco. The unresolved tannins suggested that another two years at least were needed.

E6 Jean-Christophe Piccinini

DOMAINE PICCININI
34210 La Livinière
☎ 04-68-91-44-32 **B**

Jean-Christophe's father, Maurice, was for many years president of the coopérative at La Livinière, which he transformed into one of the best in the region. Jean-Christophe has grown up with a more independent spirit. His training as an oenologist fired him to make and market his own wine. He got off to a difficult start by selecting for his *cave* and *chais* a ruin built on top of the moat of the village château, with seven metres (twenty-three feet) of water just below ground. Making a virtue out of necessity Jean-Christophe keeps some of the water exposed to give humidity to the *cave*.

Financial commitment obliged Jean-Christophe to go on selling forty per cent of his grapes to the coopérative, leaving him with fifteen hectares for his own wine. Such is its quality and reputation that this last is difficult to obtain, even at the domaine – the result of star-billing by Robert Parker and good trade shows.

Jean-Christophe uses small parcels of old ungrafted Chardonnay and Merlot to make attractive vins de pays. The Merlot★ especially is very true to its *cépage*, rich and deep after twenty days' maceration. The rosé★★ is from 100% Syrah. Jean-Christophe presses some of the grapes direct, because for him the Syrah gives too much colour when *saigné*. The bouquet suggests early summer fruits with a hint of cinnamon; on the palate the wine is fresh and quite complex.

The white AC★★★ is delicious, one of the best in the appellation. Half Grenache Blanc, with the rest made up of Roussanne, Muscat, Maccabeu, and Bourboulenc. After an initial maceration of twenty-four hours in *cuve*, it is pressed and barrel-fermented for six months with regular *bâtonnage*. The oak is very discreet, leaving a wine with delicious citrus fruit aromas and more than a hint of almonds.

The red "Tradition"★★ is not sold as La Livinière, but is excellent for all that. Typically it will be 60% Syrah, the rest from Carignan and Grenache. Deep in colour but limpid and brilliant, the first impression was of pepper with liquorice also present.

The "Clos Angély"★★★ uses the La Livinière name. The wine comes from the oldest vines and those with the best exposure: typically 70% Syrah, and 15% each Grenache and Mourvèdre. The wine's excellent "legs" promise long age. Raised only partly in once-used oak, the wood is well-handled. This is true, too, of the top *cuvée* "Line et Laetitia", diplomatically named after Jean-Christophe's sister and wife, both pillars of the enterprise. An *assemblage* of 80% Syrah and 20% Mourvèdre is raised in lightly toasted barrels from Saint-Emilion. Lovers of oak will give this ★★★.

Watch also for the latest news of a sweet late-picked *micro-cuvée* from Bourboulenc

grapes harvested in December and brought in at twenty-seven degrees. This wine is so far not available commercially. Annual production is limited to about 300 bottles.

E5 Madame Isabelle Coustal

CHATEAU SAINTE-EULALIE
34210 La Livinière
☎ 04-68-91-42-72 A

Madame's husband commutes every week to Saint-Emilion where he works in the wine-business. She has three children all at the local school and thirty-four hectares of vines to look after. You wonder how she manages, even with two full time staff in the vineyards and *chais*, and another to help about the place generally.

Madame Coustal bought the property in 1996. She has a few white Bourboulenc grapes, from which she makes a bone-dry vin de table, but otherwise the vineyard is planted entirely with red grapes. There is quite a high proportion of Carignan, some of it between eighty and one hundred years old, but she does not vinify this as so many others do, by *macération carbonique*. Fermentation here is traditional throughout, although Madame Coustal is experimenting with *microbullage*.

As so often in the Minervois, there are three red *cuvées* of which only the top one so far adopts the La Livinière flag. The red "Tradition"★★ has as much as 45% Carignan, 35% Grenache, and 20% Syrah, a very unusual balance in which the Grenache makes up in weight for the lighter style Carignan, and the Syrah gives structure and spice to the whole. This is an excellent first wine, deep in colour but completely brilliant, with blackcurrant on the nose and tobacco and cedar-wood on the palate. A gentle wine, developing notes of liquorice and eucalyptus – just the sort to go with a navarin of lamb.

The "Cuvée Prestige"★★ has more Syrah (50%), still a lot of Carignan (35%), and only 15% Grenache: a bigger wine, round but needing some ageing. Perhaps this is the best of the three reds, but oak-fanciers will

give ★★★ to the "Cuvée La Livinière": a wine that typically might be 70% Syrah, and 15% each of Mourvèdre and Grenache. This is a wine with huge potential and all the qualities to promise long keeping.

Madame Coustal's rosé, called "Printemps d'Eulalie"★, should not be overlooked. *Saigné* from Syrah and Grenache it is delicate and dangerously quaffable.

E13 Marie-Claude et Jean-Louis Poudou

DOMAINE LA TOUR BOISEE
11800 Laure-Minervois
☎ 04-68-78-10-04
ⓦ www.domainelatourboisee.com A

Allow plenty of time for a visit to colourful Jean-Louis Poudou: he's extremely voluble, given to high-flown fantasies and paradoxical statements. The hype is not intended to mislead; it is a natural way of expressing his enthusiasm. For example, if you ask him: "Which grapes do you grow?" he will reply: "Almost the entire palette of world grape varieties." This means: "I have all the usual Minervois grapes..."

His grandfather won medals in Paris as far back as 1897. The family came from Badens, so in Laure (ten minutes down the road) they are "foreigners". Marie-Claude inherited some vines at Laure so Jean-Louis moved there and together they bought some more. Self-taught and untrained, he would have been the worst possible student. He fears the scientists: "Man is there to enable the grapes to do their best for him, so he should not impose a programme of his own on them. A winemaker's job is simply (*sic*) to make the best wine he can; sales will follow." Would that life were as easy, though he admits that it took him ten years to learn his *métier*.

He worries that his property is called "Tour Boisée"; he does use new wood, but believes it is there to give roundness to the wine, and not to change its taste.

He has eighty-five hectares at Laure of which twenty-eight are used to make AOC wine. Thirty-five hectares have been replanted during the period of his and Marie-Claude's ownership. He treats each *cépage* for what it is. The idea of "*ameliorators*" is to him an abomination. "You bring each variety to full maturity so as to get the very best out of it, whether Syrah or Cinsault." All the grapes are destalked and vinified traditionally, none by *macération carbonique*.

These wines are benchmark Minervois; excellent value for money too. There is also an extensive range of vins de pays★: "Blanc Tradition"★★ (Marsanne and Maccabeu). Exotic fruits on the nose. Deep on the palate.

"Rosé Tradition"★★★. One of the biggest rosés of the South, bigger than many Tavels. A suggested partnership with roast veal, starts off a whole train of gastronomic fantasies. "Red Tradition"★★★. Usually this is a blend of equal quantities of Grenache, Carignan, Mourvèdre, and Syrah. Dark wines with excellent legs and a yeasty nose. Spices, toast, and liquorice on the palate. Tremendous fruit with good acidity and friendly but persistent tannins.

Red "Cuvée Marie-Claude"★★★ (with lots of *vin de presse*, and oak-aged). Smoke and *torrefaction* on the nose. Huge, almost Madiran-type wine. White "Cuvée Marie-Claude"★★. Dry, but with marmalade and citrus fruits prominent on the nose. Big oaky stuff. Botrytised Chardonnay★★ is made in good years, originally suggested by the accidental omission to pick until the month of December.

E15 Michel Julien

CHATEAU VILLERAMBERT-JULIEN
11160 Caunes-Minervois
☎ **04-68-78-00-01 A/B**

Château Villerambert is divided between two families, so that, whether you are looking for Villerambert-Julien or Villerambert-Moreau you wonder whether you have arrived at the right place. Fear not: Michel Julien will guide you to his tasting room at the west of the courtyard.

You will at once be struck by samples of

above Isabelle Coustal of Chateau Sainte-Eulalie at the doorway of a *capitelle*

beautiful deep pink marble, hewn from the local quarries at Caunes. This was the stone of which the Trianon and the Palais Garnier Opera house in Paris were built. Not surprisingly Michel for many years named his two red wines "Trianon" and "Opéra". The name Trianon had to be abandoned, however, because it had been previously registered as

a trademark by a Champagne house.

Today the two *cuvées* are simply called "Château Villerambert-Julien", the first wine of the château★★★, and "L'Opéra du Villerambert-Julien"★★, the second wine.

E9 Emilie Faussie

CHATEAU DE VIOLET
route de Pépieux
11160 Peyriac-Minervois
☎ 04-68-78-11-44 B

This is a three-star hotel with twenty bedrooms. The Faussiés bought the property in 1963 and Madame intended to make her life the hotel which she created there in 1966, while her husband Joseph looked after the replanting of the vineyard. Sadly Joseph was obliged to retire on health grounds in 1991.

Madame, forced to decide between selling or somehow restructuring the operation, decided on the latter. While she concentrates a good part of her time and energy on the hotel, the winemaking is in the hands of Hélène Serrano, assisted by oenologist Jean Natoli and Madame's son Jacques-Bernard.

The château is imposing. The dining room has magnificent medieval stone flags, while all the reception rooms have ornate seventeenth-century chimney-pieces. There is an old *cave* transformed into a wine museum with big old *foudres*, and an extensive collection of winemaking tools and equipment. The new *cave* was built by Madame Faussié, who has a flair and style which enable her to make her Scottish tweeds look somehow chic. She is a persuasive advocate of the virtues of her flagship dry white wine called "La Dame Blanche"★★★. This is made entirely from Marsanne planted by her husband on stoney terraces surrounding the château. A complex and stylish bouquet gives way to flowers on the palate, with spices and hints of peaches and pears. In 1998 she made a sweet wine from the same grape variety, late-picked on November 25th which will be excellent after some cellarage.

The mainstream red called "Cuvée Clovis" ★★, is half Syrah, the remainder from roughly equal quantities of Mourvèdre and old

There is no telling in advance what will go into each wine: the decisions are made on the basis of which are the best *cuvées* each year from the fifty-eight hectares under vine. In 1998, for example, the first wine was made from 40% Grenache and 60% Syrah (with a good dose of *vin de presse*), while the "Opéra" had less Syrah but a good 20% Carignan. The real difference is that the first wine is raised in oak, a quarter being new each year.

Both red wines from this property, made from grapes grown on a wide variety of soil – marble, schist, clay, and chalk – require ageing and should be opened well in advance of being drunk. Even the Opéra is quite dense and dark in colour, with a very agreeable bitter cherry element to it – an ideal partner for a cassoulet or grilled meat. The first wine is even bigger, quite grainy, suggesting a life of at least eight years before reaching its peak.

Michel plans to make white wines in due course, using Marsanne, Roussanne, and Viognier. Meanwhile his rosé★★★ is on no account to be missed. From a cocktail of all his red grapes, Michel makes by *saignage* an amazingly big and powerful wine, quite deep rose-pink in colour, short-heading even La Tour Boisée for muscle.

Carignan, the latter vinified by *macération carbonique*. The wine is delicate rather than powerful, fine and elegant. Another red, called "Vieilles Vignes en Vendanges d'Automne" ★★, is aged in once-used barrels, and is a keeper. A "Minervois à l'Ancienne" called "Le Castellas" ★ is made from old Grenache and Carignan and also keeps well: it is good value too.

vin de table

E3 Paul Durand

DOMAINE PAUL LOUIS EUGENE
avenue du Midi
34210 Siran
☎ 04-68-91-52-87 B/C

Paul's father was called Louis and his grandfather Eugène; hence the name of this domaine. For Paul Durand the Languedoc has so many possibilities that he refuses to work within any rules. Virtually all his wines are sold as vins de table, but their excellence transcends the humbleness of the labels.

With only five hectares currently producing grapes, plus another three maturing at Cassagnoles, Durand eschews all publicity and contact with the media, whose darling he nevertheless succeeds in being. He does not care much what his fellow winemakers think of him, though mention of his name to any of them usually produces a knowing smile of appreciation. He is, quite simply, a one-off.

Durand believes wine is the result of a contract between man, the vine, and nature. He is growing, or has in his time grown, at least seventeen different *cépages,* from each of which he makes small quantities of wine and then either treats them as *vins de cépage* or, more usually, blends them into unusual *assemblages*. The damp *cave* is lined with barrels, none of them new, but he uses no other material for maturing the wines. He clambers among them like a mountain goat, pipette in hand, expounding on the history and the composition of each. The wines are all given three years in barrel before bottlling. He believes that the lees re-integrate

themselves into the wine, so he spurns any racking, fining or filtration. There is, though, absolute brilliance and limpidity in the glass; this long, pure *élevage* is what he calls the clothing for his wines, to whom he has given only the frame.

As the wines are mostly blends of his multifarious *cépages*, the permutations are enormous and are rarely repeated from year to year. It would be unusual for any to fall below ★★★ standard. The Syrah he uses "like a sauce in cooking", the Mourvèdre is at its best when "tough" and it is then ideal for blending. Cabernet Sauvignon is not his favourite grape, but Cabernet Franc is another matter: he is passionate about it and the result is certainly outstanding. Equally, his Merlot is first class and could easily pass as a good Saint-Emilion. He makes a powerful, sweet Grenache, sometimes recalling tawny port in style, and his Cot is close to a Cahors. These grapes he almost always blends. His Sauvignon has just a touch of Marsanne to take the edge off the gooseberry.

Another regular, "Habilis"★★★, is pure Carignan, made by *macération carbonique* with a *cuvaison* of up to eight weeks.

other good minervois growers

Rémy Bonnet
Domaine Aimé, 34210 Cesseras
☎ 04-68-91-14-10

Jean Panis
Château de Bagnoles and Château du Donjon, both 11600 Bagnoles
☎ 04-68-77-18-33

Jérome Portal
Château de Beaufort,
34210 Beaufort
☎ 04-68-91-28-28

Robert Eden
Domaine Cathare (also Château Maris),
Chemin de Parignolles,
34210 La Livinière
☎ 04-68-91-42-63

GAEC Coudoulet
Château de Cesseras, Chemin de Minerve,
34210 Cesseras
☎ 04-68-91-15-70

Gérard Chabbert
Domaine Chabbert-Fauzan, Fauzan,
34210 Cesseras
☎ 04-68-91-23-64

Guy Vanlancker
La Combe Blanche, 2 rue du Moulin à Vent,
34210 La Livinière
☎ 04-68-91-44-82

Jean-Baptiste Bonnet
Château Gibalaux-Bonnet,
11800 Laure-Minervois
☎ 04-68-78-12-02

Gérard Bertrand
Domaine Laville-Bertrou, 34210 La Livinière
☎ 04-68-42-68-68

Christian Bousquet
Château Malves Bousquet,
11600 Malves-en-Minervois
☎ 04-68-72-25-32

Mireille Meyzonnier
Domaine Meyzonnier,
11120 Pouzols-Minervois
☎ 04-68-46-13-88

Viviane et Jean-Louis Bellido
Domaine des Murettes, 34210 La Livinière
☎ 04-68-91-62-84

André Iché
Château d'Oupia, 34210 Oupia
☎ 04-68-91-20-86

Philippe Senat
Domaine Saint-Sernin,
11160 Trausse-Minervois
☎ 04-68-78-38-17

Denis Morin
Château La Villatade,
11600 Sallelles-Cabardès
☎ 04-68-77-57-51

Caves Coopératives at Azillanet,
La Livinière★★, and Siran

cabardès and malepère

This is border country. From here you need travel only fifty kilometres (twenty-seven miles) west to reach the watershed separating the Atlantic and Mediterranean basins. Cabardès is a new vineyard area west of Minervois which has grown to prominence in recent years. Malepère is a just to the south-west of Carcassonne.

cabardès

Responding to a slightly more Atlantic climate, experiments were made as long ago as the middle of the last century to plant "Atlantic" style grapes in this region. In 1953, for example, Château Auzias-Partelongue put in Merlot and Cabernet Sauvignon vines as well as the Languedocian Grenache. The vine, however, is not a newcomer here, the vineyards stretch northward from Carcassonne into the foothills of the Montagne Noire. The Romans

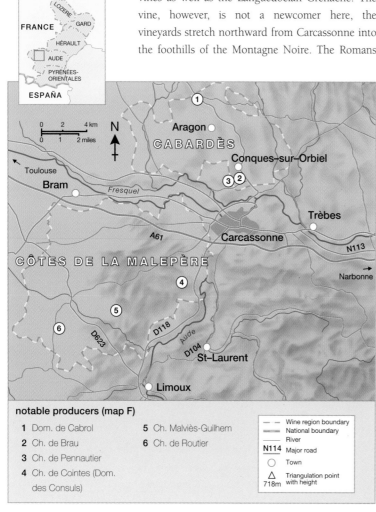

planted some in the first century BC. They also developed mining and forestry, and grew olives on the lower ground where trees would survive winter frosts. More recently, in the eighteenth century, a textile industry thrived alongside the leather-processing and the mines, and many small properties grew up beside the big estates as a result.

It was only in the late decades of the twentieth century that winemaking here took a serious commercial turn here, disowning the bad old reputation of the Languedoc. It is claimed that the blending of the two families of grapes produces balanced, complex wines, marrying the red fruits, finesse, and liveliness of the Atlantic *cépages* with the richness, body, and suppleness of Mediterranean ones. There is no white Cabardès as such, but vins de pays are made from Chardonnay, and also Maccabeu, Viognier, Muscat, Chenin Blanc, and even Gros Manseng.

The vines are grown at between ninety and 300 metres (300 and 1,000 feet) above sea-level on a variety of soils: chalky pebbles on the lower ground give way – as the vineyards climb – to granite, then schist and the more coarsely-grained gneiss, a pattern which largely repeats the soils of Minervois to the east. The climate is just that bit less Mediterranean, governed by the two winds: "*vent d'est, vent d'ouest*" is the slogan of Cabardès, echoing by implication the two cultures from which the region is derived.

There are some attractive wines made in Cabardès, but the two traditions have yet to become so completely intermingled that the appellation can be said to have its own particular style. Nevertheless, tribute is due to the enthusiasm and determination of these winemakers.

notable producers (map F)

1 Dom. de Cabrol
2 Ch. de Brau
3 Ch. de Pennautier
4 Ch. de Cointes (Dom. des Consuls)
5 Ch. Malviès-Guilhem
6 Ch. de Routier

Wine region boundary
National boundary
River
N114 Major road
◯ Town
△ Triangulation point
718m with height

côtes de la malepère

Malepère is the name given to a hilly area just to the south-west of Carcassonne, though you will not find it mentioned on the maps. Just look for the green roads marking views to the Pyrenees. In the foothills all round (at about 430 metres/1,400 feet above sea-level) lies the wine-growing area of Côtes de la Malepère, as many signposts proclaim.

The locals claim a winemaking tradition of great antiquity: a letter written by a medieval resident to a friend in the Auvergne lauds the quality of the Malepère wines. The Archbishops of Narbonne were said to be partial to the growths châteaux d'Alaigne and Routier, and in the nineteenth century vines became the dominant crop, though at that time the quality was nothing to write books about.

Gradually, from the 1970s onwards, vineyards were replanted, and the grant of VDQS status confirmed the value of the efforts put in by local growers. The vines circle the base of the *massif*, beginning almost on the banks of the Canal du Midi, following the road south nearly to the town of Limoux then turning west to the Abbey of Fanjeaux, before switching north again toward the small town of Bram.

Because the vines are not grown on the woody *massif* itself, they seem rather more extensive than they in fact are. Currently, there are but 400 hectares exploited and these are divided between 300 producers, who thus average just over one hectare each. Each of the eighteen independent producers has a great deal more than that, although only six bottle and market their own wines. Most of those who cultivate the vine have only a smallish patch which they either harvest and sell to the coopératives (of which there are four), or to the big négociants. The figures disguise the large amount of vins de pays which are produced alongside the VDQS wines. One of the coopératives claims to be the largest in France and one of the top five in the world.

Malepère is a little-known area which well repays a visit, not just for its wines. There are many circular villages, usually built around a church and a watch-tower. Defence was undertaken by the inhabitants, not by the local lords whose power was as weak as their resources. The outer walls of these villages have no windows and served as ramparts. Then there is the Cathar influence, that was very strong

hereabouts until Saint Dominic (based at the nearby Abbey of Fanjeaux), set about reconverting the locals to the "True" Church with the aid of alleged miracles.

The Languedocian grape varieties here are less important than in Cabardès. Carignan, for example, doesn't seem to ripen in this micro-climate. Some Cot is grown which also finds its way into the rosé wines in which Cinsault, Grenache Noir, and Cabernet Franc dominate. Fermentation is traditional, not by *macération carbonique*. The tendency is to emulate wines from Gascony rather than the Languedoc in the search for a yet-to-be-found *typicité*.

This is very much a crossover appellation: supple textures are balanced by power, the aromas of fresh red fruits by spices and sometimes a hint of natural vanilla. The enthusiastic *syndicat* of growers brands its wine as a perfect match for the local cassoulet of Castelnaudary – it is indeed a fine partnership.

Comparisons between Cabardès and Malepère are inevitable. It is strange that Cabardès, with its leanings viticulturally more toward the Languedoc, has a more Bordeaux flavour. In Malepère, where the Bordeaux grapes are so much the senior partners, the wine tends to be of a more Southern style.

special features of cabardès

the wines AOC since 1999 for red and rosé wines only. There is a large range of vins de pays in all three colours.

AOC area covers 14 communes to the north of Carcassonne: Aragon, Conques-sur-Orbiel, Fournes-Cabardès, Fraisse-Cabardès, Les Ilhes, Lastours, Montolieu, Moussoulens, Ventenac-Cabardès, Villanière, Villardonnel, Villegailhenc, Villemoustassou and Villedubert.

annual production 20,000 hectolitres.

grape varieties minimum 40% Merlot/ Cabernet Sauvignon and/or Cabernet Franc; minimum 40% Syrah and/or Grenache. Cot, Fer Servadou, and Cinsault allowed up to maximum total of 20%.

growers 18 independents, 4 coopératives with 280 or so members. 90% of the wine is sold in bottle; two-thirds goes for export.

the soil chalky pebbles on lower ground; granite then schist on higher slopes.

climate "Atlantic" influences; cooler and more rainy than to the east.

special features of malepère

the wines red and rosé only. Whites made as vins de pays. Currently VDQS, though elevation to AOC is in process. The area is roughly a triangle, with Carcassonne, Limoux, and Bram at its points.

grape varieties Merlot dominates, the two Cabernets making up the rest of the

predominantly "Atlantic" *cépages*. There is some Cot, Grenache, and Cinsault.

the soil chalky clay with gravel on the higher terraces.

climate wetter but warmer than Cabardès.

above view, over the vines to Aragon (Cabardès), with the pebbly soil clearly visible

above, right vines reflected on protective plastic wrapping

right early morning mists refresh the vines planted in the Côtes de la Malepère

and include Cot and Fer, and also a curiosity called Egiodola, found mostly in the Landes and valued for its deep colour. They also have some Ugni Blanc for their white vin de pays.

Their oaked Chardonnay★ is quite classy, pale but rich, dry on the palate, but somehow manages to suggest the flavour of mangoes. A lighter unoaked wine★, in which Chardonnay is tempered with a little Roussanne, is a good partner with oysters and grilled fish.

There are three red vins de pays, all based on Merlot, one being a 100% varietal★, the other two★ adding Cabernet and one of them some Fer. The one that calls for some ageing is 70% Merlot and 30% Cabernet; it is called, not surprisingly, "Mediterranean Merlot Cabernet"★, given a long maceration, some oak, and aged in cask for at least six months. The other reds are for fruity early drinking.

So too is the AOC rosé★, from 30% Cinsault, 40% Grenache, and 30% Cabernet Franc. It is given a short preliminary skin contact and a partial malolactic fermentation. The red "Tradition"★★ is from almost equal quantities of Cabernet, Merlot, Grenache, and Syrah and can either be drunk young on its fruit, or kept for longer to allow its characterful bouquet to develop. The top "Cuvée Exquise"★ is from the same grapes but is given a longer *cuvaison*; the *assemblage* is made before it is transferred to oak casks, where is stays six to twelve months, depending on the vintage. It then has a further six months in bottle before being marketed. It will keep five years or more.

These wines are attractively artisanal in marked contrast to those from...

notable cabardès producers

F2 Wenny et Gabriel Tari

CHATEAU DE BRAU
11620 Villemoustassou
☎ **04-68-72-31-92 A**

Gabriel's father, who had arrived here in 1965, replanted most of the vineyard with Merlot and Cabernet. Gabriel set out to be a lawyer, but, as with the sons of so many vignerons, the lure of the *chais* proved irresistible. Today Gabriel and his wife Wenny, a qualified architect from Belgium, have thirty-two hectares under vine of which nine rank for AOC and the rest are for vins de pays. They learnt their new calling from Professor Daniel Domergue, the didactic Minervois star. Their unusually cool *cave* dates back to 1877.

They are organic growers, all their vines having been fully "converted", the terrain now thoroughly "cleaned" by the necessary three years of purification. As organic producers they have far greater export potential, particularly in Belgium, Germany, and the UK. They exhibit at various "Bio" shows. Many of the grapes they grow are unusual,

F3 La Famille Lorgeril

CHATEAU DE PENNAUTIER
11610 Pennautier
☎ **04-68-72- 65-29**
🌐 **www.vignobles-lorgeril.com B**

This is certainly the grandest property in the Cabardès, built in the time of Louis XIII.

Ownership has descended by marriage to the Breton Lorgeril family who take a close interest in the production of the wines. Madame is in charge of the marketing and she sells 60% of the total production abroad. Bertrand Seube is the oenologist-in-residence.

There are very nearly 300 hectares of vines, of which no fewer than 120 are classified AOC and are away from the plain toward the foothills of the Montagne Noire. The vins de pays are made mainly from the grapes grown on the lower ground. All the wine is sold in bottle, a remarkable achievement for such a large estate. The wine that appears in local supermarkets is called "Château La Bastide", the name of a second property in the region owned by the Lorgeril family.

The annual turnover is estimated to be about two-and-a-half million euros, and rising. The wines are contemporary in style, with a strong leaning toward the use of new wood, although the red Tradition AOC is matured entirely in *cuve*. The Bordeaux grape varieties are never less than 70% of the *assemblage*; the "Tradition"★ has only 20% Grenache and 10% Syrah to represent the Languedoc, while another red called "L'Esprit de Pennautier"★ is 80% Merlot and 20% old Syrah, it is given a long twenty-eight-day *cuvaison*, and raised in partly new wood. The top of the range 'Collection Privée'★★ has 25% Syrah, the rest of the grapes being Bordelais; the wine is aged half in new wood and half in barrels that have already matured two wines.

There are two Chardonnay vins de pays, one oaked (quite heavily) the other not★, and a range of red and rosé★ wines sold as Vins de Pays d'Oc – or, in the case of the selection called "L'Orangerie"★, Vins de Pays de la Cité de Carcassonne.

F1 Claude et Michel Carayol

DOMAINE DE CABROL
11600 Aragon
☎ 04-68-77-19-06 A

The postal address is Aragon, a very pretty village, nestling in the lower slopes of the mountains, and well worth the visit if you have time. But this domaine is nowhere near Aragon for the motorist, who is better advised to take the main road north out of Carcassonne in the direction of Mazamet and he will find the vineyard well signposted off to the left. It is the last but one Cabardès vineyard before the highway disappears into the pine trees and the Wagnerian mists of the Black Mountain.

The Carayol family bought the property before the Second World War, but winemaking here goes back to the sixteenth century, it is claimed. Because of the altitude, the harvest is at least ten days later than in the valley. The presence of the mountain does not make the climate any wetter, but the north wind can cool the temperature substantially, suiting the Cabernet Franc grape in particular.

The Carayols have fifteen hectares in production. They make a white Vin de Pays des Côtes de Lastours★ from Grenache Blanc and a little Muscat d'Hambourg, but otherwise the production is red and rosé AOC. The rosé★ is from Grenaches Noir and Gris as well as Cabernet Franc, sometimes a little Aramon; the Cabernet is constant. There is a light red called "Requieu" from young vines, but it is the two more substantial reds which have made the name of the Carayols.

They are called, respectively, "Vin d'Ouest"★★ and "Vin d'Est"★★, reflecting the two climates which influence the terroir. The one has 60% Cabernet Sauvignon and 20% each Syrah and Grenache, the Atlantic grapes dominating the mix, even if slightly; the latter is much more Languedoc in style, 60% Syrah (by *macération carbonique*), 20% Grenache, and only 20% Cabernet. Both have much more of a sense of terroir than most Cabardès wines. They are perhaps the best reds of the appellation.

other good cabardès growers

Nathalie et Dominique Auzias
Château Auzias-Partelongue,
11610 Pennautier
☎ 04-68-47-28-28

Gilbert Rouquet
Domaine des Caunettes Hautes,
11170 Moussoulens
☎ 04-68-24-93-15

Robert Gianesini
Domaine Jouclary, 11600 Conques-sur-Orbiel
☎ 04-68-77-10-02

Jean-Régis de Civelins
Château de Rayssac,
11600 Conques-sur-Orbiel
☎ 04-68-77-16-12

Charlotte Troncin
Château Rivals, 11620 Villemoustassou
☎ 04-68-25-80-96

Anne Marandon-Maurel
Château Salitis, 11600 Conques-sur-Orbiel
☎ 04-68-77-16-10

Alain Maurel
Château Ventenac (also Domaine Maurel),
1 place du Château,
11610 Ventenac-Cabardès
☎ 04-68-24-93-42

notable malepère producers

F4 Anne Gorostis

CHATEAU DE COINTES
(Domaine des Consuls)
11290 Roullens
☎ 04-68-26-81-05
ⓦ www.chateaudecointes.com A

Cointes is in the northeast corner of the Malepère district, not far from Carcassonne. One of the former owners was a Consul of the city, which explains the name Domaine des Consuls, given to the range of vins de pays here to distinguish them from those produced under VDQS rules and the château name.

The Gorostis family bought the property in 1925 when it was planted with bad, old-fashioned Aramon, which *grand-père* Gorostis blended with imported Algerian wine; he was a négociant-grower. It was his son who started replanting with modern grape varieties, and today the family have twenty-two hectares in production, of which twelve are in the VDQS area on the higher ground behind the domaine, and ten are used for vins de pays lower down, even though all the red grapes are of the qualifying varieties. Syrah is an authorized grape, and the Gorostis have some, but they say it only grows well on the easternmost part of the region, as here, where the climate is marginally more Mediterranean and the temperatures just that bit higher.

They also have some Grenache Gris, a grape not often seen nowadays because it oxidizes fairly quickly. The Gorostis pick it before it is really ripe to avoid this problem and to make a dry white vin de pays★★, a flowery wine with a hint of aniseed and lots of wild flowers, bone dry and most refreshing. Another wine with good bite is the rosé★ from Merlot and Cinsault, the roundness on the palate balancing its good acidity. The red vin de pays★ is again mostly from Merlot, made with a short *cuvaison* and having a smokey character. The VDQS red★★ is altogether more serious, the Cabernets adding some style to the fruit of the Merlot, and the lower yields from the vineyards adding a little class to the whole.

The Gorostis' are only just starting into new oak, and are waiting to see how it succeeds for them. They also have some Chardonnay and Maccabeu coming on in some other vineyards on high ground a kilometre or so up the valley toward Roullens. Being Basque by origin, they also dream of a little Petit Manseng to make a Jurançon lookalike at some time in the future.

F5 Brigitte Gourdou-Guilhem

CHATEAU MALVIES-GUILHEM
11300 Malviès
☎ 04-68-31-14-41
Ⓦ www.chateau-guilhem.vins-malepere.com A

The château, on the edge of the village of Malviès, but well hidden from and by it,

dates from the eighteenth century. It has not been architecturally improved by two much later-built flanking towers. But the *parc à l'Anglaise*, with old cedar and umbrella pines attractively landscaped, helps give the otherwise slightly run-down buildings an air of sophistication and country-house grandeur. The property has been in Madame Guilhem's family since the 1870s, and, though she is married to a busy surgeon from Toulouse, she is still very much in charge of the wine production. He, meanwhile, loves pottering around the estate, picking up fragments of Roman vases and coins, for this was once the site of a Roman villa.

The Cinsault grape is the only evidence of Languedoc here, and it is reserved for the rosé wines. Merlot, the two Cabernets, and Cot make up the reds, while Sauvignon is the only white grape grown. The latter is used to make two quite different wines: a conventional dry one, fairly stylish, rather gooseberry-ish, but not particularly memorable; and a delicious *vendanges tardives*★★ which is as astonishing as it is unexpected. This treasure is made only in exceptional years such as 1998, and marketed in fifty-centilitre bottles at a high price. The 1998 was hand-picked on December 1st, pressed by hand, and raised in oak for twelve months. It may have fifteen degrees of alcohol with seventy grams per litre of residual sugar, and is a deep golden colour, wonderfully clear, with a bouquet of candied oranges. On the palate it is young and fresh, well-balanced, with good acidity to counteract the richness, a little vanilla and hazelnuts from the wood, and a long finish.

This is all rather a long way from the VDQS Côtes de la Malepère, which is good, if rather less poetic than the dessert wine. The red "Tradition"★, marketed under the name Château Malviès, has ripe fruit for immediate enjoyment, so drink it young. It boasts only eleven-and-a-half degrees of alcohol, but feels rather bigger than that. An oaked red, sold as "Château Guilhem"★★, is obviously intended for keeping and is a more serious affair. The wood is one third new, but

otherwise the barrels have sometimes seen three previous wines, so the flavour of the oak is held well in check.

There is a certain sophistication here which is not always to be found in other wines of this appellation. There are also some *chambres d'hôte* for those seeking the quiet life.

F6 Michèle Lézerat

CHATEAU DE ROUTIER
11240 Routier
☎ 04-68-69-06-13
Ⓦ www.chateau-de-routier.vins-malepere.com A

Madame Lézerat has been busy since she took over the reins at this property in the 1980s. She has gradually built up a proper complement of noble grape varieties, planting additional Merlot, as well as some Chardonnay and Sauvignon ready for the day when Malepère has an AOC for white wines as well as the red. She still retains, for old time's sake, some Ugni Blanc, from which she makes a vin de pays, and some Alicante whose use she does not talk about much.

The château goes back to the fifteenth century and boasts two "pepperpot" towers to prove it; sadly, it has been spoilt down the ages by the replacement of what must have been some romantic renaissance windows with fairly ordinary modern fenestration. But there is still a medieval vaulted *cave* which houses a little museum of ancient winemaking implements and some ornamental old *foudres*.

All the red wines – of which there are three *cuvées* – are made within the VDQS rules. The first, called "Cuvée Eloïse"★, is mostly Merlot with a little of each of the two Cabernets, and 20% Grenache. Otherwise the red wines come exclusively from Bordeaux grapes. The Grenache in Eloïse seems to confuse the style rather than contribute to it, but the wine is very agreeable all the same, with good fruit, and the roundness you would expect from Merlot, which also provides a soft finish.

Then there is the "Cuvée La Demoiselle" ★★, again with plenty of Merlot (50%), 20% Cot, and 15% each of the Cabernets, aged in new oak. Deep in colour and with shades of the forest floor, the wine suggests liquorice and ripe blackberries on the palate; the tannins confirm that a few years in cellar are needed.

Finally, there is a small production from Merlot, the two Cabernets, and Cot, marketed in fancy bottles under the name "Cuvée Renaissance" ★★ (50% Merlot, the balance from the two Cabernets) which is given two years and more in new wood – rather too long for some tastes perhaps, but much admired by others. An attractive rosé★ "Noces d'un Jour" features Cabernet Franc and Cot and has an agreeable bouquet of spring flowers and early summer fruits, while the white Ugni Blanc★ has been treated to a *macération pelliculaire* and seems grateful for it. The varietal Chardonnay★★ is oaked and has some round complexity. Madame suggests this as an accompaniment to scallops cooked with saffron.

other good malepère growers

Jean-Claude Turetti
Domaine de Matibat,
11300 Saint-Martin de Villeréglan
☎ 04-68-31-15-52

Marie-Hélène Hérail-Artigouha
Château de Robert,
11150 Villesiscle
☎ 04-68-76-11-86

★Cave de la Malepère
avenue des Vignerons,
11290 Arzens
☎ 04-68-76-71-71

★Cave Coopérative du Razes
(especially Château de Montclar★★),
11240 Routier
☎ 04-68-69-02-71

right Madame Guilhem, whose Château Malviès-Guilhem is built on the site of a Roman villa

limoux

The fame of Champagne is such that every other sparkling wine tends to be dubbed "Champagne substitute". To the wine growers of Limoux this is more than unjust, because it might be fairer to say that Champagne is a Limoux substitute. History is certainly on Limoux's side.

It is impossible to say how sparkling wine was invented, most probably it was by accident: wine, which had been left to winter, suddenly beginning to ferment again the following spring; the yeasts and the sugar in the grapes starting to create additional carbonic gas as the ambient temperature rose and activated the must. It certainly seems that in ancient Roman times, sparkling wine was quite well known, and there are biblical references to it. One thing is certain: Dom Pérignon, despite his mythical reputation, had nothing to do with its invention. Sparkling wine was already being produced in Limoux over a hundred years before bubbles first appeared in the cellars of Reims.

The earliest provable date that we have for the systematic production of fizzy wines in Limoux is 1531. Probably they had already been made for several centuries prior to this, as in some of the oldest parts of Roman France: Die in the Rhône Valley, Gaillac, and in Limoux itself.

The ancient abbey church at Saint-Hilaire, just northeast of Limoux, has been pinpointed as the birthplace of what is today called "Blanquette de Limoux" – the epithet "*blanquette*" deriving from the downy-white underside of the leaves of the Mauzac vine, the traditional variety in the region. It seems highly likely that Dom Pérignon did at least visit Saint-Hilaire to further both the interests of the Church and his own winemaking skills, and, back in Reims, he introduced the cork as a means of stoppering bottles, a practice which had been common in Limoux for many years previously and which perhaps had come down via the monks from the Romans.

Today, sparkling wines are made in Limoux by the old method and also the more highly developed Champagne method. The results are totally different.

In the *méthode ancestrale* the juice of white grapes is allowed to ferment in the traditional way until the advent of winter temperatures, when the fermentation is arrested by the cold; today, this is achieved by partial refrigeration. At the time of the old moon in March of the following year, and before the ambient temperatures start to rise, the wine is bottled and firmly corked. With the advent of warm weather, fermentation in the bottle resumes, creating the famous bubbles. The yeasts, which are wholly natural, sink to the bottom of the bottle and the wine is drunk young, usually before the ensuing vintage. Normally it is light in alcohol, about seven degrees, and off-dry. No sugar has, however, been added, the richness being due to the extra natural sweetness of the grapes grown in a

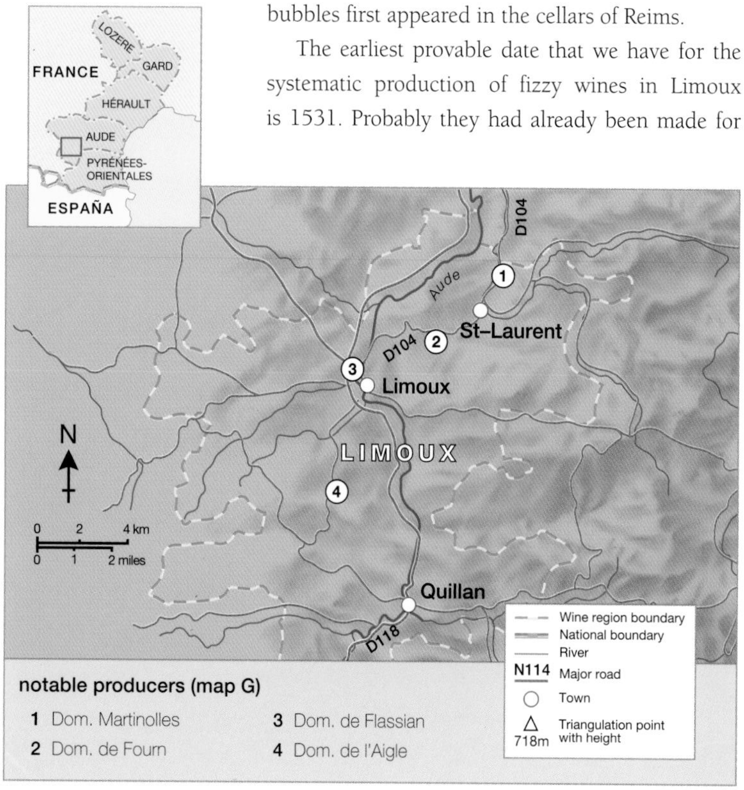

notable producers (map G)

1 Dom. Martinolles
2 Dom. de Fourn
3 Dom. de Flassian
4 Dom. de l'Aigle

southern climate, and the exhaustion of the yeasts before all the sugar has been converted into alcohol.

The *méthode traditionnelle*, the compulsory local name for the Champagne method, is quite different. Here, the wine is allowed to ferment until dry. Sugar may be added (*liqueur de tirage*) before it is bottled to offset the natural tartness of the juice, as well as addtional yeasts to encourage a second fermentation. For this, the bottled wine is stored horizontally – but so the level of the cork is below the base of the bottle, ensuring the lees fall down to the cork and settle.

After the sparkle-inducing second fermentation comes the removal of the lees from the bottle, or *dégorgement*. This is done by freezing the neck of the bottle so that the lees solidify; the cork is then deftly removed, the frozen lees being ejected from the bottle by the force of the gas inside. It is at this stage that a further sweetening material is added (or not as the case may be) to create the different styles of wine, *brut*, *sec*, *demi-sec*, *doux*, etc. It is then recorked and the cork secured by wire. Blanquette de Limoux can be assumed to have been made by this method unless labelled *méthode ancestrale*.

Blanquette by "*méthode ancestrale*" is made entirely from the Mauzac grape. The "*méthode traditionnelle*" may employ up to a maximum of ten per cent of either Chardonnay and/or Chenin Blanc, which are said to give a little extra bite to the wine (especially the *brut*), to compensate for the often low acidity of the Mauzac. The *assemblage* of the different grapes is made before the addition of the *liqueur de tirage*. Both methods have enjoyed AOC status since 1938.

There is a third style (AOC 1990), also made by the *méthode traditionnelle*, called "Crémant de Limoux" for which the rules prescribe a sixty per cent Mauzac content, the balance equally from Chenin and Chardonnay. This produces an richer style of wine, less fizzy but deeper and fruitier. It is correspondingly more expensive because Chardonnay is a lower yielding grape and the wine is required to be stored for longer before the final *dosage*. Crémant is gradually becoming the snob version of Blanquette. Is this the strategic intention of the winemakers?

A still white wine, usually high in Chardonnay and given some oak-ageing, has its own appellation, quite simply "Limoux" (1993). Often this is quite a fat wine, much in the New World style and sitting well alongside other Languedoc whites made in the modern manner. The production is relatively small – about four per cent of the total in the area.

If not all Limoux sparkles, it is all white. There is no appellation for red wines. This is because the vineyards are on relatively high ground, 200–400 metres (650–1,300 feet) above sea-level, and the climate is noticeably less Mediterranean than in nearby Corbières to the east. There are, in fact, said to be four terroirs in Limoux: the easterly vineyards on the right bank of the River Aude making full complex wines, fruity rather than flowery; those from around the town of Limoux itself (named after the hot wind called Autan) where the climate is warmer and more humid so the grapes ripen early; the mountains to the west, in the country of the Cathars, where the wines are elegant, with aromas of spring flowers and citrus fruits when young; finally, well to the south, there is the Haute Vallée where the wines are much slower to mature, and have a mineral character and some intensity.

There are 540 growers with an average of about three hectares each, but only around twenty-four actually make and bottle their own Blanquettes. This is understandable given the cost of the plant involved. There is an outstanding coopérative on the road into Limoux from the north, called Aimery Sieur d'Arques, which makes excellent wines, including a range of still Limoux called "Toques et Clochers"★★★ from each of the four terroirs.

There was a time when the *méthode ancestrale* looked as if it might die out. Bulk-producers found the process difficult to control as explosions were common during the second half of the fermentation in bottle. This was a chance for artisan growers to show their mettle, and it is good news that many have risen to the challenge. Even the giant

---

special features of limoux

the wine white only, some still, but mostly sparkling, the only such wines to be made commercially in Languedoc-Roussillon.

AOC area 41 communes around the town of Limoux on both sides of the River Aude.

grape varieties Mauzac, Chenin, and Chardonnay.

the soil mostly *argilo-calcaire*, with pebbly patches.

notable producers

G4 Jean-Louis Denois

(JEAN-LOUIS DENOIS)
11300 Roquetaillade
☎ **04-68-31-39-12 B**

Jean-Louis Denois, a Burgundian by
origin, was at the centre of a political wine
row in the year 2000, because he wanted
to plant experimentally some Riesling and
Gewürztraminer grapes, which Alsatians

claim is illegal in France outside Alsace. He
has since sold most of his vines to another
Burgundian, Antonin Rodet (q.v.), but Jean-
Louis says this had nothing to do with his
quarrels with the French authorities. He felt
he lacked the resources, physical and
financial, to go where he wanted, and that it
was better to contract than expand. He has
kept a few hectares for his own use with the
house and cellar at the top of the hill, while
Rodet builds a new *chais* away down below.

The reluctance of local growers to accept
an outsider from Burgundy does not bother

the combative Jean-Louis; he replies that the
terroir at Roquetaillade is better suited to grape
varieties other than Mauzac, all of which he
has dug up. Take the Chenin Blanc★★★, a
grape whose virtues he discovered when
working in South Africa; or the Pinot Noir★★★
from which he has been making a delicious vin
de pays in the style of the lighter burgundies;
and Chardonnay★★★ for making still Limoux.
The altitude (nearly 500 metres/1,500 feet
above the sea), the Atlantic influences on the
climate, and the good acidity of the terroir,
combine to reproduce the conditions in which

above the town of Limoux, set among the hills rising above the Aude Valley

the best burgundies are made; harvesting is late and in cool conditions. The Chardonnay is undoubtedly the best of the Languedoc. It is a keeper too; Jean-Louis has examples going back to 1989 which are still young and sprightly, but which have all the complexity and richness of the best Côtes de Beaune.

Jean-Louis has now launched a traditional method sparkling wine, made, as often in Champagne, from Pinot and Chardonnay.

This is an exciting wine★★★, at a fraction of the price of Champagne. There is also a pure Merlot★, but the Carignan★★ which he makes from grapes which he buys in from further east is more original.

G4 Antonin Rodet

DOMAINE DE L'AIGLE
11300 Roquetaillade
☎ 03-85-98-12-32 B

This is the name of the part of the vineyard recently sold by Jean-Louis Denois (q.v.), to the well-known Burgundian grower and négociant, Antonin Rodet, who was influenced by Denois' success in growing Burgundian grapes in an area where the ground and the costs are much cheaper than at home on the Côte d'Or. It remains to be seen what the *politique* of the new regime will be. The quality should be guaranteed by Rodet's own reputation. Cask samples suggest that his Pinot Noir will be bigger and beefier than Denois', but Antonin may keep the Denois style of white Chardonnay.

G3 Georges and Roger Antech

DOMAINE DE FLASSIAN
11300 Limoux
☎ **04-68-31-15-88**
Ⓦ **www.antech-limoux.com A/B**

Do not be put off by the fact that this operation is managed from within the industrial estate next to the Leclerc supermarket at Limoux; nor by the fact that half of the production derives from grapes the domaine buys in from outside. Be impressed more by the quality of the wines, the consistency of quality, the medals which they win year after year, and by the warm reception you will be given by Françoise Antech-Gazeau, Roger Antech's daughter. Françoise seems in charge of everything, including front-of-house and publicity.

Her father and uncle are the sixth generation of Antechs to cultivate the family vines at Saint-Hilaire, where the Mediterranean influences dominate. Françoise's sister and her husband look after those vines today.

At the property there are sixty hectares in production – a figure almost exactly matched by the area in the care of about thirty-five small growers from whom the Antechs buy in grapes. The juice from these is mixed in with the Antechs' own. This seems a curious arrangement, but the quality of the raw material is maintained and supervised by a contract with each grower, or rather a kind of flexible understanding. The grower is not tied to the Antechs and can leave the consortium when he wishes. However, the quality of the grapes, the hygiene at the place of harvesting, and the conditions in which they are brought in to be processed, are graded, and govern the price that is paid – and indeed whether the grapes are accepted at all.

The system is not at all like that of a coopérative, where the motivating factor of management is to find a market for the members' wines: here it is a question of the quality of the product governing the whole enterprise as well as the relationship between the Antechs and their outside partners.

The Antechs make a little Blanquette by the *méthode ancestrale*★ but perhaps more out of duty to history than to faith in the style of the wine. At present they do not make any still Limoux. They concentrate, instead, on the mainstream Blanquette made by the *méthode traditionnelle* of which they make several different *cuvées* (★ to ★★), and their Crémants (★★ to ★★★) which can also appear in various different guises. Since the presentations are liable to change quite often and new lines are introduced from time to time, it seems safer here to generalize in describing the wines. Throughout their respective ranges they are quintessentially typical of Limoux, to which they make an excellent introduction. They are widely exported, and are to be found in restaurants and shops all over France too. Not for nothing are the Antechs called "Maistres Blanquetiers".

G2 Pierre Robert

DOMAINE DE FOURN
11300 Pieusse
☎ **04-68-31-15-03 B**

Pierre Robert is convinced that the *méthode ancestrale* has a great future, and his is one of the very best examples of this wine. He has eighty hectares under AOC and a staff of twenty-seven, but the style of production is as artisanal as the philosophy of the house is rooted firmly in the terroir. It was Pierre's grandfather, a native of Corbières, who took over the property in 1938 at a time when the wines of Limoux were scarcely known outside their own area. The family, with a little help from its friends, still picks all the grapes by hand because Pierre says it is essential that they go whole into the press. The property is locked away in the hills between Limoux and Saint-Laurent. Your arrival may be greeted by an extraordinarily loud-mouthed donkey.

Most of the AOC production is nowadays by *méthode traditionnelle* but it is more fascinating to tour the *chais* with a producer like this, who has grown all the grapes himself, and to be shown the different stages of the process, than it is to see a Champagne house in Reims. *Dégorgement* is particularly interesting: the necks of the bottles are plunged into salt water at a temperature of minus twenty-five degrees; within seven minutes the lees resting on the cork have frozen to a solid cake. The *liqueur d'expédition* which is added to the *demi-sec* blends (in Limoux there are usually just the two grades, *brut* and *demi-sec*), is half wine and half sugar. Pierre has every right to be proud of this wine: his 1998★★ won a gold in Paris two years after the vintage; his 2000 shows equal promise.

The Crémant★★★ at Fourn is particularly luscious. The *dosage* is no more than is given to the mainstream Blanquette, but it imparts a round, fat style, even rich. The mousse is finer too. A wine at its best at five or six years old.

The still Limoux★★ is also one of the best in the area, not too oaky, and not having the vulgarity of many Southern Chardonnays. The range of wines here is completed by some red and pink vins de pays from a blend of Merlot, Cabernet, and Syrah.

But your visit will be rounded off with a taste of the old *méthode ancestrale*★★★, an experience not easily forgotten. A basket of flowers and honey on the nose, followed by the gentlest of sparkles, and a rich finish which leaves you beaming with contentment.

G1 Isabelle Vergnes

DOMAINE MARTINOLLES
11250 Saint-Hilaire
☎ **04-68-69-41-93 A/B**

Madame Vergnes promises you the best possible welcome and she will not disappoint you. She will also remind you that her sixty-five hectares of vines grow on the same ground from which the monks of Saint-Hilaire made bubbling history.

Hygiene, know-how, and modern technology are at the heart of the *chais* here, but Madame Vergnes insists that the family are above all growers of grapes, which they consider a noble profession. Particular attention is given to the selection of grafts which match the characteristics of the terroir;

to strictly controlled pruning and fertilisation; to yields of less than 40hl/ha (well below the average for the appellation); and above all to the health of the grapes at the moment they are picked and brought to the press.

Madame Vergnes puts a touch more Chardonnay into her Blanquette★★ than she is perhaps supposed to. It finishes pale and clear with a bouquet of ripe apples and pears. During the first two or three years, it remains young and sprightly, though round and not lacking in fruit; later, if kept, it will develop a more powerful bouquet and a toasty character.

Her Crémant★★ has typically more weight and body, but remains elegant and fruity, while her oaked Limoux★ from Chardonnay needs time to shed the wood. When young the wine has a barleysugar bouquet.

There is also a tantalising selection of vins de pays, starting with a still Mauzac★: not as appley as it is sometimes in Gaillac, a bone dry attractive quaffer, with a bouquet of white flowers and hints of vanilla, not acidic – the grape variety doesn't go that way – but a touch more so than the varietal Chardonnay: ★★. The latter is pale and fresh, not buttery at all, and a little reminiscent of a young Mâcon. It may deepen with a little time in the bottle.

The Pinot Noir★★ is, again, a real surprise to find down here in the deep South, but the altitude, the climate, and the terroir suit it very well. The lightly oaked version gets ★★★ for its extra complexity and class.

The *méthode ancestrale*★★★ is especially fine, not perhaps as rich as at Domaine de Fourn, but deliciously fresh and appley, and perhaps more typical of the grape variety. This wine is made from the oldest Mauzac vines and the grapes are the last at Martinolles to ripen. They are hand-picked, of course. After pressing, the must is protected under a layer of carbonic gas. This wine manages only about eight degrees of alcohol, but it retains seventy-five grams per litre of residual sugar.

Madame recommends it to accompany desserts, cakes, and ices. Sensible folk would accept a glass at any time of the day.

above Isabelle Vergnes of Domaine Martinolles: as sparkling as her Blanquette

other good limoux growers

Gérard Averseng
9 Impasse du Pla, 11300 La Digne d'Amont
☎ 04-68-31-27-16

Philippe Collin
Domaine Collin, Le Village, 11300 Toureilles
☎ 04-68-31-35-49

Philippe Lamouzy
11580 Alet-les-Bains
☎ 04-68-69-40-81

Michel Rancoule
Maison Guinot, 8 Chemin de Ronde, 11300 Limoux
☎ 04-68-31-01-33

★★Les Caves du Sieur d'Arques
avenue du Mauzac, 11300 Limoux
☎ 04-68-74-63-00

corbières and fitou

Corbières is the largest of the appellations in Languedoc-Roussillon, the fourth largest in France. Depending on which statistics you accept, there are either thirty-eight or forty-nine coopératives, and 301 or 411 independent growers: a record number of both in either case.

corbières

Corbières enjoys wide diversity in its terroirs and climate. On the lower ground close to the sea, the conditions are perfect for the Mourvèdre grape: hot, hardly fertile soils, Mediterranean influences such as the variety enjoys in its native Provence, and above all the slight humidity provided by the sea make for wines marked by spices, herbs, and a soft richness with gentle tannins.

In the Aude Valley, from Lézignan and Boutenac westwards to the Mont d'Alaric, the Carignan grape reigns supreme. Here the wines become more complex with a greater propensity to age well.

In Cathar country proper, in the foothills of the Pyrenees, the altitude softens the dryness and heat of the climate and the wines are powerfully aromatic, red fruits giving way to notes of ground coffee, and even chocolate. Here is a wild land of ghosts and rocks, hilltop châteaux built deliberately so as to melt into their surroundings; a country of fierce almost permanent wind and hot sun.

The western vineyards flirt with Atlantic influences but still achieve a typically Mediterranean style of big, fruity reds, and aromatic white wines.

Corbières has a pedigree that goes back to the Greek settlements in the second century BC, after which it shares a common history with the rest of Languedoc. In 1923 the present appellation area was first defined, and in 1951 it was given VDQS status. The time taken to graduate to full AC in 1985 attests to the problems of quality which then faced the area: too much bad Corbières was allowed onto the shelves of shops. This is still a problem. Although there is still a great deal of poor wine that holds the better growers back, the best of Corbières remains excellent and is improving all the time.

A spirit of adventure and a full petrol tank is all that is needed to make a thorough exploration of the area very worthwhile; and, if you strike a bad patch with the wines, the history and the landscape are endlessly fascinating.

This is Cathar country par excellence (*see* page 141). The legacy of that terrible conflict has left scars which have still not healed in the area. Not far from the surface, even among the devoutest of Catholic families, is a feeling that the so-called crusade was a profound local tragedy, rather than a victory for the Church and Crown. There is universal sympathy for those early rebels who reflect so much of the Languedocian temperament. The riots of 1907 – when vignerons took on the government in Paris – are mirrored in the spirit that has driven desperate growers in recent years to do the same: to protest violently against a perceived failure to protect them against foreign competition.

The sheer diversity of the district and the designated eleven different terroirs within it have suggested that at least some sub-appellations might be created. By 2003 it is expected that six communes within the terroir of Durban will have gained the right to add this name in some form to the generic Corbières title. Boutenac will not be far behind.

Variety and contrast is noticeable, too, in the soil-formation. The eruption of the Pyrenean mountains has resulted in layers of different types of soil and subsoil. Erosion has done its work too. In the north there is red sandstone as well as pebbly terracing, while in the heart of the mountains there is marl as well as some shale, and by the sea coral-like chalk. The hot, dry climate ensures a long growing cycle for the vines, and the winds keep to a minimum the need for chemical treatment in the vineyards.

Corbières is making a determined effort to improve its market share, particularly in terms of sales direct from growers. Tourists are attracted to this region by plenty other than its wines, which is a distinct advantage. All the same, more than half production goes to hypermarkets and the like, and twenty-two per cent is exported. The highly active Syndicat de Corbières is based at the Château de Boutenac, southwest of Narbonne. A breakaway group, "Les Crus Signés", has sprung up, attracting growers mainly from Lagrasse who want a separate identity. Others may well follow – further evidence of the perceived need for subsidiarity.

Not all of Corbières' independent growers bottle and market their own wines, many choose to sell *en négoce* or in association with the blender/producers and big-business vineyard managers.

cathar country

Visitors to the Corbières in particular cannot help noticing the fixation which the local people have with the "Pays Cathare", a fascination reflected in the amount of shelf-space in local bookshops devoted to the history and beliefs of the heretics.

Cathar faith was developed from earlier heresies emanating from Eastern Europe, founded on the concept that, although the soul of man was created by God, all physical phenomena, the world at large, was the creation of the Devil and thus evil. In rejecting the Old Testament, they also rejected the Sacraments, and thus the need for an established Church as an intermediary between Man and God. Vegetarianism and celibacy were encouraged, and indeed sexual intercourse and procreation were regarded as evil. Many Cathars rejected the doctrine of the Incarnation and the humanity of Christ. It followed that neither the death of Christ, nor his resurrection or ascension had really happened.

The spread of these beliefs was accelerated by the anger of many otherwise loyal Catholics against the corruption and worldliness of their own Church. The Cathar movement thus had a social as well as a dogmatic drive. It was not surprising that the popes in Rome were bent on exterminating this heresy.

The initial reluctance of the French Crown to head a Crusade was one of the factors which led to the emergence of the notorious Simon de Montfort as the leader of the Crusaders. In an age of cruelty

above Corbières vineyards near Lagrasse; obviously some vineyards are cultivated with more care than others

and petty war, de Montfort was one of the bloodiest of soldiers, merciless, and without remorse. He would have endorsed the verdict of the Bishop of Béziers: "Kill them all, God will look after his own." The slaughter was unbelievable. In turn Béziers, Carcassonne, and Toulouse were sacked.

Eventually Louis VIII of France was persuaded to add impetus to the Crusade, no doubt with the aim of annexing to the French Crown all the lands of the County of Toulouse, of which Raymond VI was his feudal tenant. The inevitable crushing of the Cathar forces drove survivors underground. Ultimately they were left to inhabit a few isolated fortresses in the southern Corbières, until these too were hunted out and besieged, their inhabitants slaughtered in the name of God. The fall of this heretic stronghold has been movingly told by Zoë Oldenbourg in her novel *Massacre at Montségur* (Weidenfeld and Nicolson, 1961).

fitou

Fitou is a wild region of ever-changing colours, two islands of vineyard surrounded by Corbières. On one flank the deep blue sea and its long beaches between Narbonne and Perpignan. On the other, the mountains, fantasy-inducing, with their ravines,

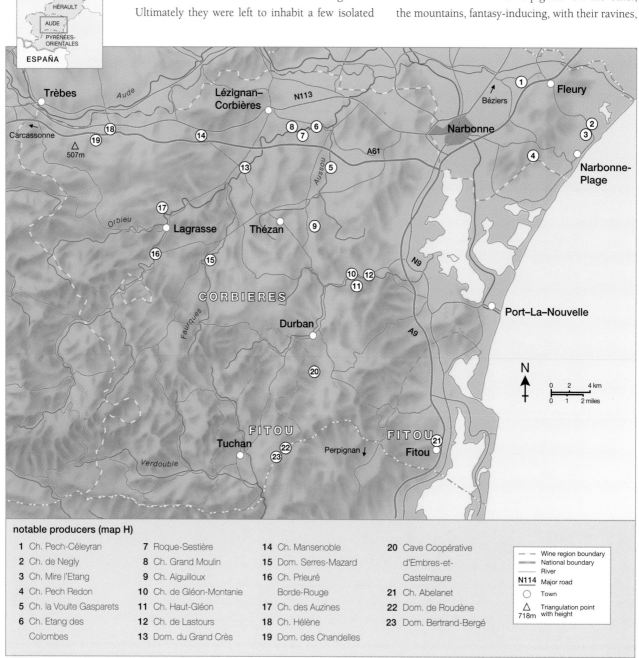

notable producers (map H)

1 Ch. Pech-Céleyran	7 Roque-Sestière	14 Ch. Mansenoble	20 Cave Coopérative
2 Ch. de Negly	8 Ch. Grand Moulin	15 Dom. Serres-Mazard	d'Embres-et-
3 Ch. Mire l'Etang	9 Ch. Aiguilloux	16 Ch. Prieuré	Castelmaure
4 Ch. Pech Redon	10 Ch. de Gléon-Montanie	Borde-Rouge	21 Ch. Abelanet
5 Ch. la Voulte Gasparets	11 Ch. Haut-Gléon	17 Ch. des Auzines	22 Dom. de Roudène
6 Ch. Etang des	12 Ch. de Lastours	18 Ch. Hélène	23 Dom. Bertrand-Bergé
Colombes	13 Dom. du Grand Crès	19 Dom. des Chandelles	

tablelands where scrub scented with thyme and lavender grow, and the dizzy medieval citadels which still watch over a magnificent, once violent countryside. The Tramontane wind blows fiercely most of the time. Not even the avenues of poplars can stand upright against it; they have been leaning since the day they were planted.

Fitou is hot, dry, and very old. The word "Fitou" itself is said to be derived from the latin *fita* meaning a boundary. It has in the past been the battleground of French and Spanish armies. Fitou was granted its AOC status thirty-seven years ahead of Corbières, who refused to join in the application for fear of having to pay higher taxes.

Its 2,600 hectare vineyard is characterized by two quite distinct wine styles from the two separated geographical areas. By the sea, the soil is typical of the chalky clay of the old sea-bed, which produces fine, more delicate, and supple wines. The hill-zone further inland is based on schist and the climate is drier, the wines more powerful. The vine is the only vegetation here which can be exploited by man.

Of the grape varieties, Syrah is gaining ground in the hills; it contributes a flowery element with accents of red fruits. Mourvèdre finds the hot seaside more to its liking, adding a characteristic tannic and aromatic structure which helps the wine to age. Nowadays the *chais* and the storage areas are temperature controlled to avoid the excesses of summer heat and winter cold. The wines are raised mostly in wood, and increasingly in new oak for the top *cuvées*, though some growers retain the old-fashioned, large *foudres*. Fitou is held by its makers to age better than many other wines from the Mediterranean.

Fitou is thus really a growth of Corbières, and it would be a bold taster who would volunteer to spot the differences blind. It can therefore be considered alongside Corbières crus such as Durban which it resembles in the Montagnée region, and Sigean where the wines are like Maritime Fitou. Like Corbières, Fitou is generally a good ruby colour, fairly alcoholic and full-bodied.

Annual production amounts to the equivalent of about thirteen million bottles of which the coopératives are responsible for eighty-five per cent. Production is dominated by the Producteurs de Mont-Tauch, a merger of several local coopératives, and they account for sixty per cent of all Fitou. They also make some Corbières from their base in Tuchan, a quantity of vins de pays, and some Rivesaltes including some Muscat. There are other "Maritime" coopératives at Leucate, Fitou itself, and La Palme, while Cascastel, in the hills, is another.

It may be thought that little room is left for the independent grower, but there are about thirty of them who compete avidly with the big boys in the annual competition called "Les Blasons"; they generally walk off with a good share of the prizes.

The object is to reward personality and *typicité*, qualities more likely to be found among the private grower, which is not to belittle the quality of the wines produced by the coopératives who were responsible, through their sheer economic clout, for the improvement in Fitou over the last decade of the old millennium. Today, they include in their range of products wines from single domaines.

above, left the wind turbines on the horizon owned by Château de Lastours supplement the profits from the vineyards

left an ancient wall and an equally well-established vine remind us that grapes are also grown for use as humble table fare

above the bunch the pickers missed... the grapes that got away

notable corbières producers

terroir montagne d'alaric

H19 Peter et Susan Munday

DOMAINE DES CHANDELLES
4 Chemin des Pins
11800 Floure
☎ 04-68-79-00-10 B/C

Of all the new arrivals in Corbières, Peter and Susan seem the most unlikely, not just because they are Welsh, but because you would not guess that they made or even liked wine. Yet, the first that they made in 1995 was awarded a *coup de coeur* from the much-respected *Guide Hachette*, and they have collected medals from competitions all over France. The problems that the Mundays have are organizational, not technical.

They live on the edge of the small town of Floure, just a few miles east of Carcassonne, but their vines are down the road at Barbaira. They moved from the UK in 1993. Peter had come to the Languedoc to pick grapes for his holiday in 1992 and immediately caught the wine bug. Both he and his wife Susan were accountants and were tired of their professional nine to five routine in the UK. Having found four hectares of vines, Peter wasted no time in going off to college before he was deemed fit to complete his purchase; but his four hectares were tied to a contract with the local coopérative with which he is still linked to this day.

He later rented a further eight hectares free of ties, so then needed to find a *chais* if he was to start making his own wine. Eventually one turned up in Marseillette, a village in the Minervois. But the authorities do not like you to grow your grapes in one appellation and vinify them in another, so they are looking for other premises closer to Floure. Meanwhile, they have built up their holding to thirty hectares, including some additional vines whose grapes they send to the coopérative.

The wine they make is either red or pink, and all AOC. The rosé★ is from Cinsault, Syrah, and a little Maccabeu. Delicate in colour, full flowery and flavoursome, it has won gold medals in Paris. There are three reds: "Chez Suzanne"★★★ is the name given to what other growers would call their "Tradition", but somehow this wine is too good for such a humble description. True, it is a classic Corbières with 50% Carignan, best drunk young for its fruit and easy-going style, but it manages a touch of class which raises it above the level of its peers. Then there is the wine named after the property, des Chandelles★★★. It will keep a long while for those who have the patience, allowing the new wood to melt into the fruit, and the tannins to soften and resolve themselves.

The top wine is called "Le Luquet"★★ and is not for the faint-hearted. Many would say it is over-oaked but it is surprising what a few years in bottle will do to bring the wood back to an acceptable level. With this wine the Mundays might consider whether they are aiming at a market that is beginning to react in favour of a more delicate use of wood.

H18 Robert Baudouin

CHATEAU HELENE
34 Route de Narbonne
11800 Barbaira
☎ 04-68-79-00-69 B

Hélène Gau, the former *châtelaine*, retired in April 2000 and sold her forty-hectare property to Robert Baudouin. Madame Gau nevertheless stayed on to help him with the millennial harvest in a year which promised well. Madame Gau had built up a reputation for making wines as well-turned as her jokes. Two of these have survived the changeover, a pair of jolly trompe l'oeil murals in the *chais*, depicting Helen of Troy and Ulysses enjoying their wine in idyllic landscapes.

Madame Gau exploited her Christian name to maximum advantage: her wines were often labelled "Hélène en Alaric", a way of linking her to the terroir named after the

mountain running behind her estate. The vines are on high terraces of chalky clay with a lot of pebbles, cultivated according to *culture raisonnée* with low yields and very little rain falling between April and October,.

The three ranges of wine all borrow their names from the Trojan story: "Pénélope"★, who appears in white with flowers and country perfumes, or in pastel pink, displaying blackcurrants, or deep velvet red featuring a powerful complex nose, a character both generous and peppery, harmonious, noble, and well-built. "Ulysses"★★ and "Helen"★★ are both nobler, after spending some time in new oak barrels – she rather longer than he, who gallantly yields to her pride of place at the top of the range.

The whites are original, suggesting preserved orange on the nose and in the mouth, the same suggestion of citrus fruit re-emerging in the reds. The wood is well-handled and all the wines deserve the high reputation which they have made for themselves among critics and connoisseurs. There is a range of vins de pays, too, a Syrah/Carignan red, a Syrah/Cinsault rosé, and a white Chardonnay/Sauvignon with a strong perfume of almond-blossom: all ★.

Robert's first vintage without Madame Gau's help was the 2001. Cask samples are excellent.

H14 Marie-Annick et Guido Jansegers

CHATEAU MANSENOBLE
avenue de Bataille
11700 Moux
☎ 04-68-43-93-39
ⓦ www.mansenoble.com B

Puns about "accepting risks" must nowadays be a bit old hat with the Jansegers. Guido is a one-time insurance broker from Belgium, whose fairy-tale meteoric success would be unbelievable were it not for the total passion

right Guido Jansegers of Château Mansenoble: the best "nose" of Belgium

which he has bestowed on his new career as a winemaker in Corbières. It takes courage for a successful businessman – even one who was voted "the best nose of Belgium" – to sell up at the age of fifty and invest the fruits of his life's work in a vineyard, a run-down one at that, producing only *vrac* wine in conditions unacceptable to a serious winemaker. It is typical of the man that he saw the property at ten o'clock one morning and was at the *notaire*'s before lunch the same day.

The deal suited both buyer and seller: Guido wanted to buy a maximum of twenty of the thirty-six hectares which went with the estate, as much as he felt he could handle personally. So the seller was able to pocket the government's reward for ripping out sixteen hectares of allegedly inferior vines (how many were priceless old Carignan, one wonders?).

Guido was an overnight star. He was able to convince his Belgian connections of the quality of his very first vintage: the Press and the wine-writers took him up and he was soon winning medals, gold at that, in international competitions. Today his market is almost entirely outside France; not only in his native Belgium, but in the USA and Germany.

The range of products is small and he has no plans to change it, just to go on making better and better wine. There are two vins de pays: a rosé★ and a blend of Merlot and Cabernet★, the latter reflecting his love of Bordeaux. Guido is not, however, interested in *vins de cépage*, because his heart lies in the excitement of blending. Visitors should not be surprised to see him hopping about in his *chais*, putting together an instant preview of his next bottling.

Mansenoble's reputation rests on its red AOC Corbières. There are no whites at all: Guido is not interested in them commercially. There are only two reds, but they are the glory of the house. "Tradition"★★ starts off where most other growers' *cuvées spéciales* leave off. Though vinification is of the simplest, the wines are given long *cuvaisons*. Guido

likes to use concrete for the more stable temperatures it offers during *élevage*. No oak is used until it is at least one wine old.

Jansegers achieves a well-judged balance of power with elegance in his wines, melding the strength of the best Rhônes with the finesse of a good claret. They need keeping, though; the "Tradition" at least five years, and the "Réserve"★★★ double that. Both will live for considerably longer. And for wines of such quality the prices are keen.

terroir de lagrasse

H17 Yves et Rémy Jaillet

CHATEAU DES AUZINES
11220 Lagrasse
☎ 04-68-43-10-13 A/B

Here is a very talented young grower, fortunate to have a father who is a professional wine-consultant to supermarkets and the like: Rémy is thus assured of links with potential customers that some winemakers take years to forge.

Rémy is a fully paid-up organic grower, his wines bearing the Ecovert logo. Having studied at Tours and done some *stages* in the Languedoc, he replanted a good deal of the land at Auzines with Grenache and Syrah; no Mourvèdre, because at a height of between 265 and 300 metres (870 and 1,000 feet) above sea-level the nights are too cool and there is not enough moisture for this grape. Rémy has, however, retained some old Carignan, and even some Alicante.

"Auzines" is the local word for the evergreen oaks to be found everywhere on the garrigue here. The four-wheel-drive tour to which a visitor may be treated is less dramatic than some but no less beautiful. As you study the vines – which have been fertilized only with old *marc*, sheep manure, algae, rotten fruit, and pigeon-droppings – do not miss the fine views over the Val d'Orbieu, and over to Rémy's organic neighbours at Château Pech Latt. This is wild country and you should not be surprised if one of

Rémy's sisters comes galloping through the vines on her horse.

Rémy's "Tradition"★★ from 1998, his first wine, was very good indeed, and his first venture into new wood the following year called "Les Hautains"★★ also exceptional. The wines here are dark in colour but brilliant, not at all soupy. There is plenty of rich ripe fruit backed by a good structure, and the wine achieves an early complexity and some elegance too. Judging by this promising début, Rémy Jaillet is tipped to go right to the top.

H16 Alain et Natacha Devillers-Quénehen

CHATEAU PRIEURE BORDE-ROUGE
11220 Lagrasse
☎ 04-68-43-12-55 B

Corbières seems to attract career-switchers, and Natacha and Alain are striking examples: she, a designer for Dior in Paris, and he a successful management consultant, suddenly abandoned their beautiful home in the Marais. Borde-Rouge was their choice from among sixty or so estates they looked at, having spent some time studying in the Rhône Valley and at the Université du Vin. They financed their purchase partly by subscription, the dividends to the lucky investors being paid in wine.

In this attractive one-time priory, Natacha has a few *chambres d'hôte*. She sees her excellent culinary reputation and talent as a hostess as means of making new clients for their wines as well as cementing the loyalty of old ones.

Only twenty-three of the estate's 130 hectares are under vine, the rest being mostly garrigue. The vines, whose average age is forty years old, include some hundred-year old Carignan and veteran Grenache too. All picking is by hand, and the *cuves* are filled and emptied by gravity, without the use of pumps. Length of *cuvaison*, the level of temperature, and the frequency of *remontage* are determined ad hoc so as to achieve consistency in style from one year to the next.

The range of wines is limited to just one white★★ and two reds. The former is a usual Corbières blend of Grenache, Bourboulenc, and Maccabeu, barrel-fermented in wood which is bought second-hand from Château Margaux after it has been used to make one wine. It combines real dryness with some *gras*. The good acidity suggests that the wine would benefit from a little bottle-age.

The red Tradition comes mostly from Carignan. It is called "Le Jardin de Frédéric"★★ and Alain describes it as a "*vin des copains*", dangerously quaffable. The more serious "Signature"★★ is a selection of old Carignan and Grenache with a little Syrah. The fine tannins need time to integrate themselves.

These excellent wines are mostly exported, the quality of good modern Corbières having not yet been discovered by the French.

terroir de lézignan

H6 Christophe Gualco

CHATEAU ETANG DES COLOMBES
11200 Lézignan-Corbières
☎ 04-68-27-00-03 **A**

A grand piano and a full-sized steam-engine are the main features of the tasting-room at this very desirable little château. They underscore the theatricality of Christophe's one-man show as guide to his delicious wines. Archeological finds link the property to the Roman era, but the vineyards as you see them today were not laid out until 1856, and the gardens were the work of a landscape-architect who had been involved in designing the Bois de Boulogne in Paris. Today, the *étang* (pond) may be dry but the *colombes* (doves) are still active, no doubt helping to manure the vineyards.

The Gualcos have been winning prizes and medals for many years, so it is surprising that their wines still represent such value for money. But their three whites, a rosé, and

right Christophe Gualco, the young winemaker at Château Etang des Colombes

three reds attest to an excellence which is indisputable. Christophe will offer you a Blanc de Blancs★ from Grenache and Malvoisie which will surprise you with its fresh spring flowers and hay; a varietal Viognier★★, again delicate but very stylish, escaping the usual clichés of apricots and peaches in a determination to avoid the commonplace; or a barrel-fermented blend of Grenache and Bourboulenc★, first given a *macération pelliculaire*, straw-yellow in the glass and with more wild flowers, but the unmistakeable flash of vanilla coming from the wood. The rosé, pale and totally translucent, suggests redcurrants with its fresh aromatic persistence on the palate.

The red "Tradition"★★ has no Cinsault but a bit of everything else; a traditional vinification followed by twelve days in *cuve* produces a deep ruby-coloured wine with spices enriched by luscious red fruits; in the mouth there are rounded, silky tannins and surprising length. The next red, from *vieilles vignes*★★, particularly of old Carignan, is made entirely by *macération carbonique*, and given eight to ten months in oak. Obviously more substantial than the "Tradition", this wine calls for food, as does the top *cuvée*, "Bois des Dames"★★★, still with 40% Carignan; a rich wine and, though oaked, showing little trace of the wood on the palate.

This splendidly traditional Corbières estate is adapting to modern tastes in the hands of its young and evangelical *patron*.

H8 Jean-Noël Bousquet

CHATEAU GRAND MOULIN
11200 Luc-sur-Orbieu
☎ **04-68-27-40-80 B**

Jean-Noël was convinced even at the age of seventeen, when he bought his first twenty-five hectares of vines, that Corbières had an enormous potential. Without the means to make and bottle his own wine, he sent his

left Roland Lagarde shares some delicious white wine from his oldest vines with his wife, Isabelle grapes to the coopérative and bided his time. In 1998 the Grand Moulin came on the market, a splendid property with twenty hectares of vineyard and a fine *chais*. Suddenly he could realize his ambition. He did much replanting, and, with the help of his *oenologue*, experimented with different aspects of vinification and *élevage* until he was able to settle on a consistent policy of production.

The terrible floods, that devastated the region in November 1999 would have dealt a death-blow to anyone of weaker stuff than Jean-Noël. With his rugby-player's physique and his gravelly country voice, he was not going to let anyone, not even the banks, get him down – even though his recently built storage *chais* was swept away by the floods and he lost most of his 1998 stock. Today, jealous tongues speak of Jean-Noël 's going too far, and too fast (he has another fifteen hectares in reserve). A more objective view is that he has already reached the top of his appellation and is destined to stay there.

Lovers of oaked white★ will go for Jean-Noël's blend of Grenache Blanc, Maccabeu, and Bourboulenc in a big way, with its limpid pale yellow colour, shot with gold, perfumed flowery nose, and rich spice. Some may find this over the top and prefer the lighter, more conventional unoaked★★ wine from a similar blend of grapes (50% Grenache Blanc, 30% Vermentino, 20% Maccabeu). Jean-Noël has recently planted some Roussanne, so the *encépagement* of the whites may change.

The reds here are even better. The "Tradition"★★ has intense fruits on the nose and is long and powerful, owing much to Jean-Noël's favourite grape, Mourvèdre. The "Vieilles Vignes"★ needs five or six years from the vintage to show its best; vinified at relatively high temperature, the wine is aged in wood, one third of which is new each year. The top wine, called "Grand Millésime"★★★, is only made in the best years: low-yielding grapes are selected on the vine and enjoy thirty-two days' *cuvaison* at thirty-two degrees, with frequent pumpings over and

délestages. The wine stays in oak, half new, half the wood of one wine, for fourteen months. The use of the wood is masterly; it does nothing to overpower the intense red fruits; the tannins are ample but soft. The wine is surprisingly drinkable after two years, but liable then to close up and be reborn like an infant prodigy after six years or so.

H7 Roland Lagarde

ROQUE-SESTIERE
11200 Luc-sur-Orbieu
☎ 04-68-27-18-00 A

Roland Lagarde is another school-teacher turned vigneron, but it is his wife Isabelle who owns this domaine, and it was her father Jean Bérail who was one of the pioneers of the still-rare white Corbières. The whites represent less than 2% of the entire production of the appellation. Roland, today, makes equal quantities of red and white.

Before Chardonnay, Viognier, and Sauvignon became the rage in Languedoc, Jean Bérail had already planted Maccabeu, Grenache Blanc, and Bourboulenc, the traditional grapes of the region. With a view to maximizing the bouquet, he introduced skin contact and temperature control. His son-in-law has proved an adept pupil because his "Vieilles Vignes"★★★ is arguably the best dry white wine in Corbières. Its 60% Maccabeu gives it finesse, 30% Grenache Blanc body, and the Bourboulenc and Marsanne which make up the balance add a bit of power. It is amazingly good value too.

There is also a less ambitious white wine★ which in Roland's own words, is "incredibly fruity, fresh, totally inviting, with the perfumes of white flowers", and he recommends it for "immediate simple pleasure" as well as to accompany seafood.

The rosé★, an equal blend of Cinsault and Syrah, has lovely sweet fruit on the palate and is very attractive even if not in the same league as the whites. To judge by the "Tradition"★★, however, the reds are also excellent: this first wine is half Carignan,

half Syrah, and is soft and velvety, though there are good tannins to support the more obvious attractions.

Roland has a problem with the layout of his domaine: the *cave* is at Ornaisons, and the vineyards themselves are in three different terroirs – at Boutenac are the famous Maccabeu and some old Carignan vines, at Fontfroide hot sandy slopes suit his Cinsault, Bourboulenc, Syrah, and Carignan, while at Lézignan, there is more Carignan and his Grenache. Small wonder that he is thinking of shrinking rather than expanding the size of the domaine; his aim is to concentrate on quality and raise the standard of his wines even higher. Furthermore, it does not appeal to him that he is still renting some of the vineyards, albeit from his father-in-law.

terroir de boutenac

H9 Marthe et François Lemarié

CHATEAU AIGUILLOUX
11200 Thézan-les-Corbières
☎ 04-68-43-32-71 B

Here are more newcomers to Corbières and another couple who have switched their careers. François is from Normandy; Marthe, a former teacher, from the Antilles. Together they bought this property, just off the road south to Durban, in 1980. The name "Aiguilloux" means in patois "the small streams" and it is these which enable the Lemariés to grow Mourvèdre. There are thirty-six hectares of vines *dans un seul tenant*, and on as big a variety of soils as Corbières can offer. Marthe will show you seven or eight carefully preserved samples to demonstrate that this vineyard contains a bit of everything. They attach little importance to the division of Corbières into eleven terroirs, perhaps because they are bang in the middle of the appellation; they say that it is the difference in micro-climates that is really important.

Some of the Lemariés' Carignan is quite old, but they replanted with a deal of Syrah when they arrived. They train all their new vines *en espalier*, and have a regular team of Spanish pickers who, Marthe says, know the vines better than she and François do.

Like so many growers, they now do not have enough space. The press lives in the open air, which makes it easier to keep the *chais* clean. And now that all their wine is sold in bottle, they have had to build a new *chais d'élevage*. Although they use oak, it is never new, due to a strict belief in "*élevage pas boisage*".

They make no white wine, but their rosé★, containing 40% Cinsault, François says is good with oriental food. Onion skin in colour, very dry, it represents 10% of their production and is much to the liking of their Japanese customers.

The red wines are made for keeping, though fermented entirely by *macération carbonique* (except for some Grenache which is made traditionally). They are surprisingly rich and very full. Often there are scents of mushrooms and forest-floor, and when mature the flavour may recall game, liquorice, or roasted coffee. The gently oaked version is called "Les Trois Seigneurs"★★ after the counts of Narbonne, Durban, and Lézignan.

H13 Hervé et Pascaline Leferrer

DOMAINE DU GRAND CRES
avenue de la Mer
11200 Ferrals-les-Corbières
☎ 04-68-43-69-08 B/C

Hervé Leferrer has the kind of curriculum vitae which few growers could begin to match; after getting his diploma at Montpellier, he worked for three years with the wine authorities in the Loire Valley before becoming *régisseur* at the Domaine de la Romanée-Conti.

But Hervé wished to be his own master. His limited savings gave Pascaline and himself the option of either buying a half hectare in Burgundy or else moving somewhere where the land was cheaper but where there were still exciting prospects of making quality wine. The answer lay in the five hectares that he bought in the Corbières,

ground which a local stonemason had planted with Grenache and Cinsault in the early 1980s. This was no picture-postcard Mediterranean vineyard, but one 300 metres (1,000 feet) above sea-level on top of a remote and inaccessible hillside where there was nothing but the garrigue, the rabbits, and the unremitting wind.

Over the years Hervé and Pascaline have acquired a further ten hectares of the same kind of inhospitable terrain. They have also created an enlarged *capitelle*, to provide shelter from the weather and to store equipment which would otherwise have to be brought several kilometres from Ferrals. The wine is made and matured in a converted *bergerie* (sheepfold) in the centre of that village, just adjacent to the school that the local children attend. Hervé explains that his training in more northerly areas, the high altitude and correspondingly cooler climate enjoyed by his vines, combine to produce a style of wine which concentrates more on reticence and understatement than on brute force.

He makes two red wines. A "Tradition" which he calls simply "Grand Crès"★★★, contains 25% Cinsault, which contributes significantly to the subtle style of the wine, is vinified traditionally; all but the Cinsault are given their second fermentation in wood and aged in not-quite-new barrels for a year. The result is a rich, fruity wine with great style and length.

The more expensive "Cuvée Majeure"★★ is mostly Syrah with a little Grenache, vinified at high temperature, and aged partly in new barrels and partly in older ones for a year. After *assemblage* it is aged a little more in *cuve* and bottled two years after the vintage. A wine which should be kept for five years or more.

Note the excellent rosé★★, made entirely from Cinsault, with its rich nose of ripe fruits, peaches, mangoes, and lychees. The excellent white AC★★★ is on a par with the reds. A blend of Roussanne, Viognier, and Muscat, it is lively, fruity and elegant at the same time, and Leferrer rightly eschews

oaking this wine so as to preserve its aristocratic style.

H5 Patrick Reverdy

CHATEAU LA VOULTE GASPARETS
11200 Boutenac
☎ 04-68-27-07-86 B

Romain Pauc is the name of an ancestor of Patrick Reverdy and also the title given to the top red wine of this estate, one of the best – as well as the best-respected – in Corbières. The vineyard goes back more than a hundred years, but it was Patrick and his father who put it on the map and started bottling their own wines in 1974. Today, Patrick works closely with his son Laurent who obviously has what it takes to succeed to the estate when Patrick decides to put away his *sécateurs*.

The age of the vineyard is reflected in its old vines, some Carignan going back to 1905, and no vine that is younger than twenty-five years going into the main red wine: the "Cuvée Romain Pauc"★★★ made from vines at least forty-five years old. All the vines are grown in the old-fashioned way, *en gobelet*, and thus the grapes are picked by hand. Legitimacy and tradition may be the keynotes here, but the entire crop is vinified by *macération carbonique*, proving, if proof were needed, that this method can produce wines that are every bit as distinguished as those made traditionally. Paradoxically, though, travelling in the reverse direction from most growers, the Reverdys are now experimenting with traditional vinification.

The Carignan grape reigns here, the red wines containing at least 60% of it, supported mostly by Grenache. There is a little Syrah, and even less Mourvèdre, the latter being largely reserved for the rosé. About seven per cent of the total output is white, from a blend of Grenache Blanc, Vermentino, and Maccabeu.

The "Cuvée Romain Pauc" is made only in the best vintages, otherwise there is just the one red called "Cuvée Réservée"★★★. The two wines have the same *encépagement*, but the grapes from the oldest and sunniest vines are naturally kept for the premium wine which receives a year's ageing in oak, 20% of it new. The Cuvée Réservée gets only seven months and then only in wood which has already been used for one or more wines.

The wines are a brilliant pomegranate colour, with a bouquet of prunes and blackcurrants; the Romain Pauc has, in addition, suggestions of spices and animal aromas. Well-structured and with a long fruity finish, the wood is discreet and control of it exemplary.

terroir de sigean

H12 CAT Château de Lastours

CHATEAU DE LASTOURS
11490 Portel-les Corbières
☎ 04-68-48-29-17 B

You would expect that a grower who offers, for forty francs (six euros), a wine which has twice been judged internationally in the same class as Cheval Blanc, Pétrus, and Daumas Gassac, would by now have little left to sell. Such is the good fortune of Jean-Marie Lignères, the *régisseur* at Lastours, which makes his 130 hectares under vine one of the biggest as well as the best vineyards in Corbières.

This estate fascinates because itis organized as a charitable foundation, a *Centre d'Aide par le Travail*, where sixty mentally handicapped people are given a new meaning to their lives as hands-on winemakers. From the beginning, Jean-Marie's policy was to aim for the top: there was no question of creating a *château pinardier* (a plonk factory). Buyers would merely be patronising if the wines of a property run on these lines were anything but first class. Harvesting is by hand, with some

right Château la Voulte Gasparets is assured of a fine future with Laurent Reverdy

reinforcement from Spain. Otherwise, all the work is done, under direction, by the patients, down to and including the bottling, labelling, and the preparation of wines for despatch. Jean-Marie, himself a qualified oenologist, has other passions in life; he has created an experimental wind-farm on top of the mountains whose *éoliennes* are a feature of the local landscape and visible for miles around between gaps in the hills.

More surprisingly, he is a four-wheel-drive fanatic. He has developed hair-raising tracks here which serve as stop-over practice for the Paris-Dakar Rally. He competed in that event in 1990 and suffered a tragic accident which leaves him without full use of his limbs. But he still gives some visitors a tour in competition conditions, driving them straight to his turbines, 300 metres (1,000 feet) above sea-level, where the ground is very stoney and porous. Here the Carignan grape, planted in pockets sheltered from the omni-directional winds, is particularly successful, and night temperatures are cool even in mid-summer. Harvesting is a month later than in the valley 275 metres (900 feet) below.

As well as being the only grape used to make a light, quaffable red called "Chatellénie"★, Carignan makes up half of the more serious red called "Simone Descamps" ★★★, named after the founder of the Centre. This unoaked wine gets better the longer you keep it, with its liquorice, deep tannins, and good fruity finish. It yields nothing in quality to the "Cuvée Fûts de Chêne"★★ from Carignan, Grenache, and Cinsault grown on lower ground. The top wine, twice the price of the other reds, is called simply "Château de Lastours"★★★, grown nearest of all to the sea on chalky clay from equal quantities of Carignan and Grenache, unobtrusively and very skilfully oak-aged.

Note the absence of Mourvèdre, as well as all but a little Syrah. Even the rosé is 100% Grenache – pale, aromatic, and scented.

left Nicolas Duhamel of Château Haut-Gléon is assisted by a friendly hound

Good unoaked whites are made from Malvoisie and Grenache, with a notably high percentage of Muscat. There is also a delicious 100% dry Muscat★★.

terroir de durban

H10 Jean-Pierre et Philippe Montanié

CHATEAU DE GLEON-MONTANIE
11360 Durban
☎ 04-68-48-28-25
Ⓦ www.gleon-montanie.com B

For vignerons who lost twelve of their fifty hectares of vines in the terrible floods of November 1999, and half of their crop to hail in June of the following year, the Montaniés are extraordinarily positive. But perhaps they are able to take a longer-term view than most, having been at Gléon since 1861. Philippe is the sixth generation there, and the family has been bottling its own wine for over a hundred years.

The floods of 1999 also nearly destroyed the old medieval bridge carrying the road which used to link the north with Durban. Today, a tunnel built about a hundred years ago takes the traffic by an easier and more direct road, but in the past Gléon defended the pass into the mountains and was besieged by the Spanish in 1503.

During the last century the Gléon estate was divided into two to meet the legal rights of the previous owner's two sons. The other property is now called Haut-Gléon (q.v.).

This estate varies enormously in altitude, like Lastours. Some vines are at a mere 50 metres (165 feet) above the level of the sea, whereas others rise to over 350 metres (1,150 feet). The high ground at Gléon is particularly favourable to the Grenache grape. All the wines here are made under AOC.

There are six hectares of Malvoisie grapes, an unusually high proportion of white in an essentially red appellation, and there is some rosé too, largely saigné from Cinsault. But it is the reds for which Gléon-Montanié is

more widely known. The "Tradition"★★ is half Carignan, and is a beautiful garnet red with excellent legs, and a high rank in its class. Syrah dominates the second red (60%) called "Combe de Berre"★★, which is given its malolactic fermentation in wood but is raised in cuve. The top of the range is "Gaston Bonnes"★★, after a family ancestor: the wine is a version of Combe de Berre but is aged in barrels that have already housed one wine – again, there's no obtrusiveness of oak.

H11 Léon-Claude et Nicolas Duhamel

CHATEAU HAUT-GLEON
Villesèque-des-Corbières
11360 Durban
☎ 04-68-48-85-95
Ⓦ www.hautgleon.com C

New investment shows results here at the twin Gléon property, bought in 1991 by Monsieur Duhamel, a successful rainwear manufacturer from Belgium. Much money has been spent on new chais, on plant to put in them, and on the restoration of the buildings and landscaping of the park. But you still need to cross the old medieval bridge past Montanié to get here, and the old road to Durban over the mountains really needs a four-wheel-drive.

Léon-Claude, though himself a devotee of wine and delighted to exchange the fogs of Belgium for the sunshine of Languedoc, must have been astonished by the fanatical vocation which developed in his son Nicolas, who took to his new life as vigneron as a duck to water. As guide to the property and its wines, Nicolas exudes a passion rare except in those whose family have been making wine for centuries. But the influence of the previous winemakers still lives on, because the oenologue is the son of the former vigneron here. This no doubt helped the Duhamels in their initiation into winemaking especially since their first vintage, 1992, was such a difficult one.

The policy was clearly to shoot the wines of this property straight to the top. 1993 put

them on the map, and they are there to stay. Their customers include such prestigious restaurants as L'Oustau de Baumanière in Les Baux-de-Provence, the Barbacane in Carcassonne, Guy Savoy in Paris, and Pierre Orsi in Lyon.

Apart from an inexpensive supermarket wine sold as "Château Glénum", the range starts with a vin de pays★ from a blend of Pinot, Merlot, and Syrah. This sounds a bizarre mixture but it works well; it makes a very fresh and rather un-Southern style of wine. The red AOC wines – ★★ and ★★★ – are a different proposition altogether: well-structured, with plenty of extraction, big fruit, loaded with alcohol, and aged in new oak, a very fashionable style. There are white wines too, the AC★★ being from a mixture of Roussanne, Grenache, and Bourboulenc, barrel-fermented with frequent bâtonnages. Outside the appellation, white blends may include Chardonnay, Viognier, and Sauvignon Blanc★.

As may be imagined, these wines do not come cheap, but they represent "New World Corbières" at its best.

H20 SCV Castelmaure

CAVE COOPERATIVE D'EMBRES-ET-CASTELMAURE
11360 Embres-et-Castelmaure
☎ 04-68-45-91-83 A/C

Exceptionally, this coopérative is mentioned because it is small and has an artisanal feel. It takes advice from the best possible sources, and most importantly the wine is excellent, definitely the best to be found as far south as this in the Corbières. The landscape has a tormented look, more evocative of the earthquakes that created the Pyrenees than the gentler countryside in the north of Corbières. There are plenty of micro-terroirs, with a chalky schist predominating. There is also a chalk plateau called "Les Grandes Terrasses".

On paper there are ninety-seven members of the coopérative, but a mere twelve own 90% of the vines, which are sandwiched in between the two parts of the Fitou appellation. Bernard Pueyo has been in charge here since 1983. He spent the first ten years mainly trying to get the members to concentrate on the vineyards. Much replanting took place, but Carignan still accounts for 50% of the total. By the early 1990s the new grapes were coming on stream so Bernard was able to switch attention to the *chais*, perfecting the vinification and experimenting with the *assemblages*. The result has been that since the late 1990s the quality here has been extraordinary.

"Tradition" here is represented by the Castelmaure range, mostly red★★, but with a little white and rosé too. The next range is called "Pompadour"★, the red version of which is oaked. Top of the tree is a red called "Le 3 de Castelmaure"★★★. The making of this wine is largely down to two consultants, Dominique Laurent from Burgundy and Michel Tardieu from Aix-en-Provence. This is a very ambitious wine from 40% Syrah, 35% Grenache, and 20% Carignan, half from schist and half from chalk. The wine is matured fourteen months on its lees without filtering or fining and ends up a wonderful dark, limpid colour, with a bouquet of flowers and candied fruits. Complex mixtures of spices and fruits, cherries perhaps, overlay a mineral base. Complexity and power are balanced by elegance and a complete resolution of all the components. The aftertaste is subtle, almost delicate, and very long.

terroir de saint-victor

H15 Annie et Jean-Pierre Mazard

DOMAINE SERRES-MAZARD
11220 Talairan
☎ 04-68-44-02-22 B

Le Cellier Saint-Damien is the name of the Mazards' tasting-room, but it is more than that: it is a treasure-house and museum where visitors can learn about the region, its

flora and fauna, local produce, restaurants, and hotels in the vicinity, as well as the wines. The village of Talairan, whose population is outnumbered by that of the wild boars (according to Jean-Pierre), hardly needs an *office de tourisme* when it has the Mazards.

You will be expected to share the Mazards' passion for the wild orchids of Corbières, where many rare and beautiful species are to be found. One of their white wines, an unusual *demi-doux* example, is called "Orchidée cuvée Marie-Pierre"★★, containing much Muscat, late-picked after the main harvest is over. It is surprisingly pale, with greenish tints, but strongly aromatic on the nose, fresh and well-balanced in the mouth. Many wines claim to partner foie gras well, but this would be exceptional because of its touch of acidity on the finish; it would also not be difficult to follow it with a red wine to accompany the rest of a meal.

In 1986 the Mazards took on Jean-Pierre's family vineyard started by his grandfather. They have fifty-five hectares of which 80% are AOC on pebbly chalky clay. Fourteen hectares are on ground much higher up the hillsides and are picked later: this is where the orchids grow in April and May.

"L'Orchidée" is not the only white wine here; there is also a "Blanc de Blancs"★ from Grenache Blanc, Maccabeu, Marsanne, and just a touch of Clairette which is very dry and floral, the Maccabeu showing through well. The Mazards make a nice rosé★ too, largely from Cinsault, the colour of rose petals and scented by the garrigue. Three reds are headed by the "Tradition", called "Domaine Saint-Damien"★★, based on Carignan: a brilliant cherry red colour with good red fruits.

The "Rouge Fût"★★ is aged in oak for six months, and the top red, called "Cuvée Henri Serres"★★★, gets twelve months. In each case the wine is assembled before it goes into the wood. They are both deeper than the Tradition, with a touch of vanilla and witch hazel from the wood. Annie suggests these wines would be at their best at five years old.

other good corbières growers

Philippe Mathias
Clos de l'Anhel, 11200 Lagrasse
☎ 04-67-43-18-12

Paul Herpe
Château Auris, 11100 Narbonne
☎ 04-68-45-17-92

Christian Baillat
Domaine Baillat, 6 rue des Monts Laurier,
11200 Montlaur
☎ 04-68-24-01-08

Suzette et André Lignères
Château la Baronne, 11700 Fontcouverte
☎ 04-68-43-96-73

Guilhem Durand
Château la Bastide, 11200 Escales
☎ 04-68-27-08-47

Jean-Pierre Richard
Château Bel Evêque, 11430 Gruissan
☎ 01-45-04-00-25

Cellier Charles Cros
(Domaine de Bellevue and Château
de Ribaute), 11200 Fabrézan
☎ 04-68-42-75-20

Brigitte Terrier
Château Blanc-Terrier, 11130 Sigean
☎ 04-68-48-40-32

Louis Max
Château de Caraguilhes,
11220 Saint-Laurent-de-la-Cabrérisse
☎ 04-68-58-11-40

Philippe Courrian
Château Cascadas, Moulin de Salles,
11220 Saint-Laurent-de-la-Cabrérisse
☎ 04-68-44-01-44

Frédéric et Patrick Roger
Château La Domèque,
11200 Lézignan-Corbières
☎ 04-68-43-81-59

Monsieur de Lamy
Château Fontarèche,
11200 Lézignan-Corbières
☎ 04-68-27-10-01

Christian et Bruno Laboucarié
Domaine de Fontsainte, route de Ferrals,
11200 Boutenac
☎ 04-68-27-07-63

Bruno et Fabienne Schenk
Domaine du Grand Arc, 11350 Cucugnan
☎ 04-68-45-04-16

SARL F L B Rigal
Château du Grand Caumont,
11200 Lézignan-Corbières
☎ 04-68-27-10-82

Pol Flandroy
Château de L'Ille, 11440 Peyriac-de-Mer
☎ 04-68-41-05-96

Roger Bertrand
Château de Longueroche,
11200 Saint-André-de-Roquelongue
☎ 04-68-41-48-26

Anne-Marie et Jean Maymil
Château Maylandie, 11200 Ferrals-Corbières
☎ 04-68-43-66-50

Véronique et Florent Cuculière
Domaine de Mingraut, 11700 Fontcouverte
☎ 04-68-43-40-01

Marie-Paule Pitt
Château Montrabech-Pitt, 10 rue Dantopine,
11000 Carcassonne
☎ 04-68-25-56-18

Jacqueline Bories
Château Ollieux-Romanis, 11200 Montséret
☎ 04-68-43-32-61

Anne et Xavier de Volontat
Château les Palais,
11220 Saint-Laurent-de-la-Cabrerisse
☎ 04-68-44-01-03

Louis Max
Château Pech Latt, 11220 Lagrasse
☎ 04-68-58-11-40

Jacques Bacou
Château du Roc,
11700 Montbrun-des-Corbières
☎ 04-68-32-84-84

right Jean-Pierre Mazard of Domaine Serres-Mazard

Claude Vialade et Jean-Paul Salvagnac
Château Saint-Auriol, 11220 Lagrasse
☎ 04-68-58-15-15

GFA Château Saint-Estève
Château Saint-Estève,
11200 Thézan-des-Corbières
☎ 04-68-43-32-34

Dominique Bacave
St-Jean de la Gineste,
11200 Saint-André-de-Roquelongue
☎ 04-68-45-12-58

Coste, Roux, et Limouzy
Cellier de Ségur la Bellevie, 11200 Ribaute
☎ 04-68-43-11-27

Bernard Sichel
Domaine Trillol,
11350 Rouffiac-des-Corbières
☎ 04-68-45-01-13

Louis Panis, Château du Vieux Parc
11200 Conilhac-Corbières
☎ 04-68-27-47-44

Gérard Bertrand
Domaine de Villemajou,
avenue de Lézignan
11200 Saint-André de-Roquelongue
☎ 04-68-42-68-68

notable fitou producers

H21 Régis Abelanet

CHATEAU ABELANET
7 avenue de la Mairie
11510 Fitou (Maritime)
☎ 04-68-45-76-50 A

The Abelanets of Fitou go back a long way.
They can trace an unbroken male line back
to 1697. Régis has searching blue eyes,
a dashing smile and the weather-beaten
face of a man who has spent his life in the
Tramontane wind.

He presides over a *cave* which is directly
opposite the Mairie in Fitou village, a position
which echoes the Abelanet reputation in this
split appellation. Régis is a man of Maritime
Fitou and some would say its finest exponent.
Much is thus expected of his school-boy
son, who has a large responsibiity awaiting
his shoulders.

The Abelanets' twenty hectares of vines
are scattered around the edge of the village
under the lee of the mountains to the west
which give some shelter from the wind. Régis
has planted an unusually high proportion
(60%) of Carignan, and, unlike others in the
Maritime sector of Fitou, he prefers to have
Syrah than the more usual Mourvèdre.

An equal quantity of Grenache goes to
make up his complement of vines. There
are two inexpensive reds, one made for

even earlier drinking than the other. The second of these is his basic Fitou red, a "Tradition"★ of which most growers would be proud.

But his pride and joy is his oaked top-of-the-range wine which cannot help winning medals all over the place. It is from his oldest vines and matured a year in concrete before being transferred to the oak for another year. The barrels are renewed on a three-year-cycle. This wine★★ manages to combine power with elegance, its silky tannins promising a soft complexity in the years to come.

To please his substantial German market, Régis also makes a sparkling vin de pays from Maccabeu. There are also white and rosé wines from Maccabeu, the pink version being "stained" with Grenache. There is also a good Muscat de Rivesaltes★.

H23 Jérôme Bertrand

DOMAINE BERTRAND-BERGE
avenue du Roussillon
11530 Paziols (Montagnée)
☎ 04-68-45-41-73 B

Young Bertrand's great grandfather started here as an independent grower in 1911. For health reasons his son became a member of the coopérative. The next generation decided to resume their independence and the young Bertrands have now taken over the reins. Their thirty-two hectares are all over the place: twenty in and devoted to Fitou, some over the border into Corbières, and they make a deal of Rivesaltes from Muscat and from Maccabeu. The red grapes lean more toward Carignan than Grenache, and the Syrah which will become obligatory in 2008 is already yielding.

The wines are raised in concrete rather than stainless steel. The Bertrands prefer this material anyway, but it was a choice that was forced upon them by the height of the buildings when they reconverted them into a cave. Like all growers, they do not have enough space, though the old stable next door is ready for conversion when the

Bertrands have the time and resources. It is intended, when that time comes, to instal their new oak barrels there, Jérôme being keen on using new wood. His first efforts in oak are too young to assess, but, judging by the standards of his wines to date, they should be very good indeed.

The high Carignan content of his "Tradition"★★ gives splendid fruit, while another cuvée, "Ancestrale"★★, is in a more modern style deriving its character from the Syrah. The most individual of the wines is a 100% Carignan called "Mégalithes"★★★ made for the first time in 1998 and which Jérôme intends to put in barrel in the future.

The village of Paziols is known for the quality of its Maccabeu, from which Jérôme makes a rather delicate Rivesaltes★, of which the oaked version★★ darkens well to become ambré; French barrels give a touch of vanilla to this wine, while some American ones add more than a suggestion of Scotch whisky. The young Muscat de Rivesaltes★★ is produced entirely from the Petits Grains variety and has an almost Sauvignon-like gooseberry style.

H22 Jean-Pierre Faixo

DOMAINE DE ROUDENE
11350 Paziols (Montagnée)
☎ 04-68-45-43-47
ⓦ www.cru-fitou.com B

Just down the road from the Bertrands, the Faixos have a similar history; they are former coopérateurs who left the coopérative in the 1980s to start making their own wine. Jean-Pierre's problem was that there was no cave to come home to, so he had to start from scratch.

The estate has twenty-five hectares, mostly devoted to red Fitou of which there are two versions: an unoaked "Sélection"★★ with Carignan prominent (Jean-Pierre says he only resorts to macération carbonique in difficult years). The other red is an oaked cuvée★★★, which is even better,

the tannins promise a longish life ahead. Madame Faixo, who comes from the wineless département of Ariège but is making up for lost time with a vengeance, thought it needed pairing up with a good civet (stew).

This property is another where the vines are divided into tiny parcels. Jean-Pierre is trying to rationalize them by inducing other growers to exchange bits of land for his own. But in a country where the ownership of a particular plot has a symbolic importance way beyond its quality or the purpose to which it is put, he is finding progress slow.

Production here is to a high standard; all harvesting is by hand, and vinification is traditional. Pickers are recruited as they knock at the door at vintage time; Faixo does not see the point in arranging for the same team to come each year or getting involved with the fixers in Spain. Arranging matters this way probably costs him less too.

The red wines here are good enough to put the vins doux naturels rather in the shade. These are good, though, even if they tend to be on the light side.

other good fitou growers

Alain Izard
Domaine Lerys,
Chemin de Pech-de-Grill,
11360 Villeneuve-les-Corbières
☎ 04-68-45-95-47

★★Robert Daurat-Fort
Château des Nouvelles,
11350 Tuchan
☎ 04-68-45-40-03

Jean-Louis Fabre
Domaine de la Rochelierre,
17 rue du Vigné, 11510 Fitou
☎ 04-68-45-70-52

★★Les Producteurs de Mont-Tauch
11350 Tuchan
☎ 04-68-45-41-08

roussillon and rivesaltes

The Roussillon vineyards go back to the days of Ancient Greece, whose sailors came from Corinth to trade in iron mined from the Pyrenees. Pliny the Elder sang the wines' virtues; he particularly liked the sweet ones. These are less fashionable today, although Rivesaltes and other vins doux naturels still have a good following.

Today Roussillon is officially known by its county and pedestrian name of "Pyrénées-Orientales". This barely distinguishes it from the Pyrénées-Atlantiques, situated at the other end of the Pyrenees to the other frontier-straddlers, the Basques. The two areas have very little in common.

Roussillon forms a large basin bounded to the north, west, and south by mountains, while the Mediterranean Sea completes the square. It is drained from west to east by three main rivers, the Agly, the Têt, and the Tech. It is largely on the slopes above these eroded valleys that the wines of Roussillon are made. Over all looms the usually snow-clad Pic de Canigou which rises to a height of 2,784 metres (9,000 feet) only thirty miles from the sea.

The climate here is truly hot, Roussillon being consistently the driest French *département*. The temperature averages nearly twenty-four degrees in July, day and night. Apart from the occasional storm, rain reserves itself for brief wet periods in spring and more especially autumn, but the ground is otherwise so dry that rainfall is largely wasted as it runs straight off the parched soil. As in the Corbières, the winds are an important climatic influence, speeding up the evaporation of moisture from the soil and the vines.

Such an environment produces grapes that are rich in sugar and deep in colour. The soil is largely acidic, and on hard rock, which has in the past made it difficult to dig underground to build cool *chais* and suitable storage facilities. The need to vinify at high temperatures and the impossibility of ageing at an acceptable level of heat led to a style of wine suitable only for immediate and local consumption. This explains why local growers concentrated on the production of vins doux naturels instead, which, with their extra added alcohol, as well as their high natural sugar content, were stable, and would not suffer from heat while stored, or during transportation by land or sea.

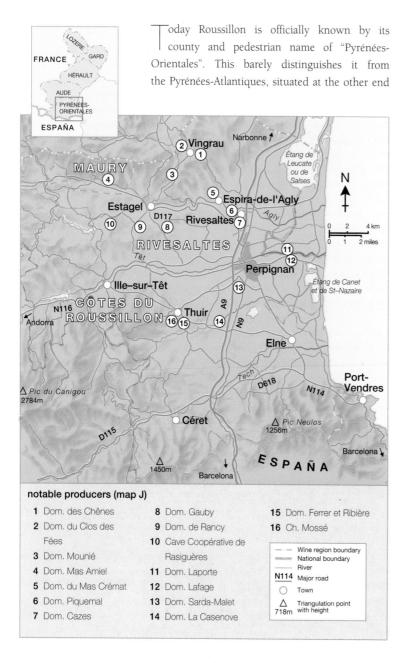

notable producers (map J)

1 Dom. des Chênes
2 Dom. du Clos des Fées
3 Dom. Mounié
4 Dom. Mas Amiel
5 Dom. du Mas Crémat
6 Dom. Piquemal
7 Dom. Cazes
8 Dom. Gauby
9 Dom. de Rancy
10 Cave Coopérative de Rasiguères
11 Dom. Laporte
12 Dom. Lafage
13 Dom. Sarda-Malet
14 Dom. La Casenove
15 Dom. Ferrer et Ribière
16 Ch. Mossé

- - - Wine region boundary
 National boundary
 River
N114 Major road
○ Town
△ Triangulation point with height
718m

It is not often realized that thirty per cent of the wines produced in the Roussillon are vins doux naturels: 450,000 hectolitres out of a total of one-and-a-half million. Roussillon produces ninety per cent of all vins doux naturels consumed in France. These are marketed as Rivesaltes, or, in the tiny appellation where the description fits, as Banyuls. In Rivesaltes, most producers of vin doux naturels also make dry table wines, as described in this chapter. (*See also* page 174.)

Of the remaining Roussillon production, 720,000 hectolitres are accounted for by vins de pays and vins de table, the former enjoying a variety of names, including Catalan, Coteaux des Fenouillèdes, Côtes Catalanes, Côte Vermeille, Val d'Agly, as well as the wider ranging Vins de Pays d'Oc and Pyrénées-Orientales. Only twenty-two per cent of the production is of unfortified table wines covered by appellation.

The production statistics hide a steep decline in both the acreage under vine and the volume of wine produced since the phylloxera era. In 1882 there were 76,000 hectares of vines, of which about half were wiped out by the disease. By 1935 the area under vine had almost recovered to former levels, and no less than four million hectolitres of wine were produced; since then both acreage and production have fallen back by more than fifty per cent. This is partly due to rapid expansion of fruit and vegetable culture. Feeding the *en primeur* markets of Europe – especially since the advent of the European Union – orchards and market gardens have largely taken over from the vine on the lower ground, pushing the vines back to their best terroirs in the hills.

The trend away from quantity and in favour of quality is in spite of, or perhaps because of, the relatively old-fashioned winemaking environment. Although the coopérative movement is long-established, and seventy per cent of all production is in the hands of the sixty or so coopératives, over three-quarters of the vineyards are worked by their owners, not by tenants or professional managers.

Machine harvesting is still the exception rather than the rule – partly because the widespread vinification of the Carignan grape by *macération carbonique* requires hand-picking, partly because the gradients of the terraces on which the vines are grown do not permit machine-working of any kind other than the smallest mini-tractors. But, the introduction of temperature-control techniques, both in the *chais* and storage areas, has revolutionized production of white and rosé, while making it easier to preserve the fruity character of the reds. There is also a growing tendency for members of coopératives to leave and make and bottle their own wines.

Roussillon comes in all three colours. Red makes up eighty per cent, seven per cent is white, and thirteen per cent rosé. In the vins de pays category Chardonnay, Sauvignon, and Viognier are the grapes most often to be found. As might be expected with wines made at this latitude, the reds are strong and full-bodied; they can be heady and sometimes soupy in texture: the Villages wines generally have a bigger structure and ageing capacity. The whites are surprisingly light, fruity, fresh, and flowery, the latter being a characteristic of the Maccabeu grape. The rosés are, on the other hand, dangerously full-bodied and misleadingly more-ish.

Roussillon, taken as a whole, has not yet made as much impact on the world's wine markets as it should do – nor as much progress as the best areas of the Languedoc. However, the way is being shown by a handful of really talented growers, some of whom are making wines of a quality at least equal to the best in the South. Perhaps, therefore, Roussillon has as much, maybe more, scope for advance as anywhere, particularly as the demand for the sweeter styles of wine seems to be in decline, and growers are responding by concentrating more on dry table wines.

pages 162/3 SNCF offers the car unbeatable views of the Roussillon vineyards

special features of roussillon and rivesaltes

the wines dry red, rosé, and white.

AOC area Côtes du Roussillon: 118 communes in Pyrénées-Orientales of which 32 are on terraces above the River Agly. The Verdouble and Maury rivers enjoy the superior AOC of Côtes du Roussillon-Villages for reds only. The four communes of Caramany, Lesquerde, Latour-de-France, and Tautavel may add their names to the Villages appellation on account of their special terroirs.

grape varieties red: Maccabeu to a maximum of 10% is allowed, except in Villages Lesquerde. No two varieties may exceed 90%. Syrah and Mourvèdre must together be at least 20%, more in the named Villages. Carignan may not exceed 60% (50% in the named Villages). rosé: Maccabeu may be used up to 30%. white: Maccabeu, Bourboulenc, and Rolle feature alongside the usual varieties.

vins doux naturels Rivesaltes and Muscat de Rivesaltes: see next chapter, pages 174–81.

the soil acidic, on hard rock.

notable producers

Growers in Roussillon are dealt with here. Producers in Banyuls and Collioure, because of their geographical separateness, have their own chapter, even though some of them make wines under the Roussillon generic appellations.

J14 Etienne Montès

DOMAINE LA CASENOVE
66300 Trouillas
☎ **04-68-21-66-33 B**

Family history here goes back several generations. Former proprietors include a navigator who served Napoleon III. Etienne Montès is himself a well-known press photographer who settled down to life as a vigneron after a hectic career which took him all over the world. His father, who is supposed to have retired long ago, is still to be seen working in the vines; he is in his mid-eighties.

The fifty or so hectares are all grouped round the pretty *mas*. In addition to the classic grapes there is some white Tourbat, a kind of Malvoisie or Bourboulenc for which grafts were brought back from Sardinia. This is, however, the sole departure from tradition of this property.

The wines, which need ageing, develop extraordinary quality after a few years. For example, a blend of Maccabeu and Tourbat★★, barrel-fermented before being aged in concrete, may take four years to reach its best and to develop its classic long, almondy finish. Time also serves well the Grenache/Carignan★ vin de pays, with its huge concentration and overripe fruit. An AOC wine called "La Garrigue"★ may have more finesse and be less rustic but it is not lacking in the same gutsiness. The top wine, called "Tradition"★★★, shows superbly after eight years, including two stored in *cuve* before bottling, to resolve some of the more obstinate tannins.

The Rivesaltes★, too, are good, but not as remarkable as the excellent dry wines.

J7 André et Bernard Cazes

DOMAINE CAZES
4 rue Francisco Ferrer
66600 Rivesaltes
☎ **04-68-64-08-26**
🌐 **www.cazes-rivesaltes.com A; vdn C**

One-hundred-and-twenty-four hectares all in one unit? Fifteen or so different vins de pays, and three AOC table wines? Machine harvesting by night? Stocks of one million bottles? This does not sound typical of an artisanal family enterprise. Nonetheless, this is very much a benchmark property for the entire range of wines to be found in Roussillon: red, white, and rosé table wines as well as some of the best vins doux naturels to be found anywhere.

The Cazes family is something of a dynasty in Rivesaltes. Great grandfather Michel sold his small production *en négoce*, but his son Aimé expanded the family holdings by buying the estate of the famous Maréchal Joffre, whose name is now borne by a range of vins de pays.

Gradually the estate grew and the next generation, brothers André and Bernard, began doing their own bottling after going to Bordeaux to study with pioneering oenologist Emile Peynaud. By then there were sixty hectares of vines, but today there are double that. Recently the Cazes have embraced biodynamic tenets, a process finally completed in 2001.

There is nothing cheaply commercial about this successful enterprise. Every wine here is marked by uniformly high standards of skill in the vineyard and *chais*, the latter today largely supervised by the charming Bruno, son of André. He rules his emporium from a campaign headquarters where every tank and barrel is monitored, not by computer, but by a giant wall-chart, the progress of each wine being studied by daily tastings at all stages of the *cuvaison,* and regularly thereafter during the maturing process.

There are wines here for all: the modest but excellent vins de pays★, a range topped by an amazing Cabernet/Merlot blend called "Credo"★★★, needing six years or so to mature. The range of AOC "Côtes du

Roussillon"★★ exemplary of its kind; and a quality range of vins doux naturels★★★ to suit all pockets, but the twenty-five-year-old "Rivesaltes Ambré"★★★ will set you back more than the vins de pays. Hardly surprising.

J1 La Famille Razungles

DOMAINE DES CHENES
7 rue Maréchal Joffre
66600 Vingrau
☎ **04-68-29-40-21 B**

At the eastern end of the main street of Vingrau this family have a lovely *mas* with

pretty adjoining outbuildings which have been converted into an attractive *chais* and tasting room. They are at the heart of the struggle to preserve the heritage of Vingrau by opposing the industry that seeks to impose a quarry on the landscape and the life of the villagers. It would dominate both. There is nothing reactionary about the Razungles, however. Their son is a research professor of oenology at the Montpellier Agricultural Institute, and a much admired wine-taster in his own right. High standards are thus the order of the day.

The range of wines starts with two white vins de pays, the first a blend of Muscat Alexandria and Maccabeu called "Les Olivettes"★, a fresh everyday wine for summer especially, and a more ambitious blend of Maccabeu and Grenache Blanc "called "Les Sorbiers★★ which is given some oak ageing. The best white is AOC "Les Magdaléniens" ★★ which probably needs three years. It goes particularly well with exotic food and with richer fish such as *coquilles Saint-Jacques*.

There are three AOC reds: the first, "Les Grand'Mères"★★★ is from vines planted after the Second World War, mostly Grenache and Carignan, with flavours of tapenade and with

plenty of good tannins. It is outstanding for its price and it is the property's best-seller by far.

Next is Les "Alzines"★★, the local name for the evergreen oaks so common on the garrigue hereabouts. It is given twelve months in oak, some new, some not. Again, the suggestion of tapenade, also peppers, spices, and even incense, heightening the fruit beneath. The top red carries the "Tautave"l★★ name because the vines are down the road in that commune, half of them

Syrah; again, the wine is aged in oak for twelve months and its weight calls out for red meats and mushroom sauces.

The fine range of vins doux naturels ends with a curiosity: a wine called "L'Oublié"★★★, which was forgotten all about for ten years and allowed to oxidize without help. Vinified completely dry from Maccabeu grapes, it is drier even than a Manzanilla, recalling nutshells, dried apples, and minerals of all sorts. It calls out to be drunk with the local anchovies from Collioure.

J2 Hervé Bizeul

DOMAINE DU CLOS DES FEES
69 rue Maréchal Joffre
66600 Vingrau
☎ **04-68-29-40-00**
Ⓦ **www.closdesfees.com C/D**

Hervé is a relative newcomer to winemaking, with sufficient confidence and passion, to aim straight for the top without apprenticeship. But then he has a career as sommelier, restaurateur, and journalist behind him, which has at least given him a fine palate; and he is only interested in the best. He aims to see his wines on restaurant lists alongside Cheval Blanc and Hermitage.

He has certainly started with much *éclat* and no doubt his professional connections have been a help. His first vintage, 1998, was made at a friend's *cave*, pressed at another, and aged at a third; all he had was a few small *cuves*, a pump and his own two hands.

Even today he has but nine hectares, partly at Vingrau where the proposal to quarry for chalk has united the inhabitants with a degree of solidarity from which Hervé has been astute to profit; and partly in the neighbouring commune of Tautavel. All his vines are old, going back beyond the memory of the most aged inhabitants of the region; some grow at an amazing height of 650 metres (2,150 feet): they include some Lladoner Pelut.

These days, Hervé has what he needs to make his own wine in his own garage; but there are still no frills. Before harvesting, the grapes are rigorously gone over by hand and eye, and again after they have been destalked; *cagettes* are used to hold the grapes, which are transported to the *chais* under refrigeration. *Cuvaisons* are long and all the wines are oak-aged, the two top *cuvées* in wood which is new each year. *Bâtonnage* and *microbullage* are carried out according to the year and the conditions of the vintage.

The results are amazing and the prices match. For the first wine, "Les Sorcières" ★★, a maceration of eighteen days is punctuated by gentle *pigeage* every day. It is aged in oak which is already partly one, partly two, and partly three years old, for eight months.

"Vieilles Vignes"★★★ is the name given to the wine made from the oldest vines of all. The *cuvaisons* are longer, about twenty-five days, and the wine is transferred to new Saury barrels for the malolactic fermentation. It is aged there for eighteen months without racking, and is bottled by gravity and hand, and without either filtration or fining.

The top wine, "Clos des Fées"★★★, is characterized by the most intensive possible control of quality in the vineyard before harvest. Fermentation is in new *demi-muids*, the wine aged in them for eighteen months. All work is carried out by hand and there is no pumping. These may be *vins de garage*, but they are already the talk of all Roussillon and only available *en primeur*, even the *micro-cuvée* – "Le Petit Sibérie", for which Hervé gets more than the opening prices of first growth claret.

J15 Denis Ferrer et Bruno Ribière

DOMAINE FERRER ET RIBIERE
5 rue du Colombier
64300 Terrats
☎ **04-68-53-24-45 B**

Many people assume that winemaking is something that has to be in the blood, requiring years, if not generations of experience. Occasionally, however, one comes across a first-class producer who has no background whatsoever in winemaking but seems born for it. Bruno Ribère is one such. He originally worked for the local Chamber of Agriculture, but was forced by poor health to seek an open air job. On the spur of the moment, he bought four hectares of vines. One day a man called Ferrer came along with his son – as members of the local coopérative they were curious about this newcomer. They all took a liking to each other and a partnership was born. They have not looked back. Today they make some of the most original and ground-breaking wines in the Roussillon.

Gradually, Denis and Bruno have been adding additional items to their portfolio of dispersed vineyards. They now have thirty different parcels in nine communes, all scattered on widely different terroirs. They are not interested in "foreign" grapes such as Cabernet, Merlot, or Viognier; nor in what the market demands, or the media dictates. They limit themselves to "wines of personality" within a certain faith which they have in common.

From the relatively unfashionable Grenache Gris★★★ they make a wine which is pale, delicate on the nose, but which explodes with fruit in the mouth and the finish seems endless. Equal quantities of Grenache and Carignan★★★ combine to make a big but wholly approachable red with perfect balance. Bruno says the secret of good balance is to get the ripeness of each *cépage* absolutely right.

These are both vins de pays, but a red AOC has recently been added, which has plenty of Syrah and will need time to age. It is surely going to be excellent. One might say that this is a property to watch, but it is already too late for that. Word has spread like wildfire among the sommeliers and *cavistes*, and stocks are always short.

J8 Gérard et Ghislaine Gauby

DOMAINE GAUBY
Le Faradjal
66370 Calce
☎ **04-68-64-34-19 B/C**

The village of Calce, hidden away in the hills to the south-east of Estagel, numbers among its 180 or so inhabitants one of the indisputably great winemakers of the South. Gérard Gauby took over the running of this estate from his father some while ago, the family having established themselves and created their vineyards here in 1983. The thirty hectares, scattered in parcels over the hillsides around the village, are cultivated in accordance with rules more bio than bio: the home-made vegetal preparations to be applied to the vineyards testify – they are brewed in vats in the courtyard and are particularly pungent on the nose.

The vines include some wonderful 110-year-old Carignan, Mourvèdre which Gérard bred himself from selected stock, Grenache of course, and some Syrah. He has tried Cabernet Sauvignon but has virtually abandoned it. Weeds are allowed to grow freely among the vine-rows: by competing with the vines for nourishment, they force the vine-roots deeper into the soil to look for nourishment. Their presence also means that yields are reduced dramatically, here only twenty hectolitres of grapes to the hectare are harvested. The age of the vines also means their output is lower, to the extent that *vendanges vertes* are deemed unnecessary.

Gérard believes that the superb qualitiy of his wines is determined more by the character and quality of the grapes that are brought in, than by what happens in the *chais*. His equipment is of the simplest: he prefers unlined cement to any other material for fermentation, and he does the *pigeage* himself. The wines are made spontaneously so that *fiches techniques* become irrelevant. There is no price-list or publicity material: there is no point, because the demand for the wines exceeds the supply.

Gérard is not interested in whether his wines comply with the rules or not; he is just as happy to sell them as vins de pays. To start with, a Chardonnay★★★ from a chalky parcel called Les Aleaux which is very gently

right Bruno Ribière, of Domaine Ferrer et Ribière, specializes in wines of character

oaked – all the wood here is at least one year old and very lightly toasted at that. From another *lieu-dit* called La Jasse★★★ Gérard makes a deliciously minerally dry Muscat; also a white Carignan and Grenache★★★ blended with some Maccabeu, Vermentino, and Viognier for a more substantial style of wine, loaded with citrus flavours (the kind of wine which would go well with sweetbreads and morel mushrooms, Gérard suggests).

Two têtes de cuvées: "La Roque"★★★ (from Grenache Gris) and "La Coume de Gineste"★★★ (from Grenache Blanc) are supreme examples of what the word terroir means; single-parcel late-picked varietal wines of rare, and very high quality.

Of the reds, "Les Calcinaires"★★★, is a big but easy to drink Grenache-based wine, while a blend from old vines★★★, Gérard compares with a fine burgundy – not everyone would agree with the comparison but no-one would dispute the quality. The summit is reached with a Mourvèdre-based wine called "Muntada"★★★, one of his few appellation wines, which has wonderful depth and spices and calls for some cellarage. Here, one runs out of stars.

Gérard has recently teamed up with the English importers Richards Walford to acquire some vineyards in and around the commune of Saint-Martin-de-Fénouillède, a leap of faith based on his intuition,

above Gérard Gauby of Domaine Gauby is referred to as the "uncrowned king" of Roussillon

experience, and alchemist's touch. Starting with eight hectares of decomposed granite, like the soil in parts of Hermitage, they expect the cooler climate at 500 metres (1,650 feet) above sea-level to achieve unusual finesse.

Their *cuvérie* in the village is called L'Abeille, and this will be the name of the wine, reflecting the organic nature of the project. They also have just over four hectares of old Grenache, Carignan, and Maccabeu vines planted on incredibly steep slopes toward Saint-Arnac.

J12 Guy et Jean-Marc Lafage

DOMAINE LAFAGE
Mas Llaro, route de Canet
66100 Perpignan
☎ 04-68-67-12-47 B

While Guy Lafage is in charge of the vines, his son Jean-Marc looks after the vinification. Jean-Marc's partner, Eliane Salinas, and he are both trained oenologists and act as consultants to overseas interests including supermarkets in London and Germany. It is perhaps surprising that their wines show as little international influence as they do, Jean-Marc's travels having taken him to California, Australia, Chile, and South Africa.

The family began its wine business in 1996 when it acquired half of the premises of the Mas Llaro coopérative, half way between Perpignan and the sea. The Lafages have just about eighty hectares of which thirty are in the hills away to the south near the village of Fourques: it is here that the grapes are grown for their red AOC Côtes du Roussillon★★, a rich, highly concentrated wine, perhaps a little hot and over-extracted, but with a new producer that may be a fault in the right direction. Guy also grows some Chardonnay★ at Fourques from which he makes a good barrel-fermented vin de pays, again a big Southern wine but not overweight.

Nearer home are the white Grenache and Maccabeu grapes which go into their white AC★★, an aromatic floral wine with surprising intensity. Perhaps even better is the dry, very muscaty Muscat★★★, fragrant despite its deceptively pale colour. Their rosé★★★ is a multi-prizewinner and deservedly so: *saigné* from a splash of all the red grape juices at the end of the *vendange* and bottled immediately. No less outstanding is their range of vins doux naturels: a Muscat★★, mostly from "Petits Grains", deep but not heavy; a Rivesaltes, *vintage style*★★, entirely from red Grenache, and an old Ambré★★★ – these last two being from grapes grown at Maury, from where the family comes. "*C'est dans le sang*," says Jean-Marc.

J11 Patricia et Raymond Laporte

DOMAINE LAPORTE
Château Roussillon
66000 Perpignan
☎ 04-68-50-06-53 B

Raymond's father bought forty hectares on the edge of this chic Perpignan suburb in 1962. Raymond took over in 1980. From a trade background in agricultural products, Raymond has no hang-ups about the kind of wines he can sell best, and his speciality is in vins de pays.

His soil is mostly clay with some chalk and his closeness to the sea enables him to profit from the cooling moisture of the Marin wind. The vines are all trained on wire, and he aims for a low yield of thirty-five hl/ha on average, achieving this by not allowing more than seven grape-bunches from each vine.

The root-stocks are chosen according to the variation in soil as well as the requirements of each grape variety. Raymond is very proud of the standards of his viticulture, and is more than happy to give visitors a conducted tour of his vineyards.

There are eight hectares of Merlot and two of Cabernet. Raymond is switching from a policy of making varietals and is concentrating on blending them. The result, which he calls "Thécle"★★★, proves that two plus two equals five; this is a real winner. He also uses Merlot to blend with Syrah and Mourvèdre to make "Ruscino"★★, to which he may add some Cabernet in years when he has some left over. The name derives from the old Roman city that used to exist on the site.

To prove loyalty to his appellations Raymond also makes a range of vins doux naturels and just one AOC Roussillon red called "Domitia"★★, which is a big Southern wine with blackcurrants and blackberries on the nose, liquorice on the palate, and good tannins to ensure a long life ahead of it. Forthcoming vintages may be oak-aged too.

J5 Mme Jeannin-Mongeard

DOMAINE DU MAS CREMAT
66600 Espira de l'Agly
☎ 04-68-38-92-06
Ⓦ www.mascremat.com B

Madame was sadly widowed in 2000, only ten years after she and her husband left Burgundy to install themselves on their twenty-four acres of dark schist. Here in the valley of the Agly, the Southern sun burns fiercely. In Catalan *crémat* means "burnt".

Madame is bravely continuing the successful winemaking which she and her late husband established, perhaps in the hope that one day one of their teenage children will want to take over one day. With a new *chef de culture* engaged to oversee work in the vineyards, Madame concentrates on the *cave*, the business side, and the upkeep of the beautiful and immaculately kept *mas*.

Mas Crémat was quick to establish an enviable reputation. Syrah, Grenache, and Carignan were already in place and yielding when the Jeannin-Mongeards arrived; Mourvèdre has been added to the red grapes, while the whites include some Carignan Blanc and Vermentino, as well as the inevitable pair of Muscats (Petits Grains and Alexandria). These last go to make a delicious dry white★★ with a bouquet of gooseberries and fresh hay; there is, of course, too, the usual Muscat de Rivesaltes★★, an unusually light and uncloying example.

Other white wines include a fragrant AOC Blanc ★, and Madame puts some of her Grenache Blanc into new wood, making a delicious *cuvée* called "La Yose"★★, enriched with flavours of exotic fruits. The reds include a vin de pays called "Tamarius"★★ from Grenache and Carignan, vinified traditionally and not by *macération carbonique*, but given only a short *cuvaison* so that the wine may be enjoyed on its fruit; this is delicious to drink with outdoor food. The AOC reds★★ are given longer; one, in which the Syrah alone is given some oaking, is chocolatey and loaded with soft red and black fruits; in the other,

Mourvèdre is also given some new wood before the *assemblage* is transferred to old *tonneaux* for a year's further ageing.

The house style strives for elegance rather than weight, surprising perhaps in an area with such a hot climate.

J16 Jacques Mossé

CHATEAU MOSSE
66300 Sainte-Colombe-de-la-Commanderie
☎ 04-68-53-08-89 A; vdn C/D

Monsieur's first love ("*plus que moi*", says Madame) is his vines, of which there are more than one hundred hectares ("far too many", she says). Madame speaks with the voice of one faced with the problem of commercializing such a large production. She is also in charge of front-of-house. Chic, blonde, with deep brown Southern eyes, full of vivacity, and her feet firmly on the ground, she is an ideal hostess at this attractive property. The views over to Mount Canigou are splendid too.

The village is a *site classé*, which means that any new construction has to be in stone, but the way round this seems to be to house some of the winemaking equipment in plastic tents. Do not be distracted by these, because the wines are of very good quality.

Try, for example, the vin de pays from old Carignan★★, with its lovely fresh fruit accentuated by fifteen days of *macération carbonique*, or the elegant red AOC called "Coume de l'Abeille"★★, from grapes grown on an unusually white schist. Even the oaked "Temporis"★★ is not heavy in style, though its high Syrah content calls for some ageing.

Of the vins doux naturels★★★, which are such a feature of this estate, you will be bowled over by the maturity of the wines. The youngest will be twenty years old, and other vintages go back to a legendary 1900. That, of course, would set you back a lot of money, but generally speaking the wines here are all excellent value – perhaps even including the 1900?

J3 Claude Rigaill

DOMAINE MOUNIE
avenue du Verdouble
66720 Tautavel
☎ 04-68-29-12-31 B

The small village of Tautavel is said to have been home to the earliest known European Man. Naturally the usual tourist paraphernalia are in evidence, but the name has also become attached to Claude Rigaill or, more accurately, to his wines.

Claude has married into the Mounié family who have a *chais* right in the village centre, built on the local rock; this means that the new oak barrels have to be stored upstairs in the attic rather than underground because it is impossible to dig down. The twenty-one hectare vineyard is mostly in the Verdouble Valley nearby, but there is also some ground nearer Maury on a pebbly schist that is particularly good for the Grenache grape.

Tautavel is one of the four Roussillon villages entitled to add its name to the appellation, and Claude does not hesitate to take advantage of this. His red "Tradition"★★ is notable for its lovely cherry-with-fruits-in-alcohol character, with plenty of concentration and soft tannins. An oaked version called "Symphonie"★★ has more Syrah and spends thirteen months in wood, one-third of which is renewed each year.

Note also a range of charming vins de pays, the red based on Cabernet Sauvignon (from which the rosé is *saigné*), and a particularly attractive white varietal from Vermentino★★ with delicious aromas of spring flowers and hay. Of the vins doux naturels, the Muscat de Rivesaltes★ is fresh and fruity without being cloying, the 'Rivesaltes Tuilé"★★ the colour of an old red burgundy, with a nutty bouquet and a palate loaded with prunes. Hurry if you want some of grandfather's "Rivesaltes Ambré"★★★, of which there is now little left: it is bottled only as required and the casks are now very low.

J6 Annie et Pierre Piquemal

DOMAINE PIQUEMAL
1 rue Pierre Lefranc
66600 Espira de l'Agly
☎ 04-68-64-09-14 A/B

This domaine, today extending to fifty-two hectares with ten more available for replanting with Grenache and a little Mourvèdre, derives partly from Pierre Piquemal's father, who sent his grapes to the coopérative, and part from his mother, whose vineyard was always independent. Pierre's tenure has seen not only complete independence but much investment in plant, notably an elaborate bottling system and two new pneumatic presses – the second of these machines particularly useful for avoiding delays in pressing the delicate Muscat grapes which are such an important part of this enterprise. Continuity is assured now that Pierre's son Franck has joined him as partner.

The Piquemals do not treat their vins de pays as a second string to their bow. On the contrary, their red "Cuvée Justin Piquemal" ★★, an equal blend of Cabernet Sauvignon, Syrah, and Grenache, has found its way onto the tables of the Elysée, the Matignon, and the Mairie of Paris. Not surprising, for its fresh crushed ripe fruit make it highly quaffable. Just as is their 100% Muscat★★ from the Alexandria variety, pale, light, delicate, and round with subtle hints of grapefruit.

The two red ACs★★ are very striking: an *assemblage* of equal quantities of all four grapes (apparently Cinsault is virtually unused in Roussillon) is quite almondy with marzipan aromas, and the Carignan is agreeably prominent. The second has 40% Syrah which is lightly oaked; one quarter of the wood is renewed each year.

A white Côtes du Roussillon AC★★ from Grenache Blanc and Maccabeu is barrel-fermented with *bâtonnage* in a manner which has now become quite usual. However, the wine is far from that, having an aristocratic style which raises it to a high plane.

J9 Jean-Hubert Verdaguer

DOMAINE DE RANCY
place du 8 mai 1945
66720 Latour-de-France
☎ 04-68-29-03-47 A/B; vdn C/D

The Verdaguers, who have been sending their black grapes to the coopérative for years, have finally taken up the making of red Côtes du Roussillon-Villages, to which they may add the name of their commune as an extra mark of quality. If it is anything like as good as their vins doux naturels, it will surely be outstanding, for their specialty is in white Rivesaltes: no Muscat, just Maccabeu, with a touch of Grenache Blanc.

The fourteen hectares of vines have been inherited by the Verdaguers or acquired by family agreement and are dotted all over the place: at Tautavel, Montner, and Estagel, as well as at Latour-de-France itself. Their *cave*, which holds a wonderful collection of old barrels ranging from demi-muids down to childrens' sizes, is right in the middle of Latour, a typically sleepy Roussillon hill-village. To make his resolutely old-fashioned wines, Monsieur Verdaguer picks by hand when the grapes are fully ripe and the sugar content is at its highest. No yeasts are added and the wines are neither filtered or fined. They are then aged for six months in concrete before being transferred to the old barrels, where they remain for at least four years, sometimes a great deal longer. In this way the wines oxidize and obtain the characteristic *goût de rancio*. They are bottled as and when they are needed for the market.

A visit here is a journey back into history. The first stop may be a young Ambré★★, which has a mere four years in barrel, and that is not unlike a Montilla – it would make a good partner with the local anchovies; back, perhaps, to 1989 for the "Cuvée Pauline"★★, which was made to celebrate the birth of the Verdaguers' daughter. This wine has spent at

right Madame Mossé of Château Mossé explains the drawbacks of a chais that is a listed building

least ten years in wood. It has overtones of figs and is quite different from the preceding vintage of the same wine★★. Now to 1974★★★, which was in cask for fourteen years, a wine which has lightened in weight with the passage of time, but has fine complexity and length.

The climax comes with the 1959★★★, matured for no less than forty-three years in old wood until it has become the colour of old Madeira. You will need your chequebook for this treasure.

J10 Cellier Tremoine

CAVE COOPERATIVE DE RASIGUERES
66270 Rasiguères
☎ 04-68-29-11-82 A

The village of Rasiguères had the good fortune for many years to count among its residents the distinguished pianist Dame Moura Lympany, who boosted the reputation of the local wines considerably by holding her own mini festival of music in the village each year. She was able to twist the arms of such celebrities as Victoria de Los Angeles to perform in the aromatic atmosphere of the *Cave* – in an ambiance far removed from that of the international concert halls to which they were accustomed.

Dame Moura still has vines in Rasiguères. The top *cuvée* of this coopérative, of which she is a fervent supporter, bears the name "Cuvée Moura Lympany"★★ to this day: a fitting tribute indeed to a great musician and a great lady.

J13 Suzy Malet

DOMAINE SARDA-MALET
Mas Saint-Michel
Chemin de Sainte-Barbe
66000 Perpignan
☎ 04-68-56-72-38 C/D; Tradition A

Madame Malet's forbears were making wine here over a hundred years ago, but during her youth it was thought that a vigneron's life was not quite the thing for a young girl, and the

wines of this region were unfashionable and hard to sell. So she was sent off to Paris where she became a law-teacher.

There she met her husband Max, who was in the business of importing and exporting fruit and vegetables. Max saw that his wife's family vineyard had enormous potential and in 1984 they took charge of it together, replanting some of the fifty-one hectares with Mourvèdre and Syrah, and for white wines Roussane, Marsanne, Malvoisie, and Viognier. The old vines that were left, dating back to the 1940s, were the traditional Grenache (both red and white versions), Carignan, and Maccabeu.

Max, sadly, died young, but Suzy and her son Jérôme finally mustered the courage to continue the domaine in his memory. Today, theirs are some of the finest wines of Roussillon. The wide spread of prices suggests disparity of quality, but this is not the case at all, the Tradition wines being excellent – it is just that the *têtes de cuvée* are more so.

The differences lie partly in the grapes used and partly in the vinification: for the red "Tradition"★★, the old Carignan and Grenache vines dominate, with the balance made up of Syrah and a little white Maccabeu; for the white★★★ the old Grenache Blanc, Maccabeu, and Malvoisie are used. For each, fermentation is short and the wines aged in tank for a few months before bottling. The results are wonderfully fruity and exotic, wines for early drinking and for enjoying with the local cuisine.

The price doubles with the "Réserve" red★★★, but the style becomes much more complex and structured. Roughly equal quantities of Syrah and Mourvèdre, with 15% Grenache. The yield from the "nobler" grapes is a bare twenty hl/ha. The *cuvaison* lasts four weeks before the wine is aged in Allier oak for twelve months. The barrels are renewed on a three-year cycle. The wine is definitely New World in style though the oaking is gentle. Pride of place goes to the red and white wines called "Terroir Mailloles" (the name of a nearby suburb of Perpignan, the word itself meaning in Catalan a young vine less than a

year old, incapable of producing fruit). The red "Mailloles"★★★ is exclusively from Syrah and Mourvèdre, given up to twenty-five days maceration, nineteen months in new oak barrels, and then bottled without racking, filtration, or fining.

The white★★★ is from Roussanne and Marsanne, morning-harvested and immediately given a preliminary maceration on the skins; it is then barrel-fermented on its lees for three weeks in part new, part one-year-old; frequent *bâtonnage* accompanies an eight-month *élevage* in cask. These are outstanding examples of modern Roussillon. If he hasn't done so already Robert Parker should give everything from this property 100/100, even the vins doux naturels★★★,

100/100, even the vins doux naturels★★★,
though they do not linger in the memory for
quite as long as the dry wines.

other good roussillon and rivesaltes growers

Maurice Conté
Château de Canterrane, 66300 Trouillas
☎ 04-68-53-47-24

Bernard Dauré
Château de Jau, route Nationale 117,
66600 Cases-de-Pène
☎ 04-68-38-90-10

Paul et Annie Favier
Domaine du Mas Bazan,
route de Saleilles, 66200 Alénya

☎ 04-68-22-98-26
(also *chambres d'hôte* and restaurant.)

Jean Gardiès
Domaine Gardiès,
1 rue Millère, 66600 Vingrau
☎ 04-68-64-61-16

Jean-Paul Henriquès
Domaine Força Réal, Mas de la Garrigue,
66170 Millas
☎ 04-68-85-06-07

Christophe Koch
Château Cap de Fouste, route d'Espagne,
66180 Villeneuve-de-la-Raho
☎ 04-68-55-91-04

EARL Mercier
Domaine Joliette, route de Vingrau,

above energy and growth, side-by-side in
the plains of Roussillon

66600 Espira de l'Agly
☎ 04-68-64-50-60

Nathalie et José Pujol
Domaine du Mas Rous, 66740 Montesquieu
☎ 04-68-89-64-91

Jean-Philippe Salvat
Domaine Salvat, Pont Neuf,
66610 Villeneuve-la-Rivière
☎ 04-68-92-17-96

Jacques Sire
Domaine des Schistes,
1 avenue Jean-Lurçat, 66310 Estagel
☎ 04-68-29-11-25

vins doux naturels

The French are a logical nation, but not always in the labelling of wines. You might think a wine called "vin doux naturel" contained nothing but the juice of the grape, but the term is used to denote wines whose fermentation has been stopped by adding enough alcohol to kill the yeasts, so the wine retains part of its natural sugar.

The process by which vins doux naturels is made is called *mutage*. By the word *naturel* the French mean that there is no added sugar.

These wines have a long history: *mutage*, it seems, was invented in the thirteenth century by a doctor of medicine at Montpellier University, to whom a patent was confirmed in Perpignan by the King of Majorca in 1299. It proved a boon, because growers could stabilize wines which otherwise would not keep long, let alone sustain voyages by boat or land.

The technique of *mutage* sounds simple, but in fact requires considerable skill, particularly in relating the operation to the fall in density of the fermenting wine. By law, *mutage* is supposed to take place in the presence of a customs official, but administratively that would be impossible. In practice, the *douanier* is satisfied if sufficient must is mixed with the alcohol (say equal quantities) to ensure that the alcohol cannot be diverted to any other purpose. Sometimes *mutage* is carried out in stages, which has the advantage of slowing down the fermentation and preventing an undue rise in temperature in the wine.

The grapes are vinified in the normal way. In the case of Muscat some of the juice may be left on the lees for a while to ensure maximum extraction of aromas. Sometimes the white grapes, again Muscat especially, will be given a *macération pelliculaire* to increase the fruit flavours. Generally, the alcohol is added when the wine has been run off the vats, but many better growers prefer to do it while the wine is still in vat (*mutage sur les grains*). This slows down the final fermentation, allows a longer period of maceration, and gives extra richness.

White vins doux naturels from Muscat are handled very carefully to prevent oxidization, a characteristic conversely much sought after in some sweet reds. To this end they are swiftly bottled and drunk young so their fruit may be enjoyed at its best.

Red vins doux naturels need varying degrees of ageing before they reach their peak. Oxidization and evaporation can play an important part. Storage may be either in wooden vats with some access to the air, even outdoors to speed up the changes in the wine. This last is called the "oxidization" method. Traditionally wines were left in large glass containers called *bonbonnes*, not quite full, out in the sun, and unstoppered. Old wines eventually acquire a highly-praised taste called "rancio" not unlike that of Madeira.

The alternative method of maturing red vins doux naturels is the so-called *vintage* or *rimage* method. In this case the wines are aged in closed vats, often under an inert gas, and are bottled early. They gradually acquire complexity with age, attaining something of the character of port. They may also be enjoyed young for their fruit, thereby improving the cash-flow of growers who cannot afford to lock up their assets in stocks of slow-maturing wine.

rivesaltes and muscat de rivesaltes

Wines of either or both these styles are made by the majority of producers in the Roussillon, as well as some in the southern part of Corbières and Fitou.

For Muscat de Rivesaltes, either or both of the two Muscat varieties may be used though the authorities are gradually increasing the presence of the Petits Grains as against the Alexandria (*see* page 21). If made from a basis of Grenache Blanc, the resulting wine is called simply Rivesaltes, which, however, is not an appellation available to growers in Banyuls who have their own appellation. The market for Rivesaltes, when it is not made from the Muscat grape, has, because of changing tastes in wine, been in decline for some years. Land within the Rivesaltes appellation is gradually being replanted, either with Muscat, or vines for dry table wines.

Rivesaltes, when it is not Muscat de Rivesaltes, may be red, white or, rarely, rosé; but if white, the Muscat grape may not exceed twenty per cent of the *encépagement*, the balance coming from Grenache Blanc or Gris, Maccabeu, and Bourboulenc. The same grapes may enter into the red wines but there must be at least fifty per cent Grenache Noir for wines aged by the oxidization method; seventy-five per cent for the *vintage* style. Up to ten per cent may be represented by Syrah, Cinsault, and Carignan.

the rules:

- White Rivesaltes may call itself '*ambré*' if aged by the "oxidization" method for at least two years.
- Red Rivesaltes may call itself "*tuilé*" if aged similarly, or for only one year if it is made by the *vintage* method.
- The additional description "*hors d'âge*" may be added for wines which have been aged at least five years.
- The suffix "rancio" may be added to the name of the appellation where that characteristic has been convincingly developed.

maury

Maury is virtually surrounded by the Rivesaltes appellation. The range of wines is identical; what distinguishes it is the terroir. The mountains to the north mark the end of Corbières and of the Aude *département*. Maury is in Pyrénées-Orientales and thus Catalan in culture. It lives in the shadow of the Cathar stronghold of Quéribus, the massive profile of whose tower dominates the landscape for miles around. If you come down from those heights the soil suddenly changes. Everywhere there is black schist, sometimes as dark as coal; the vines, brilliant green, their tufts flowing freely in the Tramontane wind, look as if they have been planted in the ashes of the Cathar martyrs who were burnt alive for their faith, in the mountains of the South.

Maury is in the valley of the river of the same name. The vineyards are undulating, except when they reach up into the mountains where they are sometimes planted in terraces. The age of the vineyard is evidenced by the fact that the vines are all trained *en gobelet*, their thick trunks gnarled with many years of hard pruning. Going east down the valley toward Estagel, the colour of the schist changes to a more conventional reddish-brown, and there are even patches of quite red *argilo-calcaire* soil.

White Maury is made from Muscat, and at this latitude the Alexandria variety is often preferred to the more usual Petits Grains. Here it seems to produce wines that are deeper and remind one of exotic fruits. Pink Maury exists but is rare; it is the red that is the mainstay of the area. It is made almost wholly from Grenache in both the oxidized and *vintage* styles. All Maury wines are vins doux naturels; if they are anything else they must be sold as Côtes du Roussillon or vins de pays.

The history of the Maury vineyard is largely that of its biggest and best-known property. Etienne Amiel, a highways engineer, won this estate on a wager with the Bishop of Perpignan in the 1870s. There were then only ten or so hectares of vines.

Later, in the time of the phylloxera, Amiel's son and heir had a friend living in the nearby village of Millas, called Camille Gouzy, an energetic grower and wine-trader. Gouzy saw that replanting

special features of rivesaltes

the wines red and white, naturally sweet, and further fortified with extra ethyl alcohol. Rosé wines of this style are rare.

AOC areas 90% of all vins doux naturels come from Rivesaltes and Banyuls in the Roussillon (plus a little in Aude). Frontignan, Mireval, Lunel and Saint-Jean-du-Minervois are in a similar style.

grape varieties the two Muscats for white wines bearing the name of the grape. Otherwise, mostly Grenache for the reds; Grenache Blanc and Gris, Maccabeu, and Bourboulenc for non-Muscat whites.

yield limited to 30 hectolitres per hectare.

alcohol content minimum 15 degrees.

special features of maury

the wines AOC Maury and Maury Rancio.

AOC area commune of Maury, and a few plots in Tautavel, Rasiguères, and Saint-Paul-de-Fenouillet.

grape varieties reds: at least 75% Grenache, Maccabeu not more than 10%, Syrah and Carignan not more than 10%. Whites: as for Rivesaltes.

ageing at least 24 months after harvest.

maury rancio the word "rancio" may be used when the wine is held to have developed this particular maderized taste (usually after exceptionally long ageing).

above, left the bonbonnes at Mas Amiel lined up in serried ranks, like soldiers on parade

left the dark schist soil typical of the land around Maury looks uninviting yet yields excellent wine

above recently filled bottles of Muscat de Mireval stand upright, neck to neck, awaiting new capsules

with immune American rootstocks would mean a necessary wait of up to four years before any return could be had on the money invested. In the village of Maury, the vine is the only viable crop and, people were dying of hunger at the time of phylloxera. In the nearby village of Millas, however, cereals grew well. Amiel and Gouzy decided to build a large mill there to make flour for the citizens of Maury. The latter, in their turn, undertook to replant their vineyards with new rootstocks, wait the necesssary four years, and promised Gouzy first refusal on their new crop of wine by way of thanks.

Gouzy's success in overcoming the phylloxera made him famous, and he was summoned by the King of Portugal to deal with the plague in the Douro Valley. The King was duly grateful and later announced that he would pay a visit to Gouzy in France. Gouzy's own house was far too modest for him to receive royalty, so he set about a crash programme of building: marble staircases and walls were erected, a two-hectare-park planted replete with fountain, all within a space of three months. But the King never came. As a négociant, Gouzy was ruined in 1907 by the collapse of the wine market. Amiel had pledged the deeds of his *mas* to a bank which itself went bust. In the liquidation Mas Amiel was acquired by a Charles Dupuy who cultivated it until his death in 1916. Charles' son Jean took over and started to produce a high quality vin doux naturel under the mark "Mas Amiel". He extended the vineyard, digging up the scrubby hillside to plant new vines.

Today the 1,700 hectares of the Maury appellation produce 48,000 hectolitres of red vin doux naturel. Two-hundred-and-fifty growers are banded together under the local coopérative and there are but ten independent producers.

saint-jean-de-minervois

Saint-Jean is a tiny area high up in the extreme north-east of the Minervois. The soil is almost exclusively chalk, the walls in the vineyards are built of chalk, and there are many chalk *capitelles*, some dating back to the time of the Druids.

The yield from the grapes is tiny, no more than twenty-eight hectolitres of wine from each hectare of vineyard, and the best wines are made from yields half the size. Seventy-five per cent of the output is in the hands of the local coopérative, whose thirty-three members share 130 hectares of vineyard. Only six private growers make up the rest of the production. The wine is drunk either as an apéritif or, like other sweet wines nowadays, with foie gras, blue cheeses, and desserts.

muscats: frontignan, lunel, and mireval

Ninety per cent of the total production of vins doux naturels comes from the Roussillon vineyards already discussed. Most of the remainder are made in these three smaller appellations. Of them, Frontignan is by far the best known, because its name was often used in the past generically to describe any vin doux naturel.

Today, the Frontignan vineyard covers only 800 hectares and most of the wine it produces is vinified by the coopérative. Sadly, this body still markets its wines in ribbed bottles which look as though they contain poison rather than wine. The market for these wines is traditionalist, above average age, and determined to fight proposals to lower the required residual sugar content of the wine. In the other corner are Château de la Peyrade (*see* page 80).

At Lunel, the AOC vineyard is even smaller (300 hectares) and once again the coopérative at Vérargues is almost all-powerful. But there are independent growers too, though one of them, the excellent Francis Lacoste at the Mas de Bellevue, is threatened with compulsory purchase to make way for the new TGV line.

Mireval is the Cinderella of this trio, limited to just two communes on the edge of the Etang de Vic. The coopérative, named after Rabelais who studied medicine at Montpellier, is the dominant grower, though the négociants Hugues and Bernard Jeanjean make Muscat at their property here.

special features of saint-jean
AOC area Confined to designated parcels totalling only 150 hectares in the commune of Saint-Jean.
grape variety Muscat à Petits Grains exclusively.
yield 28 hectolitres per hectare maximum, usually much less.

special features of the muscats
AOC area 1,350 hectares spread over 9 communes on terraces just behind the coast near Montpellier.
grape variety Muscat à Petits Grains exclusively.

notable producers

muscat de rivesaltes

Domaine Carle Courty
66170 Millas
☎ 04-68-57-21-79

Henri Desboeufs
66600 Espira de l'Agly
☎ 04-68-64-11-73

Pierre Fontanel
Domaine Fontanel,
25 avenue Jean-Jaurès,
66720 Tautavel
☎ 04-68-29-04-71

Jean Gardiès
Domaine Gardiés,
1 rue Millère, 66600 Vingrau
☎ 04-68-64-61-16

Domaine Pages-Huré
2 Allée des Moines,
66740 Saint-Génis-des-Fontaines
☎ 04-68-89-82-62

Famille Pierre-Henri de la Fabrègue
Château Rombeau, 66600 Rivesaltes
☎ 04-68-64-35-35

Domaine Rossignol
66300 Passa
☎ 04-68-38-33-17

Château de Villargeil
66490 Saint-Jean Pla-de-Corts
☎ 04-68-83-20-62

(*See also* Roussillon and Rivesaltes,
page 160.)

maury

J4 Olivier Decelle

DOMAINE MAS AMIEL
66460 Maury
☎ **04-68-29-01-02 C**

In 1998 the property was sold to Olivier Decelle, who sold his interests in the biggest frozen food business in France; the press dub him "the man who came in from the cold". Under the Dupuys, Mas Amiel was a vineyard of excellence, producing first class vins doux naturels in all three colours, including *vintage*-style reds as well as the traditional oxidized kind. The world will watch with interest what Decelle and his young *régisseur*, Stéphane Galler, are going to do.

Stocks of wine going back over many years still exist, so the Dupuy style will be with us for some time. But at least one-third of the 120-hectare estate will be made over to dry reds. Already much Syrah and Mourvèdre has been planted and, while these come on stream, some of the Grenache is being made into early drinking reds. The new owner offers his interpretation of the Dupuy Muscats: one entirely from Alexandria★★, which is deeper and more exotic than the other from Petits Grains★★. There are also two *vintage*-style reds, one oaked★★, the other not★.

The traditional Dupuy stocks offer a ten★★ and fifteen★★★ year-old, the latter showing notes of walnuts and tobacco, rather like a Madeira. Red Maury from earlier vintages are available at a price.

other good maury growers

Madame Agnes de Volontat-Bachelet
Domaine de la Coume du Roy,
66460 Maury
☎ 04-68-66-83-09

Destavel SA
Domaine de la Ferrière Destavel,
66000 Perpignan
☎ 04-68-68-36-00

Pierre Fontanel
Domaine Fontanel,
25 avenue Jean-Jaurès,
66720 Tautavel
☎ 04-68-29-04-71

Jean-Louis Lafage
Cave J-Louis Lafage,
13 rue du Docteur E Pougault,
66460 Maury
☎ 04-68-59-12-66

Jacques Sire
Domaine des Schistes,
("La Cérisaie") ave Jean Lurçat, 66310 Estagel
☎ 04-68-29-11-25

saint-jean-de-minervois

E1 Raymond Miquel

DOMAINE DE BARROUBIO
Barroubio
34360 Saint-Jean-de-Minervois
☎ **04-67-38-14-06 B/C**

The vineyards here are like a moonscape; broken up chalk with only the occasional fleck of red sandstone, lining a road that seems to lead to nowhere. Barroubio has been home to the Miquel family since the fifteenth century. The winds blow up here, and the night-breezes off the hills keep the aromas of the Muscat grapes fresh. The harvest is a fortnight behind most of Minervois; Barroubio is at over 300 metres (1,000 feet) above sea-level, almost at the limit of the vine in these arid parts.

Raymond Miquel has around twenty-five hectares planted under the St-Jean appellation. He makes a dry white★ vin de pays (as it is not *muté* and therefore does not comply with the appellation rules). Deliciously grapey, a bottle of this makes a perfect apéritif. But, the St-Jean, made in tiny quantities, is a Muscat that has been called "*le plus fin, le plus élégant, et le plus spirituel de France*".

For the "Tradition Muscat"★★, the grapes are hand-picked at the ideal moment which only long years of experience in this specialized field can determine. They are lightly pressed in a pneumatic press and then rapidly clarified by refrigeration. A long, cold fermentation follows and the wine is allowed to rest on its lees; the extra alcohol is added and in the timing and manner of this lies another secret of the wine of Barroubio. A delicate balance has to be maintained between the eventual alcohol and the amount of residual sugar. Usually the added alcohol is nearer 7% than the normal 10, which accounts for the finesse of these wines. In good years, such as 1998 and 2001, some grapes are left to shrivel on the vine and are late-picked to make an ultra-sweet wine★★★, darker in colour and from a yield of not more than fifteen hl/ha.

Miquel experimented in 1999, with a wine made from late-picked grapes vinified by *macération carbonique* and called "Cuvée Nicolas"★★★ after his young son. The results are astonishing, with a richness that one expects only in the best Sauternes, but fine acidity prevents any heaviness. The grapes for this wine were gathered in three successive pickings in December in order to ensure optimum condition, and the yield was only a miniscule 10–12hl/ha. Some years in bottle are needed before this method can be finally assessed. Even now the wine is magnificent.

other good saint-jean growers

La famille Simon
Clos Bagatelle, La Cave des 4 Vents,
34360 Saint-Chinian
☎ 04-67-93-61-63
(*see also* Saint-Chinian, page 98.)

Comte Cathare
Domaine de Montahuc,
34360 Saint-Jean-de-Minervois
☎ 04-68-91-42-63

Cave Coopérative Le Muscat
34360 St-Jean-de-Minervois
☎ 04-67-38-03-24

muscats: frontignan, lunel, and mireval

B26 Yves Pastourel et Fils

Château de la Peyrade
34110 Frontignan
☎ 04-67-48-61-19 B

Yves Pastourel believes that modern tastes call for a rather less intensely sweet version of Muscat, and that a lighter style shows off the qualities of the Muscat grape and of a vin doux naturel if the sugar levels are lower. So far he is not making any impression on the

authorities, but sheer determination will probably see he gets his way, whatever the traditionalists say.

Here is a real château with a modern *cave* and tasting room which is really more of a busy shop. It is a surprise to learn that there are only twenty-four hectares of vines.

The rather pretty and manageable château was built at the end of the eighteenth century by a Monsieur Ratié, then mayor of Frontignan. He was a fervent royalist and was eventually made a marquis by Louis XVIII as a thank you for having helped the Duc d'Angoulême escape from France to Spain when Napoleon was travelling in the other direction from Elba.

The Pastourels were winemakers before they came to La Peyrade in 1978, but they wanted to make wine in an appellation area rather than the non-appellation vineyards they already owned. Improvements were immediately put in hand. Where previously all the wine had been sold off *en négoce*. Modern methods, better clarification, separation of the second juices from the lees, were followed by new sophisticated computer equipment to control the temperature of the must in the vats. The Pastourels stress that the computers are not there to make the wine but to back up the winemakers' own judgments. However, in the conservative South, fore-fingers are wagged, berets are half-raised, and heads scratched.

Like all growers of Muscat in Languedoc, the Pastourels have discovered the attractions of a dry apéritif wine★, which of course needs no *mutage*. Theirs may retain a few grams of sugar, but it is fresh, attractive, and minerally. They also make a *moelleux*★, a big wine with a long finish. Another *vin muté*, "Solstice"★★★, one of their best products, is very pale and for drinking young: fine and elegant, not at all cloying, it typifies the house style.

Of the other fortified wines the "Cuvée Prestige" ★★★ is streets ahead of the "Tradition". It has an unusually floral, honeyed nose, is pale in colour, and on the palate exotic flavours succeed one another until they merge into a long finish.

B3 Anne et Jean-Pierre Boissier

DOMAINE DE LA CROIX SAINT-ROCH
34400 Saint-Sériès
☎ 04-67-86-08-65 C

Of the thirty hectares of Boissier vines, seven are devoted to the Muscat à Petits Grains. The vineyard is much smaller than the Pastourels', but Boissier follows the same pattern of making both dry and sweet Muscats without adding alcohol. His *sec*★★ is amazingly so, but it manages to have a most surprising nose of mangoes, and even a whiff of Alsace-like petrol.

A curiosity called "Must d'Ambrussum"★ is an attempt to create the kind of wine which the Romans might have drunk at their nearby settlement of the same name. Three parts sweet, with no extra alcohol, and just twelve degrees in bottle, Jean-Pierre devised this wine in the belief that people today reject ultra-sweet Muscat. This "Must" is made from late-picked grapes but is vinified in such a way that the fermentation is stopped late when the wine has become only half-sweet; a curiosity which has attracted a lot of media attention and is a taste to be acquired.

Whatever others say, Jean-Pierre adores the traditional vin doux naturel. From tiny yields which are allowed to shrivel in the sun, and are gone over bunch by bunch so that only the ripest fruit is selected, these luscious wines are very good. A particularly exotic version★★ is aged in *demi-muids* and has an extra complexity and depth. The unoaked wines need keeping for three years, and those aged in wood will last a lot longer than that.

B23 La Famille Maraval

DOMAINE DE LA CAPELLE
34110 Mireval
☎ 04-67-78-15-14 C

Wines that are served at the Ritz in Paris, Troisgros in Roanne, and at the Elysée itself are clearly going to be top class. Jean-Pierre Maraval is sadly no longer with us, but his charming widow, inspired by his example, warmly welcomes visitors to the *cave*. The vines are up on the garrigue, a little way toward the hill called La Gardiole, whose slope gives good drainage to the plants, while offering them up to the moisture of the sea.

There are now forty hectares of vines, the vineyard enlarged by Madame's son, Alexandre, who has taken over the bulk of his father's work. Only Muscat is made, and yields are low – as little as twenty hectolitres to the hectare overall. For the more exclusive *cuvées* yields are a good deal smaller. One of the problems with the Muscat vine is that the bunches can ripen unevenly. The grapes here are all picked by hand, usually with three *tris*, that is to say that the pickers go over the vineyards three times at different stages of the harvest.

Vinification is conventional, until the time comes for the addition of the extra alcohol, a gradual process accompanied by a thorough stirring to ensure even distribution. The wine is then aged for six to eight months in the vats. The family does not use new wood.

The Maravals have not been slow to spot the market for a dry Muscat★★. Theirs is lively and has a good mineral acidity making it an excellent accompaniment to asparagus.

Two qualities of mainstream vin doux naturel are made each year, the "Cuvée Parcelle 8"★★★ being made from selected grapes from the best parts of the vineyard and therefore having a deeper range of exotic scents and flavours than the "Tradition"★: candied oranges, roses, peaches, figs, dried fruit, melon, honey have at one time or another been detected by professional tasters.

In the best vintages, the Maravals also make a sweet wine from late-picked grapes, which has enough sugar to develop sufficient alcohol to stop the fermentation without the addition of spirit. It is made from grapes that have shrunken naturally on the vine. This exceptional wine has an elegance that more than compensates for the sweetness which is normally imprisoned in a vin doux naturel by the added alcohol.

Madame Maraval uses a special tasting glass with a small cylindrical trough at the bottom to catch wine that falls down the side of the glass. She claims this maximizes the aromas of the wine, but her daughter wryly adds this enables her mother to be extremely economical!

other good muscat growers

Francis Lacoste
Domaine de Bellevue,
route de Sommières,
34400 Lunel
☎ 04-67-83-24-83

above impressive bonbonnes at Mas Amiel, each one is covered with an old cassoulet tin

Château de la Dévèze
(*see* Coteaux du Languedoc, page 43.)

Cave de Rabelais
34114 Mireval, BP514 Cedex
☎ 04-67-78-15-14

SCA Coopérative de Frontignan
14 avenue du Muscat, 34110 Frontignan
☎ 04-67-48-12-26

Les Vignerons du Muscat de Lunel
34400 Vérargues
☎ 04-67-86-00-09

banyuls and collioure

If you drive the last few miles of the flat coast road from France toward the Spanish border, you are suddenly among mountains. This is the eastern end of the Pyrenean chain which comes to an abrupt end as it literally falls into the sea. On your left are the four port-resorts of Collioure, Port-Vendres, Banyuls, and Cerbère.

The mountains rise abruptly to your right, dotted with vines to a height of 750 metres (2,500 feet) or so above the sea.

You will notice the dry stone walls – there are 6,000 kilometres (3,240 miles) of them – that provide terraces (called *feixes*) for every two or three rows of vines. These are to prevent the vines and the soil of the hillside being washed away by storms. They need constant repair and even complete rebuilding after heavy autumn rain. Equally distinctive are the almost vertical *peus de gall* (literally "cocks' feet"), an ingenious system of canals, some vertical some diagonal, which drain the hillsides and prevent erosion. There can be few vineyards in France so spectacular.

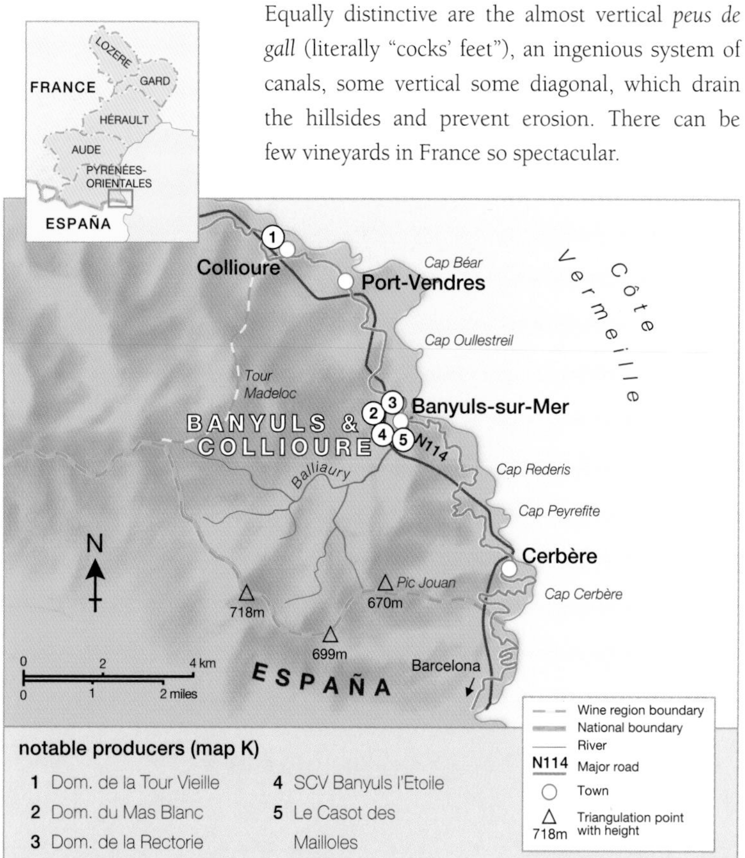

Sometimes vines are planted on slopes which fall away gently to the water's edge; just as often they are perched on cliffs overlooking the sea. The soil is red in some places, giving the name "Côte Vermeille" to the coast and local vins de pays. Higher up it is schist, a geological *millefeuille* of flaky slate.

All work in the vineyards has to be done by hand, because no machine would be viable on such gradients. The yields from the vines are very low, the norm for Banyuls being twenty hectolitres per hectare despite the legal maximum of thirty. The vigneron's life is a tough one: the *capitelles* dotted among the terraces (called *casots* in the local language), used to be lived in from Mondays to Fridays by the vineyard-workers. There was little practical access in the days before tarred roads were built to link the towns and the remote hillsides.

Equinoctial storms are a feature of the micro-climate here. They can sometimes ruin a vintage, because, in order to meet the sugar levels called for by AOC rules, picking often has to be deferred until the equinox has gone by. The sun may shine on average five days in every seven, but rain makes up in ferocity for what it lacks in frequency. Some growers therefore pick early and make table wines outside the appellation, which they market as vins de pays.

banyuls

As with other vins doux naturels there are two styles of red Banyuls. The *vintage* style (as used in Rivesaltes, *see* page 174) is here called "*rimage*" and is made only in the better years. The grapes are given a long, slow maceration for maximum extraction, and the extra alcohol is then added. To preserve

FRANCE LOZÈRE GARD HÉRAULT AUDE PYRÉNÉES-ORIENTALES **ESPAÑA**

Collioure
1
Cap Béar
Port-Vendres
Côte Vermeille
Cap Oullestreil
Tour Madeloc
2 3 Banyuls-sur-Mer
BANYULS & COLLIOURE
4 5 N114
Balliaury
Cap Rederis
Cap Peyrefite
N
Cerbère
Pic Jouan 670m
Cap Cerbère
718m
699m
Barcelona
0 2 4 km
0 1 2 miles
ESPAÑA

- - - Wine region boundary
━━ National boundary
River
N114 Major road
○ Town
△ 718m Triangulation point with height

notable producers (map K)

1 Dom. de la Tour Vieille
2 Dom. du Mas Blanc
3 Dom. de la Rectorie
4 SCV Banyuls l'Etoile
5 Le Casot des Mailloles

fruit, freshness, and impact, the wine is bottled soon after the harvest, normally within the year. Sometimes it is allowed to remain in wood for longer, in which case it is said to gain greater complexity – this style has suddenly acquired a vogue.

The oxidative style of Banyuls involves the same addition of extra alcohol at the end of a rather shorter maceration, and then long ageing in barrels, which may be of any size, or even in glass *bonbonnes* as at the Etoile Coopérative. The wine sometimes remains in wood for up to five years, or even longer, and is drawn off as it is required. It improves indefinitely, eventually acquiring the *goût de rancio* and gaining the right to add the word rancio on the bottle label.

Banyuls Grand Cru is, as may be imagined, the *tête de cuvée*: its higher Grenache content and its long *élevage* in wood give it a special cachet. Banyuls is sometimes sold as a single vintage, sometimes by blending the wines of one or more years together, and can be given fancy descriptions such as *rubis*, *tuilé*, *agé de quelques années*, or *hors d'age*; as to which there appear to be no formal rules. Sometimes it is aged like sherry in the solera manner: the wine is stored in three layers of barrels, and every two months wine is drawn off from the lowest and bottled, being replaced with wine from the middle layer, which is in turn replaced by wine from the top layer, itself replenished with new wine as required.

Banyuls, being normally sweet in character, can be drunk as an apéritif or with any of the foods associated with sweeter wines, such as foie gras, blue cheeses, and pâtisserie. It is just about the only wine that is recommended to accompany chocolate. Little Banyuls is imported into the United Kingdom where the market for this style of wine has been met by port or Madeira. In addition to the usual red, there is also a small quantity of white Banyuls made, dry and sweet, and there is a rare pink version too. All vins doux naturels.

There are three coopératives and twenty-five independent producers altogether, including some of the most passionate and dedicated growers in the South. Most make both Banyuls and Collioure.

collioure

Collioure is grown on only four hundred of the 1,700 hectares in the appellation. It used to be made by the vignerons just for themselves and their friends, with very small quantities being shipped out of Port-Vendres. Today it has become a little more fashionable now that it has achieved its own appellation.

Annual production is about 10,000 hectolitres. The wines are sturdy with good structure and concentrated aromas, powerful and tannic. They lend themselves to ageing. They are best drunk with red meats, stews, and game. It has even been said they would not be fazed by a curry of mountain goat. The rosés are delicious with fresh anchovies from the fishermen at Collioure or Port-Vendres, or with charcuterie.

The making of Collioure does not differ from that of other dry red table wines. The *encépagement*, too, is unremarkable save that, at the Domaine du Mas Blanc, they use a little of the Counoise grape, a variety that is found today in Châteauneuf-du-Pape but rarely elsewhere, and which was said to have been introduced into France by a Spanish legate serving at the papal palace in Avignon. Because the yields from the vines are so low, Collioure – like its cousin the AOC Irouléguy at the other end of the Pyrenees – is not as cheap as other wines of the region.

page 184 some of the best vineyards in Banyuls face south-west

page 185 others not so blessed are criss-crossed with ditches as protection against erosion and flooding

special features of banyuls

the wines red, white, and rosé. The name Banyuls is limited to vins doux naturels, Collioure to dry table wines.

AOC areas Banyuls and Collioure are co-extensive, both covering the four communes of Collioure, Port-Vendres, Banyuls, and Cerbère.

grape varieties Banyuls, red, and rosé: Grenache Noir (min 50%), Carignan, Cinsault, and Syrah. Grenache Gris allowed in rosé. white: Grenache Blanc, Maccabeu, Bourboulenc, and the two Muscats.

vine age minimum 4 years old.

yield maximum 30 hectolitres per hectare.

alcohol content as Rivesaltes, see page 175.

additional rules for "Banyuls Grand Cru" red: Grenache Noir min 75%. White: with less than 52g of sugar at the end of the vinification may be called Sec, Brut or Dry.

ageing "Banyuls Grand Cru" must be aged in wood for at least 30 months.

the soil red sand on lower ground; schist and slate further up the slopes.

special features of collioure

grape varieties Grenache, Syrah, Mourvèdre, which must together constitute at least 60% of AC vineyards. Grenache Gris allowed for rosé. Carignan and Cinsault may make up complement. No AOC for white.

yield maximum 40 hectolitres per hectare.

vinification grapes not crushed or destalked before pressing. There are controls over kinds of press used.

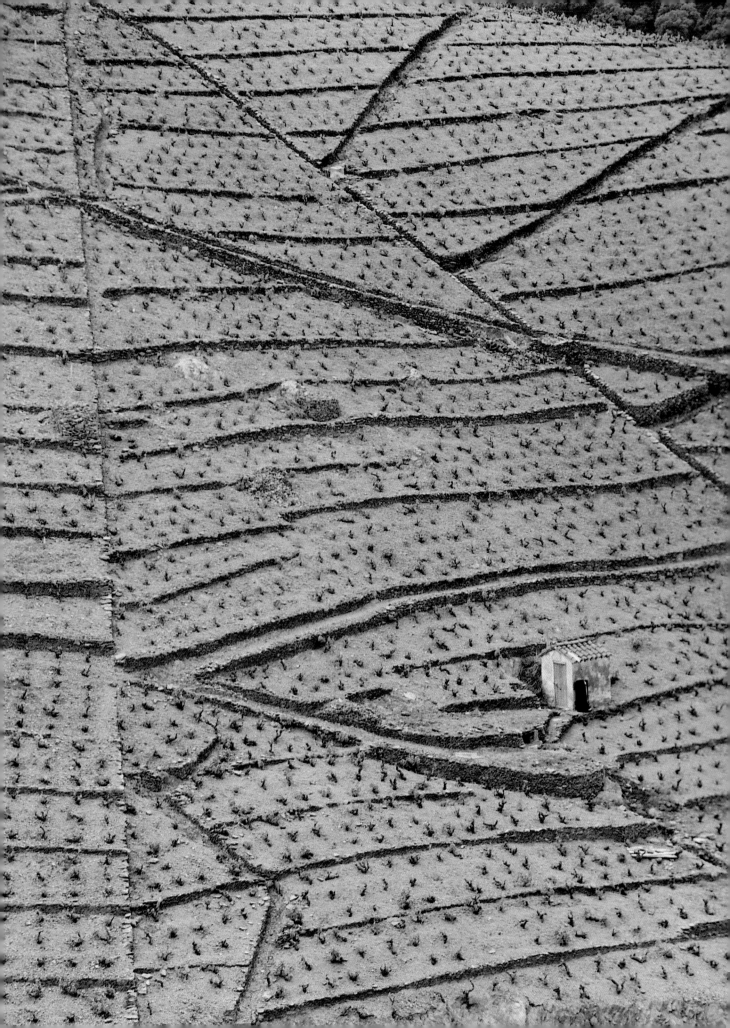

notable producers

K5 A Castex et G Magnier

LE CASOT DES MAILLOLES
17 avenue du Puig del Mas
66650 Banyuls
☎ 04-68-88-59-37 C

Who but gluttons for punishment would choose the precipitous terraces of Banyuls as the site for a wholly biodynamic vineyard? Miniscule parcels of vines, reaching to the very tops of the mountains, have to be worked only with a pickaxe, here called a *chadique*; the offerings of spraying by helicopter have to be refused because their chemicals are forbidden. Yields are down to fifteen hectolitres per hectare, and there are only five of those anyway. The gradients are so steep it takes a year to learn how to keep your footing. The grape varieties are all jumbled up and grow together as they did centuries ago.

Nothing daunts this cheerful couple of Spartan growers. They do not seem to miss the comforts of their former life in Corbières. Their greatest pride is the micro-vineyard of one third of an hectare where they have planted Syrah. It took them ten months, with their single employee, to dig this ground just near the mountain ridge and build the terraces with their own hands.

They have acquired somewhat legendary status, to the extent you'll be lucky to find them with any wine to sell.

Whatever you taste will amaze you; perhaps a dry white from a mixture of Grenache Blanc and Gris, with touches of Muscat, Ugni Blanc, and Clairette? Or a red from Grenache and Syrah, given a long *cuvaison* of a month with regular *pigeage* in the Burgundian manner, and aged in old wood. Whatever it is, it will be ★★★.

And if you are invited up into the mountains to inspect the vines, do not hesitate; nor be put off by the climb. From the top you look over the ridge into Spain.

K2 Jean-Michel Parcé

DOMAINE DU MAS BLANC
9 avenue du G de Gaulle
66650 Banyuls
☎ 04-68-88-32-12 C/D

Jean-Michel Parcé, unlike his namesakes at the Domaine de la Rectorie, represents the Banyuls establishment. His grandfather Gaston was a doctor, who loved hunting; he would go off to the Gers to shoot wild boar, bringing back with him white armagnac with which to dose his Banyuls. Father was a doctor too, as well as a hands-on winemaker: he was president of the local syndicat of growers and largely responsible for getting Collioure its own appellation. Jean-Michel has a brother who is also a doctor, but he himself confines his activity to wine. He finds his twenty-one hectares, some of which he rents, as much as he can handle. He makes roughly equal quantities of Collioure and Banyuls, including some Rimage★★ in good years.

Jean-Michel likes to make a wide range of wines. There may be up to four Collioures (★★ to ★★★): an early maturing version largely from Grenache perhaps; or a Syrah-based wine for the medium term with some Grenache and a little Counoise; a keeper from Syrah almost exclusively; or another from Mourvèdre and Counoise. In the traditional Banyuls style, he makes a dry★★ version, with just a little extra Mourvèdre – a long-lasting wine. The best-selling *cuvée*★★★ is named after Jean-Michel's father, André, and you should not miss his Solera-style wine★★★. Half this dedicated producer's wine is exported.

K3 Parcé Frères

DOMAINE DE LA RECTORIE
54 avenue du Puig del Mas
66650 Banyuls
☎ 04-68-88-13-45
Ⓦ www.la-rectoire.com C

Vincent Legrand, Marc Parcé's son-in-law, is the young manager of this controversial estate: controversial not with wine-lovers who will often rate it top of the Banyuls tree, but with the authorities, due to the unconventional, even iconoclastic nature of the wines. The owners believe quite logically that a grower's best wines come from the best use of grapes and the best understanding of terroir.

Here, terroir means no less than thirty inherited parcels of vines totalling 25 hectares in all. Marc took control in 1976, leaving the coopérative in 1982, his vision already far exceeding the conventional, although in a long war of attrition with the wine Establishment, peace has recently broken out.

More important to the wine lover is that these wines are wonderful: a varietal from the rather despised Grenache Gris★★★, lightly oaked and with an incredibly long finish, is sold as a vin de pays, but who cares? There are three quite different Collioures: early-drinking "Col del Bast"★★ (Grenache 80%, Carignan 20%); and keepers "Séris"★★ and "La Coume Pascale"★★★.

There is a range of sumptuous Banyuls, starting with an ultra-dry, manzanilla-style "Cuvée Pédro Soler"★★★; an ambré "Cuvée Elisabeth"★★★; and the wine named in honour of grandfather "Léon Parcé"★★★ made in the *rimage* style and aged in *foudres* for one year.

K1 Christine Campadieu et Vincent Cantié

DOMAINE LA TOUR VIEILLE
66190 Collioure
☎ 04-68-82-44-82 B

At last, these passionate growers have realised their dream to build outside the overcrowded town of Collioure a new *cave* where the rhythm of life is more in keeping with the essentially artisan nature of their enterprise.

They have twelve hectares, divided into as many separate parcels, scattered over the precipitous hillsides above the sea. Christine and Vincent both have roots in the coopérative movement, but both determined, during the 1980s when the future for vins doux naturels looked bleak, to expand the vineyard that Vincent had already begun. Christine had

good access to expertise; her uncle was the oenologist at the Cave de l'Abbé Rous in Banyuls, and her brother *maître de chais* at Château Branaire-Ducru in the Médoc.

The accent here is on dry table wines rather than vins doux naturels. A red "Classique"★★ is based on Grenache and Carignan – and Mourvèdre when good quality. Characterful rosé★★. And an astonishing "Banyuls Solera"★★★.

K4 SCV Banyuls L'Etoile

26 avenue du Puig del Mas
66650 Banyuls
☎ 04-68-88-00-10 C

This is more a coopérative than a club, whose wines are among the most remarkable of the region. Few estates can match this range of old wines. The director, Monsieur Ramio, and his oeonologist Monsieur Terrier, have all the fire and passion as well as the skills of the finest independents. L'Etoile was founded in 1921 by a few families and friends, each

member bringing something to the enterprise like a dowry to a marriage, whether old barrels, stocks of wine, pressesor whatever. Many of the venerable old *foudres* here date back to the beginning. The group still only handles wine from 150 or so hectares.

A collection of glass *bonbonnes* are stored on the terrace built out at first floor level so as to catch the maximum of sunshine. As at Mas Amiel, the only other vineyard with a comparable assembly, these are used to hasten oxidization and to contribute a certain oriental exoticism to the best *cuvée*, the *doux paillé*★★★, so called because of its pale straw colour, like that of an Amontillado.

One of the wonders of this establishment is the sense of stepping back into history; this is as far from the New World as you can get. The essential mission is to preserve the intimate relationship between the *cave* and its members, the emphasis still on making old-fashioned Banyuls. They do make a little red Collioure, aged miles away in the mountains.

above Alain Castex and Ghislaine Magnier of Le Casot des Mailloles picnic in the mountains

Wines range from dry to ultra-sweet, with up to a dozen different gradations, depending for their individuality largely on the point where vinification has been stopped by *mutage*. All are aged in old wood. There are as yet no new barrels and the wines are bottled as and when they are needed for sale. The longer they are aged the better they become. It would be harder to find a better example of the appellation than the Select-Vieux 1983★★★.

other good banyuls and collioure growers

Estelle Daure
Les Clos de Paulilles,
66190 Collioure
☎ 04-68-98-07-58

Domaine du Traginer
66650 Banyuls
☎ 04-68-88-15-11

glossary

agrumes citrus fruits whose character is sometimes found on the aroma of white wines

ambré amber, the colour acquired by old white vins doux naturels

appellation d'origine contrôlée (AOC) a statutory, legally controlled area of production

argileux composed of clay

argilo-calcaire clay mixed with chalk or limestone

assemblage the creative blending of wine from different *cuves* by the same winemaker

ban de vendange official permission to start the grape harvest

barrique barrel or cask, nowadays usually containing 225 litres

bâtonnage breaking up with a stick (or similar) the solid matter developing in a cask during fermentation

bidon plastic container for holding liquid, from five litres upward

bonbonne a demi-john, a glass measure of ten litres or more

botrytis a fungoid disease which rots the skins of grapes, rare in Languedoc-Roussillon but a pre-condition of fine sweet wines in damper climates

bouquet the aromas produced by wine when poured, other than the basic smell of wine; often called "nose"

bourbe the deposit from the juice, pulp, stalks, and skins of grapes during the first stages of vinification

brut bone dry (of sparkling wine)

calcaire chalk or limestone

cagette a small container for carrying the grapes to the *chais*

capitelle a small stone building constructed in vineyards to house implements and to shelter vineyard-workers in bad weather, in Catalan called a *casot*

cartagène an apéritif made from unfermented grape juice and fortified with eau-de-vie

casot see *capitelle*

cassis blackcurrants

cave wine cellar

caviste a specialist wine retailer

cépage grape variety

cépage améliorateur a grape variety, usually Syrah or Mourvèdre, encouraged by the authorities to replace older less-valued vines

chai(s) winery, for vinification and/or storing

Champenoise as in Champagne

chapeau the cake-like solid mass consisting of matter (grape skins, etc.) thrown to the surface of a vat during fermentation

chef de culture vineyard manager (c.f. *maître de chais*)

chêne oak

clairet a red wine, pale in style, but deeper than a rosé

climat a subdivision of a vineyard, either of a whole vineyard or any area of vineyards

clos a vineyard, strictly: enclosed by a wall

collage the process (also called "fining") of forcing to the bottom of a tank or barrel all solid particles suspended in a wine

coulure a disease of the vine inhibiting the young grapes from developing and ultimately causing them to rot and drop off the plant

crachoir a spittoon

cru a specially selected wine

culture raisonnée the voluntary practice of neo-organic principles but without obligation

cuvaison the period, including the time following the end of fermentation, during which the wine remains in contact with the stalks, skins, and pips of the grapes

cuve a vat of whatever material

cuvée the wine drawn off one or more vats

dans un seul tenant one continuous vineyard

débourbage the racking or settling of the must prior to fermentation

délestage the draining of a vat during vinification, the re-homogenisation of the must, then its return to the vat. An alternative to *remontage* (q.v.) and *pigeage* (q.v.)

demi-muid a barrel, larger than a barrique, usually containing 300 or 400 litres

eau-de-vie the distilled juice of grapes/fruits

effeuillage the removal of surplus leaves from a vine to promote maximum exposure of the grapes to the sun

égrappage the stripping of the grapes from their stalks before vinification

égrappoir a machine for removing the stalks from the bunches of grapes

élevage the maturing or ageing of wine

en cordon royat a way of training the vine so it produces two principal stems, the maximum shoots on each prescribed by local rules

en espalier grown as if on a trellis

en gobelet grown in bush form, the shape reminiscent of a goblet

en palissage the training of vines on wire as opposed to growth in the shape of a bush

encépagement the balance of different grape varieties in a vineyard, or in a finished wine

feixe (Catalan) the stone wall of a vine terrace

fine de Languedoc Languedoc's eau-de-vie

finesse the opposite of roughness; a quality of subtlety, elegance, and softness

floraison the flowering of the vine

foudre a large old-fashioned barrel, a tun

fouloir a machine for crushing grapes, often combined with an *égrappoir* (q.v.), when it is called an *égrappoir-fouloir*

fût a cask, often denotes a new oak barrel

galet a large, round pebbly stone like those found beside river-beds

garrigue a heath-like terrain valued for its wild herbs and flowers

gouleyant easy to drink, quaffable

goût du terroir a taste deriving from a combination of soil, locality, grape variety, and climate that is exclusive to a particular wine

gras rich, buttery, fleshy, literally fat, a term applied to white wines

grave (of the soil), gravelly, of tiny stones

greffe a vine graft

Gris a vin rosé which is so pale that it is called grey rather than pink

guyot the training of vines on one main shoot

hectare an area of 10,000 square metres, about 2.5 acres

hectolitre 100 litres

INAO French National Institute for wines of Appellation d'Origine

liquoreux the sweetest grade of wines, not to be confused with liqueur

macération the leaving of the grape skins, stalks, pulp, and juice in contact with each other either before, during, or after fermentation

macération carbonique a winemaking technique where the grapes are not crushed but allowed to disintegrate by themselves under a protective layer of carbonic gas

macération pelliculaire maceration at cool temperature before fermentation begins

madérization excessive oxidization of wine, producing an effect not unlike the smell and taste of Madeira

maillole (Catalan) a young vine not yet capable of producing fruit

maître de chai(s) cellar-master

malolactic (fermentation) a second fermentation of wine after the first alcoholic fermentation has finished, which converts the malic (harsh) acid in wine into lactic (milder) acid; often called "malo" for short

mas the southern word for a farm, sometimes a group of farm buildings

méthode ancestrale the original method of making sparkling wine as in Limoux

méthode champenoise the way of making sparkling wine as in Champagne

méthode traditionnelle the name by which the *méthode champenoise* is obliged to go outside Champagne

microbullage the introduction of tiny quantities of oxygen into a maturing wine, so as to avoid the necessity of racking the wine and thus disturbing the lees

moelleux mellow and full, usually denoting a degree of sweetness

mono-cépage a wine made from a single grape variety, a varietal

must the contents of a *cuve*, liquid and solid, during fermentation

mutage the "silencing" of fermentation by the addition of alcohol

négociant a dealer in wine

nerveux vigorous and lively (of wine)

oxidization chemical effect of oxygen on wine

pain grillé an element in the bouquet, reminiscent of well-toasted bread

passerillage over-ripeness of grapes attained by leaving them to shrivel and partly evaporate in the sun

peus de gall (Catalan) a system of combined vertical and diagonal vineyard drainage in Banyuls and Collioure

phylloxera a rapidly multiplying aphid feeding on and destroying vine roots; first appeared in the Languedoc in the 1870s

pierre à fusil the smell or taste of gun-flint

pigeage the breaking up of the *chapeau* (q.v.) to give fermenting juice access to the solids

porte-greffe root-stock

racking transferring wine from one *cuve* to another to aerate it, and then returning it to its original cask; when during the ageing of the wine this shortens the period of maturation

rafle the wood and fibre, as opposed to the fruit, in a bunch of grapes

rancio the character of an old oxidized vin doux naturel, Madeira-like

récolte harvest, crop

régisseur the over-all manager of a vineyard

réglisse liquorice

remontage the circulation of the wine in the vat by pumping it back into the top of the container to submerge the *chapeau* (q.v.)

rendement the yield of a vineyard, quantitively

rimage *see* vintage

robe colour, appearance of a wine

sable, vin de wine grown in very sandy soil

saignage drawing off ("bleeding") pink juice from fermenting red grapes to make *vin rosé*

schist/schiste shale, a flaking brittle soil

sommelier head wine-waiter, often a restaurant's wine-buyer

soutirage the racking of wine, by drawing it off its lees to clarify and oxygenate it

stage a period of apprenticeship or study, usually a year or so and with a top winemaker, who gets the benefit of free keen labour

tête de cuvée the top wine of a producer

tonneau a large cask, a hogshead

tonnelier a cooper, barrel-maker

torréfaction the smell of hot, dry roasting, as of the coffee bean

tri(e) the selective picking of well-ripened grapes; also the hand-sorting of grapes prior to vinification ("*triage*")

tuilé the colour of old tiles, often a feature of old red vins doux naturels

typicité the individual character distinguishing one wine area from that of another

vendange the grape harvest

vendange tardive the late-harvesting of overripe grapes, a term legally permitted only in Alsace but used colloquially elsewhere

vendange verte the picking of bunches of unripe grapes in July, to promote quality and concentration in the remaining bunches

vigneron a grower of vines, a winemaker

vin de cépage a wine made from a single grape variety, a varietal

vin de garage wine, usually from a small property, made in tiny quantities, to the highest specification, sold at inexplicably high prices

vin de garde a wine that requires ageing

vin de pays a wine from a recognized locality but not within an area of AOC; also a wine made within an AOC but which does not comply with the rules of the appellation

vin de presse the wine that results from the pressing of the solid matter/grape skins at the bottom of the *cuve*

vin de table a wine conforming to no rules

vin délimité de qualité supérieur (VDQS) a statutory legally controlled area of wine production not so highly rated as AOC areas

vin doux naturel a naturally sweet wine of any colour, fortified by the addition of pure alcohol

vintage a style of red vin doux naturel which is bottled young and allowed to mature like port (also called "*rimage*")

vrac in bulk; large containers other than bottles

bibliography

Clive Coates, *The Wines and Domaines of France*, Cassell, London (2000)

Roger Dion, *Histoire de la Vigne et du Vin en France*, Paris (1959)

Rosemary George, *The Wines of the South of France*, Faber and Faber, London (2000)

Dr Jules Guyot, *Etude des Vignobles de France*, reprinted by Jeanne Laffitte, Marseilles (1982, from the original Paris edition 1876)

André Jullien, *Topographie de Tous les Vignobles Connus*, Slatkine, Geneva (1866)

Alain Leygnier and Pierre Torrès, *Les Vins Doux Naturels de la Méditerranée*, Editions Minerva, Geneva (2000)

Pierre Rézeau, *Le Dictionnaire des Noms de Cépages de France*, CNRS Editions, Paris (1997)

Jancis Robinson, *Vines, Grapes and Wines*, Mitchell Beazley, London (1986)

Jean Sagnes, Monique, and Rémy Pech, *1907 En Languedoc-Roussillon*, Editions Espace Sud, Montpellier (1997)

André L Simon, *History of the Wine Trade in England*, Holland Press, London (1964)

Various, *Catalogue of Selected Wine Grape Varieties and Certified Clones Cultivated in France*, Ministry of Agriculture, Fisheries, and Food (1997)

Various, *Le Transport du Vin sur Le Canal du Midi*, Editions Causse, Saint-Georges-d'Orques (1999)

Various, *Atlas des Terroirs du Languedoc*, APE Editions, Montpellier (1996)

index